Alexander's Lovers

by

Andrew Michael Chugg

2006 & 2012

Second Edition

© 2006 & 2012 by Andrew Michael Chugg. All rights reserved.
ISBN 978-0-9556790-4-9

Preface

Alexander's Lovers is a factual, historical account of the various individuals with whom Alexander is believed to have conducted romantic relationships. It incorporates much new research and presents a more complete version of their biographies than has previously been published.

The issue of Alexander's personality has been called the hardest problem in history. This new book takes up the challenge by investigating the king's character through the mirror of the lives of his lovers. Foremost among these relationships was that with Hephaistion, the companion of Alexander's youth, who later rose to become his official deputy. Yet also of key importance were Roxane, the king's fabulously beautiful Afghan queen, Barsine, his Persian mistress, and Bagoas, the young eunuch who entered Alexander's service near the shores of the Caspian Sea. There were others, including Pankaste, the Thessalian courtesan, Thalestris, Queen of the Amazons, Stateira and Parysatis, the Persian princesses and Cleophis, Queen of Massaga, but these liaisons were either unconsummated or essentially political in nature or merely mythical.

Alexander's Lovers is aimed at the large range of Alexander enthusiasts who have been frustrated to find his rather intriguing love life relegated to little more than embarrassed footnotes in the conventional histories of his career. It is also rendered accessible to the wider audience of filmgoers who have seen Oliver Stone's *Alexander* movie or others who are freshly fascinated in the subject by the incorporation of an 18,000-word prologue providing a concise introductory biography of the king.

To understand Alexander well, it is necessary to follow his heart more carefully than his policies. Anyone who wants to know the full truth about Alexander need merely read on.

This second edition is completely revised and updated and has been extended by the incorporation of new sections on Alexander's deification and the funeral of Hephaistion.

Alexander's Lovers
Contents

	A Note on the Sources	1
1.	Prologue: A Concise Biography of Alexander	3
2.	"A Philosopher in Arms"	53
3.	Hephaistion, The Chiliarch	67
4.	Barsine, Daughter of Artabazus	138
5.	Bagoas the Eunuch	152
6.	Thalestris, Queen of the Amazons & Cleophis, Queen of Massaga	165
7.	Roxane, The Starlet	174
8.	Stateira & Parysatis, The Persian Princesses	196
9.	Epilogue	211
	Appendix A: The Nature of Alexander's Divinity	214
	Appendix B: The Structure and Decoration of Hephaistion's Pyre	223
	Bibliography	230
	Index	235

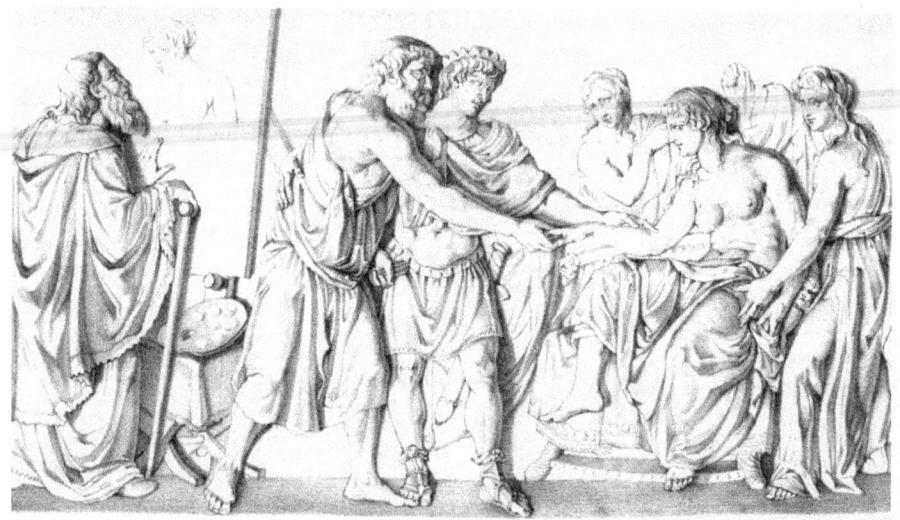

Frontispiece: Alexander gifts Pankaste/Campaspe to Apelles the painter (1820's)

A Note on the Sources

Principal Primary Sources (All Now Lost Except for Fragments)

Callisthenes of Olynthus – Alexander's official historian and a great-nephew of Aristotle, his work may have been published in Greece in instalments during the course of the expedition, but he was arrested early in 327BC and died in captivity; however, his account probably extended at least as far as the beginning of the Bactrian campaign in 329BC.

Onesicritus of Astypalaea – Alexander's helmsman on the Indus river voyage and chief pilot of the fleet for the return voyage from India; also a pupil of Diogenes of Sinope, the Cynic philosopher; his work *On the Education of Alexander* is mentioned in the *Liber de Morte*, which Heckel assigns to 317BC; it is relatively certain that he wrote before 310BC.

Nearchus of Crete – the admiral of Alexander's fleet for the voyage back from India, he wrote partly to refute aspects of Onesicritus' account, probably between 320BC and 310BC.

Cleitarchus of Alexandria – an immigrant to Egypt under Ptolemy, it is doubtful whether he participated in Alexander's campaigns, but his history of Alexander's expedition was colourful and generally accurate; it proved especially influential in Roman times; he evidently made use of Onesicritus and Nearchus and he probably mentioned the death of Cassander and the fate of his sons, so he probably wrote after the mid-290's BC, although Pliny thought that he wrote before Theophrastus; there are also indications that he used some stories given by Megasthenes, who wrote in the 290's BC; a date around 280BC is likely.

Aristobulus of Cassandria – an engineer in Alexander's service, he is said to have written his account of the expedition when aged eighty-four; his work is later than 301BC, since he mentioned the battle of Ipsus, but he probably wrote before Ptolemy.

Ptolemy Soter – a senior commander and Bodyguard in Alexander's army, he may have been the king's illegitimate half-brother; he later became pharaoh of Egypt and died in 282BC; he probably wrote his history in the last decade or so of his life; it is likely that it was not published during his lifetime, but rather during the reign of his son, Philadelphus, and then only in an edited form.

Apart from these six authors, numerous other contemporaries of Alexander wrote accounts of his campaigns, but they have proved relatively less influential and none survives in more than a handful of fragments. The most important of them may be identified as follows: Chares of Mytilene, who was Alexander's chamberlain, Medius of Larissa and Marsyas of Pella, who were among Alexander's Friends and Ephippus of Olynthus, who may have served as a

A Note on the Sources

commander of mercenaries in Alexander's army. It seems that Alexander's official journal, known as the Ephemerides and compiled by his secretary Eumenes of Cardia, was also published after the king's death.

Principal Surviving Ancient Sources

Diodorus Siculus – Greek historian of the mid-first century BC; Book 17 of his universal history (*Bibliotheca*) is dedicated to the period of Alexander's reign and is essentially a greatly abbreviated version of Cleitarchus.

Curtius – Roman historian most probably writing under Claudius in the mid-first century AD; he was largely translating Cleitarchus into Latin, but he was also aware of other primary sources and interjected various personal comments.

Plutarch – Greek essayist and biographer active around AD100; author of a life of Alexander based on over twenty primary sources; he also wrote two substantial essays and a few other articles on the king amongst his *Moralia*.

Arrian – governor of Cappadocia under Hadrian between AD130-138, his *Campaigns of Alexander* is predominantly a synthesis of Aristobulus and Ptolemy. It is accurate on military dispositions but suppresses biographical anecdotes. He also wrote the *Indica*, which is substantially an epitome of Nearchus, and a history of *Events after Alexander*, which only survives in fragments and a cursory epitome by Photius.

The Alexander Romance (Pseudo-Callisthenes) – version of Alexander's career attributed implausibly to Callisthenes by some manuscripts, but actually compiled from a diverse collection of earlier legends and propaganda in Egypt in the third century AD; it nevertheless preserves some authentic information lost from the orthodox historical tradition.

Justin (Epitome of Trogus) – epitome made by Justin in the 4th century AD of a universal history by Trogus, a Roman of republican sympathies, who probably wrote at the end of the first century BC or very early in the first century AD; Trogus nursed an antipathy towards Alexander, leading him to augment Cleitarchus with several other hostile and defamatory sources; Justin was a careless epitomiser, introducing many flagrant errors.

Metz Epitome – Sections 1-86 are an episodic Latin epitome of Cleitarchus between the death of Darius and Alexander's arrival in the Indus delta; the rest, known as the *Liber de Morte*, is derived from a 4th century BC pamphlet describing Alexander's death (also the source for the end sections of Pseudo-Callisthenes); the epitome dates from the late 4th or early 5th century AD; the sole manuscript was destroyed by Allied bombing in 1944.

Other ancient writers provide important supplementary information, especially: Strabo, Athenaeus, Polyaenus, Aelian, Polybius, Lucian and Pliny the Elder.

1. Prologue: A Concise Biography of Alexander

Birth

In the late summer of 356BC news of three happy events was brought by courier to Chalcidice and presented to Philip of Macedon as he celebrated his recent capture of the town of Potidaea. His general Parmenion had won a great battle against the Illyrians on the northern border. His horse had been victorious in the races at the Olympic games. Most significantly, his queen, Olympias, had given birth to an heir for his throne on the 6th of the Attic month Hecatombaeon, approximately 20th July in the Julian calendar. The boy was named Alexander, after brothers of both his mother and his father.

The putative ancestry of the newborn prince equipped him with an exalted pedigree. His mother, Olympias, famed for her pet serpents, was a daughter of the Molossian royal house from Epirus, known as the Aeacidae. They traced their family tree back to shining Achilles, the foremost hero of Homer's Iliad. Neither was Philip's genealogy any less illustrious. The kings of Macedon claimed descent from Argeas and from Temenus, a ruler of Argos in the Peloponnese, and thence back to Heracles of the twelve labours. Therefore they are called Argeads and Temenids or else more generally Heraclids. Whereas we might be suspicious of the authenticity of the more exotic of these relationships with the mythological paragons of Greek heroism, Alexander will probably have accepted their literal truth with the same unflinching credulity with which we still embrace our own family fables.

Youth

The most celebrated and illuminating parable of Alexander's youth is the taming of Bucephalus ("Oxhead" in English - Figure 1.1). The story goes that Philonicus of Thessaly offered a fabulously handsome horse to Philip at the correspondingly illustrious price of thirteen talents (325kg of silver). But the horse seemed wild and unbroken. Alexander, though, had noticed that the beast was starting at the dancing of its own shadow. So he wagered with Philip for the price of the horse that he could tame the thrashing stallion. Patiently, he calmed the animal and turned him to face into the sun, then, quietly casting off his chlamys, he vaulted lightly onto its back, and successfully galloped Bucephalus down the field and back again to rejoin his exultant father.

Though superficially mythological in tone, this tale is full of authentic detail, such as Alexander coaxing Bucephalus via pressure from his legs, which is a notably correct technique for bareback riding. We also know from the hunting mural above the façade of Philip's tomb at Aegae, that a chlamys-style mantel and little else was the standard garb of the teenage pages of the Macedonian king's entourage. Furthermore, Aulus Gellius tells us that Chares, Alexander's chamberlain, mentioned Bucephalus' price of thirteen talents. The taming is therefore in all probability an authentic incident, which illustrates the exemplary horsemanship skills that were to prove a key feature of Alexander's subsequent career. Most of his great victories were won with dashing cavalry charges, which is astonishing, because the stirrup was not invented for almost another thousand years. Lacking stirrups a cavalryman cannot grip his lance rigidly through its impact, else he would be unseated by the reactive force. Yet Alexander's cavalry managed successfully to charge enemy infantry formations with lances time after time. The implication is that their horsemanship had been raised to such a pitch that it compensated for their lack of stirrups.

Figure 1.1. Alexander taming Bucephalus (by F. Schommer, c. 1900)

In about 342BC when Alexander was fourteen Philip invited Aristotle, already ranked among the leading thinkers of the age, to Macedon to become Alexander's tutor. The philosopher charged a royal fee: the restitution of Stagira, his place of birth, which Philip had himself previously destroyed. The precinct of the nymphs near Mieza was assigned to be their academy and here they were joined by a select group of Alexander's comrades and contemporaries. Aristotle is said to have educated the Prince in certain esoteric arts of philosophy, such as eristics, in addition to the standard curriculum. He also inculcated a knowledge and love of herbal medicine in his pupil and edited a special version of Homer's Iliad as a present for him, which is known as the recension of the casket, since it was later kept beside Alexander's bed in a fabulously ornate coffer captured among the treasures of the king of Persia.

There is an ancient legend that Alexander and his friend Hephaistion attended the Olympic games at Pisa in the Peloponnese in 340BC. More certainly we know that later in the summer of that year Alexander was appointed Regent in Macedon, whilst his father was away besieging Byzantium. Fortuitously, it seems a neighbouring tribe called the Maedi chose this opportunity to launch an uprising, which Alexander took great satisfaction in quashing. Having captured their city, he drove them off the land and founded a Macedonian colony on the site, which he was pleased to name Alexandropolis, the city of Alexander. It was the first of many such foundations.

Chaeronea

Philip was a master politician as well as a consummate strategist and general. He deployed these abilities unremittingly in the cause of uniting the Greeks under his leadership. But there was resistance, stirred and incubated by the demagogues of the Athenian Assembly, so on the 2nd August 338BC Philip's policies culminated in a fateful battle against the Athenians and the Thebans near the town of Chaeronea in Boeotia. It seems that Philip had already learnt to trust in the talents of his precocious heir, for he gave Alexander command of his left wing (probably cavalry). Philip himself led the Macedonian right, which confronted the less experienced Athenian troops. The king retreated his phalanx formations in good order and the Athenians surged forward in pursuit. The effect was to thin the centre of the Greek allies, where the Athenian and Theban lines met. Alexander charged precipitously into the gap and turned upon the flank of the battle-hardened Theban levies. The sources assert that it was Alexander who effectively won the battle when the Theban lines gave way and broke under the pressure of his assault. Only the most resilient Theban regiment stood its ground. This was the Sacred Band, composed entirely of pairs of lovers and generally believed to have been the toughest troops in the world at this time. These were the soldiers who had destroyed the supposedly invincible Spartans at Leuctra and Mantinea a few decades earlier. Since they disdained to surrender, Alexander was compelled virtually to annihilate them:

only a handful were captured and survived the battle. The particular significance of Alexander's role at Chaeronea is that it lends the lie to the view promulgated by some that Alexander's victories were exclusively over the decadent forces of tottering oriental empires, such that he never vanquished truly tough opponents.

In the aftermath of the battle Philip sent his son as his emissary to the Athenians, ably assisted by his veteran commander, Antipater. The king was already planning a campaign to free Ionia from the Persian Empire, so it was essential to pacify his Greek opponents in order to secure his rear. The young prince was fêted by the anxious populace once they were confident of Macedon's mercy. They seem to have commissioned a commemorative portrait sculpture of their guest, of which a version has been found in the Acropolis. During this, his sole recorded visit to the city of the owls, Alexander probably visited the Academy, Plato's school, of which Xenocrates had recently become the head. This philosopher had previously acted as an Athenian envoy to Macedon and he maintained close ties through correspondence with Alexander, who later sent him a present of money, though Xenocrates accepted only half a talent (thirteen kilograms of silver), just one percent of the gift.

Estrangement and Reconciliation

In the next year relations between Alexander and his father were fractured by Philip's amorous pursuit of Cleopatra, the virgin niece of his general Attalus. The affair culminated ineluctably in Philip's marriage to the object of his desire. Perhaps in an attempt to persuade Alexander that his position remained secure, the prince was invited to the wedding feast. But this diligent plan went horribly awry, when the drunken Attalus toasted the newlyweds with the wish that their union should provide a true-born heir for the kingdom. The erstwhile brooding prince was suddenly incensed. Casting his cup at Attalus, he yelled, "Wretched man, are you calling me a bastard?" Philip was furious at this disturbance of his nuptials. Though much the worse for drink, he staggered towards Alexander with sword drawn, but stumbled and fell. Alexander mocked his father, observing, "This is the man who would cross from Europe to Asia, yet cannot walk from one table to another without losing his balance."

Alexander promptly collected his mother and fled into exile. He left Olympias in her homeland of Epirus. Then he pressed on northwards into the wild kingdoms of Illyria. But he was soon reconciled with Philip through the medium of Demaratus of Corinth, a family friend, so he returned to the court at Pella.

Nevertheless tension and distrust persisted between father and son. In 337BC Philip entered into negotiations to arrange the marriage of his imbecile son Arrhidaeus to the daughter of Pixodarus, the Persian satrap of Caria. This diplomatic manoeuvre was probably intended to support Philip's prospective invasion of Asia Minor, but Alexander felt sufficiently estranged that he was credulous of the allegation that Philip was trying to sideline him from the succession. Consequently, the prince sent the actor Thessalus as his own envoy to Pixodarus offering himself as the groom instead. Pixodarus naturally preferred a union with the heir apparent, but Philip blocked the scheme as soon as he learnt of it. He berated Alexander in the presence of Philotas, the son of his general Parmenion and as further punishment he sent a group of four or five of the most senior members of Alexander's faction at court into exile.

The Assassination of Philip

Olympias had probably been stirring up antipathy towards Philip in her homeland of Epirus. Her marriage had been a key element in the political alliance forged between Macedon and Epirus by Philip, but she may even have been formally divorced at this time. Her brother Alexander was then king in Epirus and the breakdown of his sister's marriage might have been seen as constituting a personal affront to him. Philip empathised with his brother-in-law's predicament and astutely offered the hand of his daughter Cleopatra in marriage to her Epirote uncle. So it was that on the occasion of the Autumnal Equinox in 336BC the two royal families gathered in Aegae to celebrate the nuptials. But it was above all to be a celebration of Philip's virtual apotheosis. The pinnacle of hubris was surmounted when a statue of the king was displayed in the procession accompanied by sculptures of the twelve deities of the Olympian pantheon. Philip himself chose to flaunt his popularity by entering unescorted by his bodyguard into the theatre, but death stalked in his footsteps.

A youth named Pausanias had formerly been beloved by the king, but, when displaced by another boy, had accused his rival of effeminacy and promiscuity, which led to the other's virtual suicide in an attempt to vindicate his machismo during the next battle. Attalus, who had been a close friend of the slaughtered rival, invited Pausanias to a party, got him thoroughly drunk, then had him raped by his muleteers. Pausanias sought to retaliate by charging Attalus before the king, but Philip refused to punish a man who was not only a key figure at court, but also his uncle-in-law. Pausanias thus came to blame the king himself for his disgrace. Nurturing a cold and implacable anger, he awaited such an opportunity as that presented by the marriage festivities to wreak his revenge. He stabbed and killed Philip as he walked through a narrow passage into the theatre, then fled towards horses posted to assist his escape, but tripped and fell before he reached them. He was caught and cut down by a group of the bodyguards, who had chased after him. These men included Perdiccas and Leonnatus, who were close associates of Alexander. Some have suspected that Alexander was implicated in the plot and that his friends killed Pausanias to silence him. But this makes no sense, because Diodorus says that Pausanias would have reached the horses and escaped had he not had the misfortune to stumble. Justin claims that Olympias organised the steeds, but this is also likely to be malicious rumour, because Pausanias was a high-ranking Macedonian and could easily have arranged mounts for himself. Significantly, Aristotle effectively absolved Alexander of responsibility for his father's death in his treatise on Politics.

Alexander was promptly proclaimed as the new king and quickly moved to secure his throne through the elimination of his most prominent enemies. In particular, Attalus, who was in joint-command of an expeditionary force in Asia Minor at that juncture, was summarily executed.

Quashing the Rebellions

The Greek city-states were impelled towards rebellion by the news of Philip's demise, for few imagined that his supposedly callow successor might prove an even tougher adversary. But in the autumn of 336BC Alexander undertook a forced marched southwards in full battle array and appeared before Thebes barely preceded by the rumour of his approach. Athens was intimidated into quiescence and even the ferocious Spartans stopped short of outright opposition, being satisfied merely to declare themselves aloof from the Macedonian hegemony. Most cities were supine in their obeisance to the young king. An Assembly in Corinth elected Alexander to replace his father as general plenipotentiary of the prospective Panhellenic expedition to free the Ionian Greeks from the Persian Empire.

In the late spring of the following year (335BC) Alexander marched north against the Illyrians and the Triballians, for Philip's death had stimulated unrest among these traditional antagonists of the Macedonian nation. Alexander first defeated a Thracian force, which sought to thwart his advance by occupying a key ridge. The defenders rolled carts down towards Alexander's army, but he ordered his men to break formation to allow them to career harmlessly through the ranks or else to crouch low beneath their shields, such that the carts were deflected over them. Having thus gained access to enemy territory, he crushed the Triballians and pursued them to the river Danube, which he crossed by night using small fishing boats and rafts made from leather tent covers stuffed with straw. The Getae, the tribe that occupied the northern bank, were intimidated into headlong flight. Hearing of disaffection among the Illyrian kings, formerly subjugated by Philip, Alexander marched southwest to invest the city of Pellium, which had been occupied by the enemy. The Illyrians sought to break the siege, but Alexander repulsed them and chased the survivors into the mountains.

In August news reached Alexander of a fresh revolt in Thebes. A group of banished Thebans had returned in secret and murdered two members of the Macedonian garrison, who were based in the Cadmeia, the Theban Acropolis. Afterwards, they had roused their compatriots to renewed rebellion at a public meeting by proclaiming that Alexander had been killed in Illyria. But the king, still very much alive, immediately instigated a lightning march southwards through the mountain passes with his field army. He was within a day's march of Thebes before the citizens learnt of his approach and many refused to believe he was anywhere near until he actually appeared before its walls. Though the city had twice risen against him when sworn to peace, Alexander nevertheless demanded only that they should surrender the leaders of the revolt, whom he held accountable for the murder of his men. He promised an amnesty for all others who came over to his side, but the Thebans responded with an insolent demand that Alexander should hand over two of his officers, Antipater and Philotas, to them.

It would seem that Alexander was minded to allow the citizens a space of time to contemplate the seriousness of their predicament. However, a synthesis of the accounts of Diodorus and Arrian suggests that the defenders foolishly left a small postern gate unguarded in plain view of a Macedonian regiment led by Perdiccas. This officer, probably conscious of Alexander's policy of encouraging initiative, determined to assault the weak point before the opportunity should lapse. This small action escalated rapidly as both sides threw more and more troops into the fray. Ultimately, the Theban forces gave way and jammed their gates wide open with the flood of retreating soldiers. The Macedonian garrison, which had been walled-up within the Cadmeia, chose this moment to sally forth and assault the Thebans in their rear. From this point the fall of the city was assured, despite a final stand near the Ampheum. The Theban cavalry fled into the countryside, abandoning their infantry to be largely annihilated by Alexander's allied troops, who came from surrounding cities that had long been oppressed by Theban dominion. Thebes fell in early September 335BC.

Alexander convened a session of the Council of the League of Corinth to determine the fate of the city and its captured populace. At this meeting the Phocians, Plataeans, Thespians and Orchomenians, whose own cities had been destroyed by Thebes during her glory days in the preceding decades, were implacable in moving that Thebes herself should now be subjected to the same treatment. They won the vote, so Alexander implemented their sentence: enslaving the citizens and razing the city, though he took care to spare the holy shrines and the house and descendants of the poet Pindar.

Alexander, as leader of the League, clearly bears the ultimate responsibility for the destruction of Thebes. However, the Thebans had proclaimed an alliance with the Persian Great King against Macedon, which Alexander would have considered a particularly despicable act of treachery against himself as a fellow Greek. Moreover, Thebes had been condemned by due legal process, so Alexander could hardly overthrow the decision without undermining the Council. Nevertheless, there is evidence that the king felt some remorse, not only in the stories that he intervened to save various Thebans such as Timocleia, but also because he is said later to have released Theban mercenaries, whom he caught fighting for the Persians, despite imprisoning Greek mercenaries from other cities. Plutarch relates that Alexander excused them with the words, "These alone, because of us, have neither city nor land left to them."

The city-states of the south were readily pacified and reconciled with Alexander in the aftermath of the catastrophic downfall of Thebes. Alexander returned northwards, but took time on the way to visit the oracle at Delphi, for he was keen to seek signs of divine favour for his expedition against the Persian Empire. The priestess, known as the Pythia, was initially uncooperative and insensible to Alexander's charm. But when in frustration he sought to drag her to the temple, she simpered, "You are invincible, my son!" Hearing this, Alexander was satisfied and declared he had no need of further prophecy (Figure 1.2). He left a present of 150 gold coins minted by Philip at the shrine.

Figure 1.2. Alexander coerces the Pythia at the Delphic Oracle (by A. Castaigne 1898)

'Tis mute, the word they went to hear on high Dodona mountain
When winds were in the oakenshaws and all the cauldrons tolled,

And mute's the midland navel-stone beside the singing fountain,
And echoes list to silence now where gods told lies of old.
I took my question to the shrine that has not ceased from speaking,
The voice within that tells the truth and tells it twice as plain;
And from the cave of oracles I heard the priestess shrieking
That she and I should surely die and never live again.   A. E. Housman

The Invasion of Asia and the Battle of the Granicus

All was now set to begin the great adventure (the course of which is traced in the map of Figure 1.3). In about May of 334BC Alexander crossed the Hellespont into Asia with an army of Macedonians and Greek allies nearly 40,000 strong, including around 5000 cavalry. On approaching the eastern shore at Abydos Alexander cast a spear onto the beach, an Homeric gesture symbolising that the Asian conquests should be considered spear-won land.

Alexander's first objective was the ancient citadel of Troy, steeped in poetry and myth. It had much the same resonance for Alexander as Jerusalem has for a Christian. Here at the tombs of the heroes Achilles and Patroclus he offered a highly symbolic sacrifice jointly with his companion Hephaistion.

Meanwhile, the Great King, Darius III, had spared no expense in employing the most renowned mercenary general of the age to organise the Persian defences against Alexander's expedition. This man was Memnon of Rhodes and he was forthright in his advice to the Persian governors of the region that they should on no account risk a battle until a relative deficiency in infantry of the Persian forces could be made good, for they numbered merely 20,000. But it offended against the honour of the Persian lords to refuse to contest Alexander's advance, especially when they possessed a clear numerical advantage in their 20,000 cavalry. Consequently, they deployed their army across Alexander's path in what they hoped was a readily defensible position along the steep further bank of the river Granicus. Between around late May to early June of 334BC the first major engagement of the campaign was fought at this spot when Alexander launched a head-on assault across the river.

He led the attack with his crack cavalry squadrons against the position of the key Persian commanders in the centre of their line, but for a while the outcome hung in the balance as the Macedonians were almost thwarted by the steep and slippery bank as they clambered up out of the rushing stream. Alexander himself might have been decapitated from behind by Spithridates, Persian Governor (Satrap) of Lydia, except that Cleitus the Black sundered the offending arm from its shoulder at an opportune moment (Figure 1.4). Nevertheless, the Persian cavalry eventually fell back and Alexander's forces crashed on into the enemy's exposed infantry, who were mostly Greeks themselves. Many mercenaries were slain, such that resistance soon disintegrated and Memnon fled the field with the remnants of his forces.

A Concise Biography of Alexander

Figure 1.3. Alexander's Empire

Figure 1.4. Cleitus saves Alexander at the Battle of the Granicus (after Charles le Brun)

The Ionian Littoral

Sardis and Ephesus quickly surrendered to Alexander in the wake of his victory at the Granicus, but Memnon now sought to bolster a stand by the Persian commander at Miletus by sending in the Great King's Mediterranean fleet of 400 ships. However, Alexander's smaller fleet managed to reach the area first and were able to blockade the approachs, whilst the Macedonian army stormed the Milesian citadel. The Persian armada attempted to entice Alexander's fleet into a naval engagement in open waters, where their numerical superiority could be deployed to good effect. But Alexander refused to risk the likelihood of defeat and instead elected to disband his navy. He was short of cash to pay them at the time and he had become reconciled to the fact that he could not hope directly to challenge the powerful Persian fleet to win control of the sea-lanes. Out of expediency, the king declared an intention to defeat his enemy's naval forces by capturing their bases on the land: specifically, the ports of the eastern Mediterranean seaboard.

Towards the Autumn of 334BC, as Alexander advanced southwards down the Ionian coast, Memnon next determined to check his progress at the port of Halicarnassus in Caria, which offered the advantages of a readily defensible location, imposing ramparts and an excellent harbour. A protracted and bloody siege ensued. Alexander employed sophisticated engines progressively to level a long section of the city wall, whilst the defenders vigorously opposed his assaults by making sallies in force with the aim of destroying his engines. Eventually, however, Memnon was forced to conclude that the extent of the damage to the walls and the attrition of his forces made it inevitable that the city would soon fall, so he evacuated most of his troops to the island of Kos, whilst setting fire to large sections of Halicarnassus to cover his retreat. Following the consequential capitulation of the city, Alexander pursued a policy of appointing local rulers by making Queen Ada of the Carian royal dynasty the satrap of the liberated city. She in her turn did him the honour of formally adopting him as her son. This was one among numerous vaguely Oedipal relationships, which Alexander enjoyed with a succession of older women, though they seem all to have been Platonic affairs.

As the winter of 334-333BC set in Persian resistance along the Ionian littoral effectively collapsed. The cities of Caria and Lycia willingly surrendered to Alexander, lured by his restitution of self-government in the form of local democracies to the Greek inhabitants and persuaded by the accumulating evidence that Persian power in the region had genuinely been broken. Callisthenes, Alexander's court historian, seems to have popularised a story that the sea itself did obeisance to Alexander as he marched along the coast of Pamphylia, though others wrote that it was merely blown aside from his path by a stiff northerly wind. Nevertheless, the Macedonians encountered sporadic opposition in Pisidia, where most of the local inhabitants were not ethnically Greek. For them, Alexander's Pan-Hellenic crusade held less allure. In this region the cities seem to have sided with either the Persians or the Greeks according to local tribal rivalries. Though ignored by many modern histories, a fairly significant battle was fought at Sagalassus, in which Alexander overwhelmed his Pisidian opponents.

Gordium and Tarsus

Early in 333BC Alexander invaded Phrygia and in May he reached Gordium, where he was met by several thousand reinforcements from Macedon. In the temple on the acropolis Alexander was confronted by an ancient conundrum. A knot made of cornel bark fibres tied a wagon pole to its yoke (Figure 1.5). Legend foretold that he who should succeed in unravelling the knot would also succeed to the throne of Asia, an irresistible incentive to Alexander's ambitions. However, the end of the rope in the knot had been tucked back into its core, making it impossible to know where to start. Some say that in frustration Alexander hacked the knot apart with his sword. But Aristobulus wrote that he simply extracted the pole-pin, a bolt that had run through the knot, and that this enabled him to remove the yoke, thus satisfying the stipulation of the prophecy.

Figure 1.5. Cutting the Gordian knot (by A. Castaigne 1898)

Meanwhile back in the Aegean, Memnon was leading a naval counter-offensive, in which he seized the islands of Chios and Lesbos, but he fell ill and died whilst blockading Mytilene. His nephew Pharnabazus continued to prosecute the war in the islands and intimidated Tenedos near the mouth of the Hellespont into expelling Alexander's mercenaries. However, Alexander had by now ordered Antipater to re-assemble his fleet to meet the burgeoning threat to his supply lines and communications. The defence of the islands was championed by Proteas, who led a flotilla in a victorious surprise attack upon a Persian squadron anchored at Siphnos.

Meanwhile Alexander marched on via Ancyra and through southern Cappadocia, crossing the Taurus Mountains into Cilicia in about September of 333BC. From amidst the mountain passes Alexander led a detachment of cavalry and his most mobile troops in a lightning dash to Tarsus, for the city had been threatened with plunder and destruction by a Persian garrison commanded by Arsames, who was now forced instead to flee without doing serious harm. However, Alexander had seemingly contracted a fever in the mountains, which he now sought to allay by bathing in the chill waters of the river Cydnus, where it ran through Tarsus. Instead he caught a cramp and his illness worsened until his life seemed threatened. At this point one of his doctors, Philip of Acarnania, proposed to administer a purgative potion. But Alexander now received a letter from Parmenion, which warned that Darius had bribed Philip to poison him. Though some ancient accounts (probably deriving from Cleitarchus) exercise dramatic licence in claiming that Alexander handed the letter to Philip and simultaneously drank his medicine, it would seem more plausible that the king showed the letter to the physician to test his reaction a little prior to actually swallowing the drug. Alexander seems to have lost consciousness for several days after imbibing this remedy, so some suspicion lingers regarding its nature and effectiveness. However, the king subsequently recovered rapidly. Philip was consequently credited with his cure and was appointed as one of Alexander's inner circle of Companions.

Some have inferred that Alexander's illness was malaria, apparently because serious symptoms were manifested following bathing and mosquitoes are associated with still water (which they need in order to reproduce). However, malaria has an incubation period of at least a week, whereas we are told that Alexander had only just arrived in Tarsus after a hectic descent from the mountain passes. Rather the evidence is suggestive of a feverish gastro-intestinal illness, resembling typhoid and attributable to consumption of contaminated food or drink either before or during the gallop down from the mountains.

The Battle of Issus

News of the death of Memnon had spurred Darius into raising an imperial army, which he now led in person to confront Alexander. The Great King entered Cilicia in November via an inland pass, but Alexander had just marched south into Syria by the well-trodden coastal route. Despite the evidence that Alexander was surprised when the Persian army was suddenly manifested in his rear, straddling his communications, this turned out to be an advantageous predicament for the Macedonians. It compelled Darius to fight in a relatively narrow coastal strip, where he was unable to deploy his superior numbers to outflank Alexander. Some features of the timing of Alexander's movements suggest that he may have been manoeuvring to achieve such an outcome, for he seems to have dawdled in Cilicia after hearing of the approach of Darius, despite having recuperated from his illness. However the Persians' capture and butchering of the invalids that the Macedonians had left behind at the town of Issus argues against Alexander having foreseen the exact direction of his adversary's approach.

Alexander retraced his route northwards whilst Darius advanced fifteen miles south from Issus to the north bank of the river Pinarus. Here in November 333BC the armies clashed in a major engagement known to history as the battle of Issus. In this fight Alexander's forces were seriously outnumbered, probably by at least four to one, although figures in some sources numbering the Persian horde at above half a million are likely to be exaggerations. Ironically, there were probably more ethnically Greek troops on the Persian side than fought for Alexander. For instance, a contingent of thirty thousand Greek mercenaries made up some of the toughest of Darius' regiments near the centre of his ranks.

Darius had stationed some of his weaker troops in the rough, rising ground on the inland side of the battlefield. He also positioned a large section of his archers in this area, in order to compensate for the relative fragility of his main battle line there. The Persian forces were drawn up behind the river Pinarus, which in ancient times flowed diagonally in a northwesterly direction across the coastal plain from the foothills to the sea on the western flank of the battlefield.

Among the Macedonian ranks Alexander took the traditional post of the king commanding the right wing. He interpreted the opposition of the Persian archers upon this wing as an indication of the poor quality of Darius' infantry in the vicinity. Furthermore, the obliquity of the river made it relatively inevitable that first contact between the armies would occur on the Macedonian right. Alexander therefore opened the battle by personally leading a charge against the Persian left, which panicked the archers into fleeing back through the Persian ranks and rapidly collapsed the entire Persian left wing.

In the centre, the Macedonian phalanx found that the rough ground tended to break up their formation, creating gaps that were eagerly exploited by the Greek mercenaries opposing them. Similarly there was vicious fighting towards the coast where the Persian horse were confronted by Alexander's Thessalian cavalry. Judiciously, on perceiving the pressure upon his own centre and left, Alexander abandoned his pursuit of the Persian left and wheeled his powerful right wing around to roll up the Persian flank, ploughing towards their centre, where Darius now found himself assailed from two sides. Eventually, as the Macedonians steadily fought their way to within yards of his position, he turned his chariot and began to retreat. The sight of their leader abandoning the field instigated a general rout of the Persian forces, in which many of them were overtaken and killed by the relentless Macedonians.

Darius switched from his chariot to a cavalry mount and escaped through the mountain passes. However, his camp was quickly overwhelmed and there the Macedonians captured most of the Great King's close family, including his mother, his wife, a pair of daughters and an infant son. On returning late in the evening from his abortive pursuit of Darius, Alexander retired to the Great King's former tent, but was afterwards rudely disturbed by a freakish caterwauling of women's voices emanating from close at hand. On being advised that these were Darius' ladies mourning his assumed demise, Alexander dispatched Leonnatus to reassure them and to promise them respectful treatment. The next day Alexander himself decided to pay his respects to the Persian queens, so he approached their tent in the company of Hephaistion. On account of the latter's superior stature, Sisygambis, the mother of Darius, mistakenly did him obeisance and was much embarrassed when the error was pointed out by her eunuchs. Alexander sought to put her at ease with the words, "You were not mistaken mother, for he too is Alexander."

Damascus and Sidon

Alexander dispatched Parmenion with an advance party on a mission to capture Damascus. He was successful in securing the treasure from Darius' war chest and also in apprehending the wives and families of many of the Persian lords. The former was instrumental in alleviating the financial strain upon Alexander arising from the maintenance of a large army in the field. Among the latter was Barsine, Alexander's future mistress.

In December 333BC many of the Syrian coastal cities and also the island of Cyprus transferred their allegiance to Alexander. At the ancient port of Sidon the local petty king was a Darius loyalist, who was only persuaded to surrender by pressure from the populace. Accordingly, Alexander determined that he should be replaced and delegated the task of appointing his successor to his companion Hephaistion, whose choice eventually alighted upon an impoverished gardener, Abdalonymus, who was distantly related to the Sidonian royal family. This tale of rags to riches would be of incidental interest, were it not for the discovery of a marble sarcophagus of astounding magnificence in the Sidonian royal cemetery in 1887. It currently resides in the museum at Istanbul, where it is known as the Alexander Sarcophagus, but this only refers to the presence of an unambiguous depiction of the king wearing the lion-scalp helm of Heracles amongst the sculptural masterpieces adorning its sides. It is probably the tomb of the humble Abdalonymus, through the medium of which the grateful monarch paid homage to his benefactor.

The Siege of Tyre

A little further south the impregnable fortified islet of Tyre tried various gestures of appeasement towards Alexander as he approached, sending him a golden crown, provisions and envoys promising allegiance. Alexander smiled upon these gifts and salutations, but to test the fidelity of the city he requested that he should be admitted to its ancient temple to sacrifice to Melqart, the Tyrian Heracles, since Heracles was also the legendary founder of the Macedonian royal house. The envoys demurred, suggesting that Alexander might care to visit an alternative temple on the mainland. Sensing duplicity, Alexander issued an ultimatum that either he should be allowed to visit the island or else he would destroy Tyre. The envoys withdrew to consult with their compatriots, who, thinking their island unassailable, opted for defiance. By this decision in January 332BC there began the most epic siege in all of ancient history.

The Macedonians were confronted by the intimidating prospect of assaulting a heavily fortified island situated some seven hundred metres offshore, the inhabitants of which were still masters of the sea at the outset. Lacking sufficient ships for a naval engagement, Alexander initially prosecuted the siege principally through the construction of a gigantic mole designed to link the mainland with the island-town. This was easily extended through the shallows within covering range of the Macedonian artillery, but progress slowed to a crawl in the deep part of the channel, where also the Tyrian ships were able to attack the construction crews. Alexander erected towers at either corner of the leading edge of the mole to protect his workers, but the Tyrians sent fire ship to incinerate them and a storm assisted in the partial demolition of the causeway. Dauntless as ever, Alexander broadened the mole, so that it could accommodate more towers and he set about collecting a great fleet to maintain a blockade on the Tyrian harbours. Matters began to tip decisively in Alexander's favour, when large sections of the Persian fleet in the Mediterranean went over to him, mainly because he now held most of their homeports.

In the course of the siege Alexander sent envoys to the Tyrians, seeking to persuade them to surrender on reasonable terms, but the defenders foully murdered these men in violation of sacred law and threw their bodies into the sea. It is also recorded that the Tyrians captured a Macedonian ship sailing from Sidon and executed its entire crew, casting these men from their parapets too. The Macedonians were incensed, but eventually their mole came within spear range of the walls of Tyre and they assembled a sufficient fleet to confine the Tyrian vessels to their port. The Tyrians now resorted to tactics that further provoked the Macedonians. They poured red-hot sand down upon their attackers, which, seeping between the soldiers' mail and their skin, virtually flayed its victims alive.

After seven months of tireless endeavour and dejecting setbacks, in July 332BC Alexander placed catapults and ramming engines aboard some of his ships and succeeded in battering the south-facing walls of Tyre until a wide section crumbled. Then the Macedonians launched a general attack, using ships with gangways, which were lowered across the breaches (Figure 1.6). Simultaneously, Alexander's Cyprian and Phoenician allied fleets attacked the Tyrian harbours and forced their mouths. A ferocious sack of the city ensued in which some 6000 of the Tyrians were slain. Alexander may have crucified up to another 2000 of the leading male citizens in retribution for the summary executions of his own men during the siege. The surviving Tyrians, between 13,000 and 30,000 of them, were sold into slavery. Only envoys from the Tyrian colony of Carthage and a few who had sought sanctuary in the temples were freed.

Figure 1.6. The Siege of Tyre (1696)

Although the mole may not have been quite complete when Tyre fell, it subsequently silted up forming an isthmus, which permanently connected the islet with the mainland. The modern condition of Tyre as a peninsula is one of the most tangible legacies of Alexander's campaigns.

At around this time letters were exchanged between Alexander and Darius, the latter offering the western half of the Persian Empire, his daughter's hand in marriage and 10,000 Talents worth of treasure (250 tonnes of silver) in settlement of the war. However, Alexander insisted that Darius should acknowledge him as his overlord, which Darius refused to accept. Josephus, a 1st century AD Jewish historian, recorded that Alexander paid his respects at the temple in Jerusalem as he progressed southwards through Palestine. Although uncorroborated by other sources, the claim is plausible, since Alexander generally took great care to respect local religious sensibilities.

The Siege of Gaza

The last serious opposition that Alexander encountered on the Mediterranean seaboard came at the fortress of Gaza, where a eunuch called Batis had remained loyal to Darius, recruiting a force of Arab mercenaries to defend his citadel. In besieging the town during October of 332BC Alexander constructed a wide ramp against the south-facing walls and undermined the battlements in other sectors, since the earth was friable and easily dug. Alexander sustained minor wounds to his shoulder and his leg in various assaults. The king was often found in the thick of the fighting. That he shared in their dangers and hardships was one key reason amongst others that his men loved him and were eventually prepared to follow him to the ends of the Earth.

According to a fragment attributed to Hegesias of Magnesia writing about 30 years after the events, the leaders of Gaza plotted to assassinate Alexander. During a sally they sent forward an Arab who pretended to surrender to the king. However, on kneeling before Alexander, the assassin drew forth a sword concealed beneath his corselet and stabbed at the king, who just barely managed to twist aside, such that the wound was slight. When the Macedonians finally forced their way into the city, they killed many of the defenders and the women and children were sold into slavery. Specially tough treatment was reserved for Batis, who was dragged behind Alexander's chariot in imitation of Achilles, when he dragged Hector's body behind his chariot before the walls of Troy. Alexander always made a point of dealing harshly with those guilty of treacherous behaviour.

Egypt and the Oracle at Siwa

In late November of 332BC Alexander entered Egypt. Some have been surprised by this apparent diversion from the theatre of the war against Darius, but this overlooks the fact that a general state of warfare and unrest still prevailed throughout the eastern Mediterranean. Egypt itself had recently been attacked by Amyntas, a Macedonian renegade, though the natives had slain him and wiped out his mercenaries. Alexander must have been anxious both to complete his control of the major Mediterranean ports and to secure the richest of all the nations that had thus far fallen within his grasp.

Egypt and Alexander found one another equally beguiling. The ancient civilisation of the Nile desperately needed a powerful champion, who would honour and respect its religion and preserve its temples and sacred monuments from pillagers and aggressors in a hostile world. Conversely, the yet intact Egypt of the Pharaohs appealed strongly to Alexander's senses of culture, style and mysticism. It was nice to be appreciated and even better that Egyptian sensibilities required that Alexander should be considered an honorary god, for apotheosis in emulation of the Homeric heroes was always an ardent ambition at the back of Alexander's mind. The Alexander Romance states that the Egyptians set Alexander on the throne of Hephaistos as king of Egypt, when he reached their capital at Memphis. Hephaistos is the Greek equivalent of Ptah, the chief god of Memphis. Arrian mentions that at Memphis Alexander sacrificed to the Apis bull, which was considered a manifestation of Ptah, and that he organised festivities. All this supports the view that Alexander underwent formal coronation as Pharaoh. Certainly, he was subsequently recognised as such in hieroglyphic inscriptions and temple reliefs.

Alexander was notably fond of oracles, so the relative proximity of one of the most famous of them all at the oasis of Siwa, just a few hundred miles west of the Nile valley, proved an irresistible temptation, especially since it was dedicated to the sun god Ammon-Re, whom the Greeks associated with Zeus, and was said to have been visited by Heracles and Perseus in their travels. The king led a small expedition of his companions along the Mediterranean coast to a point almost opposite the oasis, then the party struck south across the desert. They all but ran out of water, but were saved by a rare rainstorm. However, the weather also obliterated the signs, which had marked the route, so that the group became disoriented. Fate intervened again when a pair of ravens was spotted overhead, providing a bearing for the oasis by the course of their flight.

At the temple Alexander was greeted by the chief priest with the salutation "O pai Dios", which means "O son of Zeus". Plutarch suggests that this was an error for "O paidion" ("O my son"), but in Egypt "Sa-Re", which means "Son of the Sun", was the standard title preceding the Pharaoh's birth name, so "O pai Dios" seems more likely to have been a translation of this title into Greek.

Cleitarchus wrote that Alexander asked the oracle whether he was destined to rule the entire world and that he was assured that it was so fated. Also Alexander enquired whether all the murderers of his father had been punished. The oracle disputed the form of the question, asserting that his divine father could not be slain, but affirmed that all those responsible for the assassination of Philip had been dealt with. However, Callisthenes wrote that Alexander went alone into the temple of the oracle and Plutarch cites a letter from Alexander to Olympias, which stated that the king had received secret responses, so there is some doubt as to whether Cleitarchus' version is accurate. Arrian says only that Alexander received the answer that his heart desired.

Most probably on his return journey from Siwa in early February 331BC, Alexander founded the city of Alexandria, which later became the capital of Egypt and the greatest city in the Hellenistic world. Alexander's purpose was to connect his new realm of Egypt more intimately with the rest of his Mediterranean empire. He chose a site on a rocky isthmus between the sea and a large lake just to the west of the marshy Nile Delta. Here he found a natural harbour between the shore and the island of Pharos, which he probably recalled having been mentioned in Homer's Odyssey. The story is told that Alexander lacked supplies of chalk with which to mark the outlines of the future city, so he resorted to using barley meal from the army's rations. Flocks of birds alighted to feast on the meal, but Aristander the seer interpreted this omen as foretelling that the future city would be abundant in resources and would feed a multitude from many lands.

The Battle of Gaugamela

Curtius has a curious comment that Alexander planned a trip up the Nile to visit Karnak and wished to go as far as Ethiopia. There is also a strange story in the Alexander Romance about a meeting between Alexander and Queen Candace of Meroe in Ethiopia, but this might be an insertion from the Augustan age when a Roman Prefect of Egypt really did receive the submission of a Queen Candace of Meroe. At any rate, Alexander soon received word that Darius was gathering a vast host near Babylon, so he set forth from Egypt to confront the resurgent threat in the spring. He reached Thapsacus on the Euphrates in late July 331BC. Darius had entrusted Mazaeus, the Satrap of Babylon, with the defence of the river crossings, but either by accident or cunning design he failed to impede Alexander in traversing either the Euphrates or the Tigris. Darius carefully groomed a wide plain on the eastern side of the Tigris at Gaugamela about sixty miles north of Arbela as his chosen site for the climactic battle, thinking he would enjoy the full advantage of his superior numbers in such open terrain. Nevertheless, the Macedonians grimly advanced upon the Persian position, approaching from the northwest. On the 20th September by the Julian calendar just after 9pm local time there was a total eclipse of the Moon, which overawed the superstitious Macedonian troops, but the seers restored their confidence by declaring the Moon to be symbolic of the Persians, so its disappearance assuredly heralded their defeat.

Battle was joined eleven days after the eclipse on October 1st 331BC (Figure 1.7). The Persian horde numbered at least a quarter of a million men, including around 40,000 cavalry, and incorporating 200 scythed chariots plus a few elephants. Arrian tells us that Alexander's forces, though superior to Darius' troops in quality and experience, comprised no more than 7000 cavalry and 40,000 infantry. It was therefore inevitable that Alexander would be outflanked, so his dispositions were designed specifically to counteract this threat. Firstly, he put a strong second line behind his front line with orders to wheel about and confront any attack appearing in the rear of his advance. Secondly, he placed substantial units on both of his flanks trailing back obliquely from his main line. Both the Greek and the Persian cavalry units were concentrated upon the wings of their respective formations.

Alexander stationed himself on his right wing and advanced his ranks into the ground prepared by Darius. Well before the two armies closed, he began to march his entire force obliquely towards the right-hand edge of the groomed turf, simultaneously retarding the progress of his left wing such that his right would contact the Persians first. Darius was concerned lest his chariots be rendered useless in the rough, so he countered by rapidly extending his left wing to encompass Alexander's right and inhibit further lateral drift. He also attacked the Macedonian lines with his chariots, but they were rendered ineffectual by the disciplined response of the Macedonian troops, who shouted to frighten the horses and felled the charioteers in a hail of spears. A major engagement was then instigated on Alexander's right as his flanking cavalry charged the encompassing Persian horse and both sides reinforced. Consequently, a weak point developed in the Persian line between Darius in the centre and his left wing. This was the opportunity that Alexander had been manoeuvring to develop. The king led a charge of the entire Companion Cavalry in wedge formation into the weak area, then swung around towards the Persian centre and attacked Darius' position directly. As the Macedonians came within missile range of Darius, his charioteer was slain by a spear and, as his soldiers started to give way around him, he wheeled his chariot about and once again fled the field with Alexander in hot pursuit.

Figure 1.7. The Battle of Gaugamela (1696)

Meanwhile Parmenion, commanding Alexander's left wing, was fighting a desperate defensive action supported by the Thessalian cavalry, who were opposed by some of the best Persian mounted units led by Mazaeus. Concerned at one point that his line was close to collapse, he sent a messenger to

Alexander with a desperate plea for reinforcement. Alexander therefore broke off his pursuit of Darius and charged back to rescue his own left wing. On the way the Companions fought the most deadly engagement of the battle, when they inadvertently obstructed the retreat of a large contingent of Persian cavalry. By the time Alexander broke through to his left, the pressure on Parmenion had already been alleviated, since the Thessalians had counter-attacked and the rumour of Darius' departure had sapped the will of the Persian forces.

The Metropolis of Babylon

Alexander revived the pursuit, but Darius escaped into the mountains. Alexander had himself proclaimed King of Asia at Arbela and decided to march on Babylon, whither Mazaeus had withdrawn with his troops in good order, in preference to following Darius into difficult terrain. This city was at that time the greatest in the world, crammed with spectacular temples and palatial architecture, including the Tower of Babel, its 7-storey ziggurat and the famous Hanging Gardens on terraces above the river. It also enjoyed the protection of the strongest fortifications of any town in the Empire, so it must have been a matter for relief that Mazaeus came out to Alexander as a suppliant and surrendered his city into the hands of his new lord. Alexander in gratitude reinstated him as Satrap of Babylonia.

Figure 1.8. Alexander's entry into Babylon after a painting by Charles Le Brun.

A Concise Biography of Alexander

Alexander entered Babylon in a chariot and drove down the processional route, which had been strewn with flowers and garlands by the enthusiastic citizens, who cheered him from the walls and buildings. It was a moment of sublime triumph, nicely recaptured in a painting done for Louis XIV by Charles le Brun (Figure 1.8). Alexander was profoundly impressed by the magnificence of the city and the effusive welcome he received from its inhabitants. He determined to make Babylon the capital of his empire, as is shown by the mu-tau-rho monogram on those of Alexander's tetradrachm coins minted there: this stands for Metropolis, which is "mother-city" in Greek. Alexander's fêted reception in Babylon is rendered all the more poignant by the fact that it was also fated to be the scene of his death just seven and a half years later.

Alexander's army passed a relaxed month at Babylon in feasting and other more exotic entertainments, before moving on to Susa, which had also surrendered to Alexander's envoys shortly after Gaugamela. In this city, which he reached during December 331BC, Alexander took possession of a treasure equivalent to about 100 tonnes of gold. Such vast financial resources were an important enabling factor for the vast extent of Alexander's subsequent campaigns. He could now afford to make his dreams a reality.

The Invasion of Persia

In early January of 330BC Alexander was finally in a position to assault the province of Persis, the ancient heart of the Persian Empire. En route certain Uxian mountain tribes had the temerity to demand a toll from him in exchange for unimpeded passage through a pass. He requested that they meet him to accept payment within the pass, and then unobtrusively deployed several regiments of his own troops among the surrounding crags via mountain tracks. When the Uxians eventually showed up, they were routed and compelled to pay tribute to Alexander.

Ariobarzanes, the satrap of Persis, attempted to block Alexander's advance at a pass known as the Persian Gates. He constructed a wall across the narrowest part of the gorge and defended it stoutly against Alexander's initial assault. However, Alexander found among those locals rounded up by his troops a Greek-speaking man, originally from Lycia, who knew of a precipitous goat track that wound through the mountains to emerge behind the Persian positions. The king led a substantial force twelve miles along this route in the dead of night and appeared in the Persian rear at dawn. Bugles signalled the remainder of Alexander's forces simultaneously to launch a frontal attack upon the wall and Persian resistance collapsed in panic.

As Alexander approached Persepolis, the capital of Persis, in January of 330BC a horrible and pathetic sight confronted him. Up to 4000 mutilated Greeks approached his cavalcade waving fronds in supplication. They had been enslaved by former kings of Persia and compelled to labour at various crafts.

Figure 1.9. Thais inveigles Alexander into burning the Palace of Persepolis (G. Simoni)

Those limbs and other extremities, such as ears and noses, which were not required for the performance of their assigned individual duties, had been amputated to make the control and confinement of them easier, and they had been branded with Persian insignia. Alexander was deeply moved and burst into tears. He offered them repatriation to Greece with substantial presents of money, but they feared the reactions of their families and countrymen to their disfigurement and preferred to accept gifts of land and livestock amidst the Persian countryside.

Alexander's experience in encountering these men must have resembled that of the liberators of the Nazi concentration camps in Europe at the end of the Second World War. It is more than likely that it influenced Alexander's treatment of Persepolis, which was unusually harsh. Having captured the palace at the site together with another immense sum of treasure, Alexander burnt this spectacular edifice to the ground shortly before he left Persis in the spring of 330BC. The Vulgate sources tell us that at a drunken party Thais, an Athenian courtesan, encouraged Alexander to raze the building in revenge for the Persian sack of Athens 150 years earlier (Figure 1.9). However, Arrian states that Alexander claimed that he destroyed the palace at Persepolis symbolically to avenge the sacking of Athens and the burning of temples and also *to exact retribution for all the other injuries the Persians had done to the Greeks*. This might well originally have been an allusion to the mutilated Greek craftsmen and have indicated a desire to eradicate the scene of their degradation. Nevertheless, Alexander is said later to have regretted the conflagration.

The Macedonians also captured the old Persian capital at Parsagada, where Alexander made a special point of paying his respects at the tomb of Cyrus the Great, the founder of the Persian Empire.

The Pursuit of Darius

In May 330BC, once the passes were clear of snow, Alexander resumed his pursuit of Darius, who was holed up in Ecbatana amidst the mountains. The Persians lacked the strength to make another stand against Alexander, so Darius fled northeast towards the Caspian Gates when word was received of his approach. Initially, Darius had a lead of a full week, but Alexander was relentless in chasing after the former Great King, so he began to close the gap. Nevertheless, Darius got through the Caspian Gates ahead of the hunt, though many of his remaining followers were beginning to desert him. At this point a very curious situation transpired. Alexander suddenly halted before the Gates for five days, whilst on their far side Darius was dramatically deposed and fettered by a group of his satraps, led by Bessus, the lord of Bactria.

Alexander's sojourn seems out of character, because he was normally inexorable in such pursuits. A way of making sense of these events would be to postulate that Darius had sent a message to Alexander offering to surrender on terms and that Alexander had decided to accept the offer. This would also explain just why Darius was deposed at that point, for he would have had to announce the deal to his senior courtiers and they might well have found it unconscionable. According to Arrian the next thing that happened was that Alexander received word that Darius had been deposed. Instantly, Alexander resumed the chase.

In his letters Alexander had already implied that Darius could retain the throne of Persia, if he agreed to become Alexander's vassal. Had Darius publicly bowed down to Alexander and blessed his daughter's marriage to him, Alexander could have appointed him Satrap of Persis with little risk. Actually, this arrangement would have been invaluable to Alexander as a means of legitimising his rule with his new subjects. The practice of reappointing local magnates had already been established, for example, in the case of Mazaeus. It was to become one of Alexander's central policies in the following years.

In late July of 330BC, with Alexander hot on their trail, Bessus and his cronies murdered Darius. Our antique sources speak of Alexander's disappointment and anger on discovering Darius' corpse. If Bessus had believed that Alexander would have killed Darius, then he surely would have handed him over instead of criminalizing himself as a regicide. The implication is that Bessus had reason to think that Alexander would have employed a subjugated Darius further to legitimise his authority. This Bessus could not allow, for he had decided himself to lay claim to the throne of Persia.

Hyrcania and the Caspian Sea

Alexander now advanced his army into Hyrcania, a luxuriant land on the southern shores of the Caspian Sea, which fascinated the Greeks with its novel flora and fauna. One by one many of the dispossessed Persian lords surrendered to him and a beautiful and talented teenage eunuch entered Alexander's service on one such occasion, but Bessus had fled east towards his own satrapy of Bactria. In the meantime Alexander took steps to win the loyalty of those Persians whose hatred of Bessus made them his natural allies. For example, Oxathres, the brother of Darius, was appointed as one of Alexander's Friends and joined the Companion Cavalry.

In August, a local tribe called the Mardi disdained to offer their fealty to Alexander, insolence that provoked the king to attack them. In the course of skirmishing in the mountains the Mardians succeeded in stealing Bucephalus. The king was distraught and issued a proclamation threatening obliteration for the Mardi, if his beloved steed were not promptly returned. Cowed by this threat, the Mardians duly surrendered the illustrious beast accompanied by rich gifts and soon after they themselves capitulated to Alexander.[1] It was always

---

[1] Note however that Arrian, *Anabasis* 5.19.5 places this incident in the land of the Uxians.

unwise to come between Alexander and those persons, creatures or things for which he was passionate.

By this time, Alexander had dismissed the Greek allied forces from his service, since their mission to support him in the campaign against Darius had been fulfilled. However, as many as were willing were re-enlisted in Alexander's personal service, for now the king envisaged a new campaign, eastward-bound with Bessus as his quarry. It was clear now that he was no longer acting on behalf of the Synhedrion of the League of Corinth, but was tracking down a declared usurper in defence of his own throne as King of Asia. At this time too the sources report that Alexander was starting to adopt some of the pomp and ceremony of the ousted Persian monarchy. The accusations include frequent and lavish state banquets and the adoption of supposedly Persian royal attire in the form of a diadem, a gold-trimmed tunic of purple with a broad white stripe down its front, a matching knee-length cloak and a decorative sash-belt worn just beneath the breast. In fact, since Alexander refused to wear the trousers or the long-sleeved jacket, that were the most distinctively Persian feature, there were only subtle differences between this raiment and contemporaneous Greek apparel. More significantly perhaps, Alexander was now sleeping with both a Persian mistress and a Persian eunuch. The more conservative elements among the Macedonians were beginning to feel estranged by this "orientalising" behaviour.

The Philotas Affair

Just how dangerous such undercurrents of discontent might prove for the king was amply demonstrated by the events of October 330BC. Alexander had advanced into the territory of the Zarangians (a.k.a. Drangians) with a task-force of the army in pursuit of Satibarzanes, Satrap of Areia, who had first sworn fealty to the king, then promptly revolted. Soon after the main body of his troops had caught up with Alexander at the Zarangian capital, the tensions in camp shattered the veneer of unity when a plot to assassinate the king was betrayed to him. Several previous Macedonian kings had fallen to the treacherous knife and javelin thrusts of trusted courtiers, so it was important for Alexander to be alert to any hints of such plotting. The conspirators in this case seem to have been middle-ranking men of no special influence, but the seriousness of the scheme was underlined by the fact that one of them, a certain Dymnus, fell upon his sword when guardsmen were sent to arrest him.

The crucial aspect of this plot was the manner of its betrayal. Cebalinus, the brother of Dymnus' lover, Nicomachus, had sought to inform Alexander by alerting Philotas, who was the commander of the Companion Cavalry and the second ranking officer in the army. But Philotas failed to communicate the information to Alexander, making excuses to Cebalinus, until the latter in desperation brought the matter to Alexander's attention through one of the Royal Pages. Alexander was initially minded to forgive Philotas, but a council of the king's Friends urged his interrogation and trial, because his conduct had self-evidently been treasonable under the law. The Assembly of the Macedonians heard Philotas confess to having failed to mention the plot to Alexander, his defence being that he had considered the matter a triviality. However, the Assembly nevertheless condemned him for the dire significance of his silence and he was executed in a hail of missiles.

One problem remained. Philotas was the son of Parmenion, Alexander's most venerable general, who was sitting astride the army's supply lines at Ecbatana in command of a large garrison force. Alexander's camp was sealed and a small party of trusted men was sent out on camels, the fastest available means of transport, on a successful mission to eliminate Parmenion before he could revolt. Whereas the law allowed that relatives of a traitor could be executed, it was a provision that Alexander rarely enforced. In this case, however, Alexander seems to have harboured some genuine suspicions against Parmenion and, anyway, necessity dictated the measure, since the safety and security of the entire expedition relied heavily upon the integrity of its supply lines.

The Capture of Bessus

The army weathered a harsh winter in northern Arachosia, then crossed the Khawak Pass moving northwards through the Hindu Kush in the Spring of 329BC. Provisions were in short supply, so the Macedonians were reduced at one point to slaughtering the pack animals. In a desert region in Bactria, Alexander famously refused water brought to him in skins, because the rest of the army had to go thirsty and he preferred to share in their hardships. Bessus was alarmed by Alexander's inexorable advance, so he retreated further northwards across the Oxus into Sogdiana. This wrecked his credibility and his own commanders, led by Spitamenes, arrested him. They offered to surrender him to Alexander, who sent Ptolemy with a detachment to secure him (Figure 1.10). Afterwards Alexander handed Bessus over to Oxathres and the family of Darius, who had him ritually torn to pieces at Ecbatana.

The Branchidae

At around this time events conspired to persuade Alexander to submit another legal dilemma to the ruthless judgement of some of his troops. The army was astonished to be welcomed in the wilderness by a Greek-speaking tribe living peacefully in an isolated valley. However, their initial pleasure rapidly turned to horror and repugnance, when they discovered that these sociable folk were the descendents of the Branchidae.

This clan had been priests and guardians of the temple and oracle of Apollo at Didyma near Miletus when the Persians had invaded their region 160 years beforehand. They had shamelessly collaborated with the enemy in the pillaging and destruction of their shrine, such that their memory continued to be reviled throughout the Greek world. The Great-King Xerxes had settled them in this remote region to keep them safe from the bitter reprisals of their fellow Greeks, for religious law demanded that the Branchidae and their descendents should be wiped from the face of the Earth.

Figure 1.10. The punishment of Bessus (by A. Castaigne 1899)

Alexander, it would seem, felt himself poised upon the horns of a dilemma. In his soul he felt deep respect for the purification demanded by religious law in respect of this most heinous crime, but in his heart he doubted that the extirpation of the innocent and cheerful descendants of the desecrators could possibly be ethical. His solution was to refer the decision to the Milesians in his army, Miletus being the nearest large town to the shrine of the Branchidae. Tragically they seem to have been of the majority opinion that religious law should be upheld and applied. Of course, by modern standards this was an atrocity, but by ancient standards the case is much less clear-cut. Plutarch felt the tradition was immoral, although he conceded that it was a stipulation of religious law. Conversely, Aelian in a Suda fragment asserted that the Macedonians had acted honourably in the matter.

The Insurrection of Spitamenes

In the summer of 329BC Alexander advanced to Samarkand and thence to the River Jaxartes (the modern Syr-Darya, mistakenly thought to be the Tanais by Alexander's expedition), where the king founded another city to be known as Alexandria Eschate (Alexandria the Furthest). At this juncture the entire region rose up in a ferocious revolt, annihilating Macedonian garrisons and wiping out foraging parties. The insurrection is said to have been incited by Spitamenes and his allies. Their precise motive is unclear, but suspicion tends to alight upon Alexander's new civic foundation. The local people may have been quite happy to acquiesce to the notional sovereignty of a distant throne, but a king who founded colonies of his own people in the heart of their territory was another matter.

Alexander successively subdued seven rebel cities in quelling the first fires of the rebellion and despatched a relief column to Samarkand, when news reached him that it was besieged by Spitamenes. Thereupon a vast host of Scythians arrived on the far bank of the Jaxartes, shooting arrows across the stream and yelling insults at the Macedonians. Alexander's troops crossed the river on inflated hides under covering catapult fire and began a furious pursuit of these uncouth riders from the steppes. The weather was hot and the territory barren. Exhaustion and thirst led Alexander to drink from a stagnant pool, but the water was bad and the king rapidly fell dangerously ill with dysentery. The chase was abandoned and the Macedonians returned to their camp, where Alexander gradually recuperated.

Spitamenes had meanwhile abandoned his siege of Samarkand upon news of the approach of the relief force. The Greek troops chased incautiously after him towards the most remote corner of Sogdiana, but they were ambushed by their quarry and over 2000 of them were slain. It was the greatest military disaster of Alexander's career, though he was not himself present. Spitamenes resumed his siege of Samarkand, but this time Alexander marched against him in person, obliging him to retire hastily once again. Though Alexander pursued him keenly, Spitamenes got across the border to take refuge with the Scythians. Alexander and his army settled down to weather the winter of 329-328BC in Bactra (a.k.a. Zariaspa).

The Rock of Ariamazes

The campaigning season of 328BC saw many rebel lords holed up on various crags and eyries, which they fondly supposed to be impregnable. However, Alexander generally took the attitude that the more forbidding the difficulties, the more attractive and worthy the challenge. The pinnacle occupied by a local potentate called Ariamazes (in the Vulgate sources) represented a particularly challenging prospect.

Nevertheless, Alexander initially engaged its defenders in negotiations, offering that they might leave in peace and unmolested if they voluntarily gave up the rock to him. They responded with raucous laughter, confiding that Alexander would require winged soldiers to take their stronghold. This merely strengthened the king's resolution and inspired him to resort to psychological tactics. He gathered a large team of about 300 Macedonians with rock-climbing skills and offered huge prizes, if they should manage to ascend to a crag, which rose up behind the main rebel base upon the Rock. The climbers ascended through the night using tent pegs as makeshift crampons. About thirty of them fell to their deaths, but the great majority duly appeared along the crest of the crag the next morning, waving linen flags. Alexander sent a herald to indicate to the defenders that he had found his airborne assault troops and pointedly to reiterate his invitation to surrender. Thoroughly cowed, the occupants of the Rock slew their outmanoeuvred commander and duly flung themselves upon the king's mercy.

Just a month or two later Alexander assaulted another ostensibly unassailable pinnacle named the Rock of Sisimithres after the tribal leader whose forces were its occupants. In addition to the usual sheer cliffs an impassable ravine protected this fastness, but Alexander set about filling up the gorge with such gusto and made such marvellously rapid progress that these rebels were similarly intimidated into surrendering. On this occasion Sisimithres himself had the wit to instigate the capitulation and he consequently remained in post as Alexander's subject ally.

The Decapitation of Spitamenes

In the late summer of 328BC the Macedonians needed to flush out adversaries who were pursuing highly mobile hit-and-run tactics in the field. Hence Alexander swept his army through Sogdiana in five separate columns under different commanders. At about the same time Spitamenes invaded Sogdiana with the assistance of a freshly recruited force of Scythian cavalry and he seems to have penetrated behind Alexander's lines as far as Bactra, but was then attacked and driven off by Craterus. Finding that Alexander's armies were all about him, Spitamenes engaged the column led by Coenus, since it seemed the weakest of the Greek battle groups. After a fierce tussle, Coenus drove the Scythians into the desert, where, as some say, his own wife decapitated Spitamenes and delivered his head to Alexander to forestall further aggressions.

Alexander spent eighteen months campaigning in Bactria and Sogdiana, a period that included some of the toughest fighting of his career before the area was sufficiently pacified for him to move on. Some have questioned whether he had any lasting impact, despite these exertions. But in fact, he was succeeded by a dynasty of Macedonian kings who continued to dominate the region for the next three centuries. They are almost absent from the surviving accounts of antique writers and historians, but we know them from the classically Greek and lustrously lovely series of coins, which they minted and distributed to advertise their power over a realm of wildernesses.

Figure 1.11. The killing of Cleitus (by A. Castaigne 1899)

The Killing of Cleitus

In the autumn of 328BC Alexander was based at Samarkand. At this time the command of the Companion Cavalry was shared between Hephaistion and

Cleitus, a member of the Macedonian "old guard". Alexander now chose to honour Cleitus by appointing him as Satrap of Bactria. A little later, at a drinking party of Alexander's Friends, as everyone sank into inebriation, the king indulged in the usual reminiscences of recent campaigns, comparing his successes favourably with those of his father Philip. Cleitus was feeling disgruntled at the prospect of remaining behind when the army moved on and his mood was further inflamed by these remarks. He launched an astonishing diatribe full of fervent and increasingly cutting insults that deeply wounded and angered Alexander. Eventually, the king threw an apple at his tormenter, then sought his sword and might have attacked the delinquent except that those around him held him back, whilst Ptolemy dragged Cleitus out of the hall. There the matter might have rested as a drunken squabble, but for the fact that Cleitus shortly after returned yelling fresh calumnies. Alexander snatched a spear from a sentry, met Cleitus as he surged back through the curtain across the doorway and ran him through (Figure 1.11).

Alexander's rage evaporated into an equally intense orgy of contrition. Some say he had to be restrained from stabbing himself with the same spear. He was inconsolable for three days, refusing to eat or drink or have any care for his person. The Assembly sanctioned the killing retrospectively, but it was the dishonour rather than the illegality of the act that Alexander found hard to endure. Firstly, Cleitus had been a member of the official group of his Friends, who seem to have enjoyed special discretion to speak frankly to the king on occasion. Worse, he was the brother of Alexander's nurse, Lanike, who was especially dear to the king. Worst of all, he had saved Alexander's life at the Battle of the Granicus. Eventually, Alexander's companions and Anaxarchus, a court philosopher, managed to persuade the king to abandon his grieving, although it seems that Alexander continued to regard the killing of Cleitus as his most regrettable deed.

Matrimony

Alexander was based at Nautaca fifty miles south of Samarkand during the winter of 328-327BC. In the early spring of 327BC the army conducted mopping up operations against the dregs of Sogdian resistance in the mountainous regions to the south and east. At this time the king visited the Rock of Chorienes, a local potentate whose base happened also to be harbouring the wife and daughters of Oxyartes, a prominent rebel baron.

Alexander became enamoured of one of Oxyartes daughters, when Chorienes presented her, in company with his own daughters, as a dancer for the entertainment of his mighty Macedonian guests. To everybody's astonishment, the king proclaimed that his intention was a formal marriage. The prospect of becoming the father-in-law of the king was a more than sufficient incentive for Oxyartes to reconcile himself with Alexander. He attended a splendid nuptial ceremony and was rewarded with appointment as governor of his region. The surprise that this move caused at the time has been shared by many modern commentators. Why did Alexander concede the honour of matrimony rather than merely make Roxane his mistress? Certainly, the conservatives in the Macedonian army were displeased that Alexander's heir might to their thinking be born half-barbarian. And yet Alexander could be seen merely as emulating a policy perpetually pursued by his father of allying himself through marriage with particularly troublesome nations. Furthermore, both Alexander and his senior courtiers were probably naggingly concerned that, since the execution of Alexander Lynkestis in the context of the Philotas affair, there was no competent heir to the throne available. After all, we have seen that Alexander had already several times been in acute personal danger in the course of the expedition up to that point and there were no eligible Greek princesses anywhere nearby.

The Proskynesis Experiment

At around this time Alexander was suffering some minor embarrassment from the fact that his new subjects from the former Persian Empire were habitually prostrating themselves before him as the new Great King, whilst the Greeks continued to greet him with just a cursory salute. The political dilemma was that his new vassals were liable to lose respect for his status if obeisance were abolished, whereas the Greeks were resistant to gestures that they regarded as decadent oriental excesses. Alexander and his closest advisors were minded to seek a compromise. They seem to have formulated a hybrid ritual involving kneeling, bowing and blowing a kiss, then receiving a kiss from the king in return. This is termed *proskynesis* in our sources, though its exact details remain obscure. Hephaistion arranged a formal banquet to which all the leading courtiers were invited on the understanding that each in turn would perform the new ceremonial greeting. However, Callisthenes, the son of Aristotle's niece and Alexander's official expedition historian, refused to kneel, asserting that such obeisance was due only to the gods. Alexander in turn refused him the answering kiss. This had the effect of miring the matter in a manure of controversy, so Alexander quietly dropped his introduction of *proskynesis*.

The Conspiracy of the Pages

In the late spring of 327BC Alexander's forces assembled at Bactra. By tradition the Macedonian king was attended by a group of the teenage sons of Macedonian nobles commonly termed the Royal Pages (although they were probably aged between 14 and 18). These youths were destined to fill senior positions in the army and administration, so Alexander was keen to provide them with a liberal education during their service to him. The duty of their tutelage fell upon Callisthenes, who became a great influence upon them. In the course of a royal hunting expedition Hermolaus, a Page who was particularly close to Callisthenes, had the temerity to kill a charging boar before Alexander himself had the opportunity to strike it, which was a huge breach of etiquette. Alexander had him whipped in front of the other Pages. In consequence, it seems he began to nurse a foetid hatred of the king. At Bactra he formed a conspiracy with five other like-minded Pages including his lover Sostratus. The plot was hatched that they should murder Alexander in his bed on an evening when they were collectively appointed to keep guard over his tent. However, when the opportunity of a common shift arose, Alexander happened to stay away all night at a party. Soon after, another of the conspirators, Epimenes, leaked the plot to his lover and the details rapidly reached Alexander's ears. The Pages were tried before the Macedonian Assembly, where Hermolaus openly confessed and delivered a ringing denunciation of the king's "orientalising" policies. All six were stoned to death by the Macedonians and Callisthenes was arrested. Both the degree of Callisthenes' guilt and his ultimate fate are matters of great inconsistency in our sources. Some say the Pages implicated him, others that they did not. Ptolemy wrote that Alexander had him hanged, but it is more likely true that he died of obesity, disease and an infestation of lice whilst still imprisoned during the Indian campaign, which was the version recorded by Chares, Alexander's chamberlain.

The Invasion of India

In the early summer of 327BC the army re-crossed the Paropamisus Range, the modern Hindu Kush, via the Kushan Pass, heading first south then east towards India. Hephaistion took command of the greater part of the army and led it on the direct route into India through the Khyber Pass with orders to bridge the Indus. He was assisted by Taxiles, the Indian ruler of Taxila, who had submitted to Alexander in the hope of securing his support against Porus, a powerful neighbouring rajah. Alexander himself took a more mobile force on a roving campaign through the steep valleys of Swat to the north of the Khyber Pass. Many minor engagements were fought in the course of these operations, but Massaga, the greatest city in the region, put up the stiffest resistance. It had engaged 7000 Indian mercenaries to provide a professional core for its army. Alexander lured them into the open by pretending to retreat at their first onslaught, then counter-attacked, driving them back into the city with significant losses. After a short siege, just at the point when the Greeks had almost breached their ramparts, an Indian herald sued for surrender on terms. Alexander's principal demand was that the mercenaries should agree to serve in his own forces. To this end they marched out of the city and encamped on a nearby hillock. However, the king received credible intelligence that the mercenaries intended to creep away under cover of darkness, so he surrounded their mound with his own forces in the night. Most of the mercenaries were killed in the course of their ensuing stand and the survivors were taken prisoner. It was always dangerous to break faith with Alexander.

Not all the tribes in this region proved hostile. The citizens of Nysa welcomed Alexander and requested and received generous treatment on the grounds that Dionysus, the Greek god of wine and revels, had purportedly founded their city.

Aornus

Early in 326BC some of the Indians sought to hold out on the summit of a mountain overlooking the upper reaches of the Indus River. The Greeks called it Aornus, the birdless rock, but we are fairly sure that it was the peak now known as Pir Sar. A legend was related to Alexander that Heracles had failed in an attempt to storm Aornus, which filled him with a special longing to outdo his mythical ancestor. Local people told him that the easiest approach to Aornus was via a second mountain that rose up behind it and which might in turn be scaled by means of a narrow and precipitous path. Guides led an advance party under Ptolemy to seize the crest of this peak. A few days later Alexander managed to bring his main force up to join them. A deep ravine still separated Alexander's position from Aornus, but he set his troops to filling it in order to forge a pathway for his assault. Progress was rapid, so the defenders opened negotiations with a view to covering their evacuation of Aornus, but Alexander adroitly transferred his troops onto the vacated area of the summit ridge and harried the Indians' retreat.

In the spring of 326BC Alexander crossed the Indus on a bridge of boats constructed by Hephaistion. The army steadily advanced eastwards into the Indian plains, reaching the allied city of Taxila around April. Ahead lay the territory of the powerful rajah named Porus, who was an antagonist of Taxiles and therefore Alexander's enemy by association.

The Battle of the Hydaspes

In May 326BC Alexander marched forward to the Hydaspes river, which is nowadays the Jhelum. Here the forces of Porus confronted him, arrayed as for battle on the far bank and incorporating a large herd of powerful war elephants. For once Alexander was thwarted, for it was impossible for the Greeks to cross over without being cut to pieces and trampled as they came ashore.

Alexander split his forces into detachments and began to march them up and down his side of the river, so as to probe Porus' defensive strategy and establish any weak spots. Over days and weeks Porus' troops wearied of the game and grew noticeably complacent. Finally, on a dark and wild night under cover of a thunderstorm, Alexander led a large contingent up the river, whilst leaving the bulk of his army under Craterus camped opposite Porus. Just before dawn the king forded the river on a bend where an island filled the middle of the stream and his forces reached the far shore in large numbers before Porus could bring up substantial contingents to oppose them. In the first instance Porus sent his son with 2000 cavalry and 120 chariots, but Alexander easily smashed this formation and killed the prince.

Figure 1.12. The surrender of Porus (by A. Castaigne 1899)

Porus now chose to deploy his main army against Alexander with up to 200 elephants in its front line and 2000 cavalry on each wing. Alexander attacked Porus' left wing with his own cavalry, feinting a flanking charge, which dragged Porus' cavalry away from his centre. Following a pre-arranged plan, two regiments of Alexander's cavalry led by Coenus charged into the gap. The cavalry on the Indian left wing broke and retreated, but at this juncture Porus' elephants reached Alexander's troops. Alexander's infantry ringed these beasts and cast a hail of missiles upon them, seeking especially to kill the mahouts astride their necks. The elephants became maddened and indiscriminate in their trampling, which inflicted as much damage on the Indians as on the Macedonians. Alexander's flanking charge had enabled some of his forces to get behind the Indian lines causing their formations to become compressed and depriving them of the ability to manoeuvre to avoid the monstrous rampaging beasts. At the same time Craterus had managed to cross the river and was bringing substantial reinforcements into the fray. A large part of Porus' army was destroyed with terrible carnage, but the rajah himself fought on desperately whilst any of his troops stood their ground. However, after he was wounded in the shoulder, he wheeled his elephant and sought to retreat, though virtually completely surrounded. Alexander sent Taxiles to persuade him to surrender, but Porus charged at his bitter adversary, so instead the king sent forward Meroes, an old comrade of the rajah. At last Porus placed himself at Alexander's mercy. The king with his usual sense of theatre rode up to accept Porus' submission, asking him how he desired to be treated (Figure 1.12). "Like a king", Porus retorted. "That I grant for my own sake, but ask what you wish for yours," Alexander responded, but Porus assured him that everything was covered by his first request.

Alexander founded a city called Bucephala in the spot at which he had crossed the river in memory of his horse, which died at this time, either of exhaustion or from battle wounds. The king commemorated the battle with an issue of silver medallions, which he distributed as presents among his soldiers. The obverse shows Alexander on Bucephalus attacking Porus' elephant with a long Macedonian lance (*sarissa*). More interestingly, the reverse depicts Alexander in full armour wielding a thunderbolt, which was the special attribute of Zeus. However, it was probably intended to allude to Alexander's use of the thunderstorm to conceal his river crossing. The handful of these coins which have survived are among the most valuable numismatic relics from antiquity. Also around this time Alexander made a present of silver embossed shields to his crack infantry regiment, the *hypaspists* or shield bearers. Afterwards they acquired their more famous appellation as the *argyraspides* or Silver Shields.

The Mutiny on the Hyphasis

The battle of the Hydaspes was fought either in mid-May or shortly after the summer solstice in late June 326BC. In the ensuing months Alexander progressed ever further eastwards, negotiating the crossing of two more great tributaries of the Indus. But this was the season of the monsoon, which meant virtually continuous heavy rains. The army's clothing and equipment began to rot and morale plummeted as rumours of vast native armies ahead, furnished with thousands of war elephants, began to percolate through the ranks. A mutinous mood seized the troops as the army reached the banks of the Hyphasis River and there was a growing consensus that they should advance no further.

Alexander called a conference of the senior commanders and implored them to support a continuation of the campaign, but Coenus made an emotional speech in support of retracing their steps, which carried the day. Alexander shut himself in his tent and sulked for three days, at one point even threatening to march on with only his native levies. On the third day he relented and commanded that sacrifices should be performed to test the disposition of the gods towards a crossing of the river. To nobody's surprise, the auguries proved unfavourable, so Alexander conceded that he would lead the army back to Persia. Thus Alexander's greatest defeat was inflicted at the hands of his own men. Nobody else ever acquired sufficient influence with him as to persuade him to abandon his objectives.

Altars dedicated to the gods of the Greek pantheon were erected on the bank of the Hyphasis, and then the retreat began with a march back to the Hydaspes.

The Brahmins and the Mallian Arrow

A large fleet awaited Alexander at the Hydaspes, the construction of which he had ordered after his victory over Porus with the intention of exploring downstream in the Indus river system at some convenient juncture. There were eighty large warships of Greek design and perhaps around a thousand lesser vessels, many of which had been requisitioned from the natives. Alexander sailed downriver on board the flagship of this motley fleet in early November 326BC, whilst Hephaistion advanced down the eastern bank in command of the main body of the army and Craterus led the baggage train and some lesser troop contingents down the western shoreline.

The Brahmin caste of priests and holy men had whipped the Indians into a fanatical frenzy at the news of Alexander's approach. The nations of the Mallians and the Oxydracae controlled the territory near the confluences of the Indus with its great tributaries. Alexander heard that they intended to mount a united resistance, but his armies fell upon the Mallian towns before they could join forces with their neighbours. Nevertheless, they often fought bitterly against the Greeks and sometimes preferred suicide to surrender, inspired by the reckless religious zeal of the Brahmins.

The Greek soldiers were dispirited to find themselves engaged in further deadly fighting, when they had believed themselves homeward bound. At one Mallian town in the early months of 325BC, Alexander perceived that his men were hanging back from engaging in the assault. He personally seized a siege ladder, propped it against the town's wall and scampered up onto the parapet closely followed by Peucestas, Leonnatus and Abreas. There he stood for a while, the focus of a hail of Indian missiles in full view of his laggard troops, who were shamed into rushing up the ladders to support him. But so many clambered upon the rungs that they collapsed beneath them, leaving Alexander and his three comrades in yet more splendid isolation (Figure 1.13). The king decided to leap down the inside face of the wall, since that location appeared to offer better shelter from the rain of missiles and there might at least be an opportunity to strike back at the enemy. Abreas was shot and killed by an arrow in his face. Alexander himself was struck in the chest by an arrow and, though he fought on whilst he had strength, he eventually fainted from loss of blood. However, Peucestas and Leonnatus bravely defended the king's recumbent body until the rest of the army had managed to improvise means to scramble over or bash their way through the defences to mount a rescue.

Though Ptolemy wrote that air and blood escaped from Alexander's wound, implying a punctured lung, he also admitted that he had been elsewhere during this action. The other ancient sources imply that the arrow merely lodged in Alexander's breastbone or rib cage, which was a less threatening injury and is far more consistent with the reports that Alexander mounted his horse and walked among his thronging troops just a week after sustaining this injury. It had nevertheless been a close call. The king heaped honours and rewards on Peucestas and Leonnatus, his trusty bodyguards.

Figure 1.13. The ladder breaks at the Mallian town (by A. Castaigne 1899)

The Treachery of Musicanus

Alexander and his fleet swept on down the swiftly flowing river swelled by the melting snows in the distant mountains. In the early summer of 325BC they came ahead of the news of their approach into the kingdom of Musicanus, who was rumoured to be the richest rajah in India. He was panicked into a hasty submission to Alexander, though he had been reticent whilst the Greeks were still far upriver. Alexander was nevertheless disposed to be magnanimous, especially in view of the rajah's royal gifts to him, and so he reappointed Musicanus to the rule of his kingdom. But this was the season in which the Brahmin fanatics stirred up their worst trouble, for they persuaded Musicanus to rebel almost as soon as Alexander had left his city. Too soon indeed, for the Greeks returned in a vengeful anger and the rajah was captured and hanged as an example to his recalcitrant subjects.

Figure 1.14. The fleet is wrecked in approaching the Indian Ocean (1696)

The Visit to the Ocean

Later in the summer Alexander's expedition reached Patala at the apex of the Indus river delta, where two great branches of the stream split for the final stages of their journeys to the sea. Alexander was entranced by the prospect of an encounter with this mythical ocean, so he set off down the western channel with a sizable flotilla of his larger ships in July 325BC. A storm blew in wrecking some of his vessels, which had to be rebuilt, but still he pressed on. Without visible warning the fleet arrived upon the tidal reaches of the river. The phenomenon of tidal ebb and flow was virtually unknown to the Greeks, because it scarcely exists in the Mediterranean Sea. Alexander's crews were astounded to find their galleys suddenly stranded in the mud by a rapidly receding tide, and equally astonished when they were refloated as the waters flowed back in a tidal bore. Some ships were driven ashore and others damaged when dashed together by the turbulent stream (Figure 1.14). Undeterred Alexander sailed on beyond the river mouth and out into the vacant vastness of the Indian Ocean. On reaching an island, the fleet anchored and went ashore to perform sacrifices and religious ceremonies in honour of Poseidon.

The March through Gedrosia

Alexander returned to Patala after completing the exploration of the delta. Craterus had already departed with a large fraction of the army including the veterans, the elephants and the greater part of the baggage train. He led them west to Persia by an easy but circuitous route through Arachosia and Areia. However, Alexander had learnt that a more direct march through Gedrosia would considerably shorten the journey. He was also warned that this route traversed harsh and dangerous terrain and that previous expeditions had suffered great losses in pursuing it. Nevertheless, Alexander enjoyed such challenges, thinking they would enhance his reputation with posterity. Furthermore, he wished to bring the larger vessels in his fleet back with him. Nearchus and Onesicritus were charged with sailing it westwards along the coast into the Persian Gulf after emerging from the western mouth of the Indus and Alexander hoped to keep the army near the coast so as to re-supply the fleet at regular stages on its voyage. These carefully laid plans began to go awry from the start. When Alexander marched west in early September 325BC, Nearchus was still trapped in India by unfavourable winds and the fleet failed in fact to make significant progress westwards until Alexander had almost completed the journey by land.

At first progress was straightforward for the land forces with little hint of the perils which lay ahead, but soon the king's column entered searingly hot desert territory and the worst of the terrain lay closest to the coast, so that Alexander's persistence in trying to keep the army in communication with the fleet placed the expedition in particular jeopardy. The baggage animals began to die and the wagons had to be abandoned when their wheels sank into deep drifts of sand, so it became impossible to rescue those who fell behind due to illness or exhaustion. On one occasion the army camped in a dried up streambed with a barely a trickle of water to entice the parched troops. But a sudden storm over the mountains upstream caused a torrent to sweep through the camp in the second watch of the night, drowning many and sweeping away much of the expedition's remaining equipment.

In desperation Alexander was compelled to march further inland to save the survivors. It was a terrible decision, for in his mind he was condemning the fleet to starvation on the barren coastline, but in ensured that the bulk of his army survived. After sixty days of hunger, hardship and suffering they reached the relative safety of Pura, the Gedrosian capital. The magnitude of the disaster is sometimes overstated in modern accounts. Plutarch implies that over thirty thousand soldiers emerged from the Gedrosian desert, which was surely the majority of those that embarked on this march and we do not hear of any deaths among the senior men.

Festivities in Carmania

In December of 325BC Alexander's army is said to have cavorted in a weeklong Dionysiac *comus* as they processed through Carmania. This was banqueting on wheels, for Alexander led the festive procession in an enormous chariot drawn by a team of eight horses. Additionally, Athletic and artistic contests were held to celebrate the deliverance of the army from the ravages of the desert march and the king's victorious return from the east. The rejoicing climaxed when Nearchus unexpectedly arrived at Alexander's camp in Carmania bringing the tidings that the fleet had survived its voyage virtually intact and now lay safely at anchor in a river mouth on the Strait of Hormuz at the mouth of the Persian Gulf.

The Purging of the Satraps

By January of 324BC Alexander had accumulated substantive evidence of maladministration by his satraps whilst he had been absent in the east. Charges were brought against several of these governors, both Greeks and Persians, by their own troops as well as by the subject peoples and there was tangible evidence of the desecration of temples and tombs. The king was particularly distressed by the looting of the tomb of Cyrus, the founder of the Persian Empire. Cyrus seems to have been a personal hero of Alexander, probably because he had read the Cyropaidia or Upbringing of Cyrus. Xenophon, an Athenian pupil of Socrates, had penned this work shortly before Alexander's birth. He had represented Cyrus as a paragon of monarchy and there are indications that Alexander sought to emulate Xenophon's exemplar of kingship, especially in his treatment of vanquished enemies. Following investigations and summary tribunals a number of satraps and key officials were executed for turning to criminality when they had believed Alexander's expedition to be permanently diverted in India. Arrian comments that Alexander won deep respect from the common people, because he would not allow his senior officials to maltreat any of his subjects.

The Exiles Decree & Divine Honours

By the early spring of 324BC Alexander had reached Susa at the heart of his Empire. At this point he began to implement a series of plans and policies, which were profoundly controversial at the time, but which nevertheless hint at the magisterial scope of his vision for the future government of his world. In around March 324BC he formulated a decree, which stipulated that those who had been exiled by their cities would have a right of return unless they had been proscribed for murder or sacrilege. This edict was announced to the Greeks at the Olympic games in early August 324BC. Most exiles repatriated by the decree were victims of political disputes in their home cities. They had been creating a degree of instability within Alexander's domains by hiring themselves out as mercenaries to any local potentate who cared to resort to violence to resolve a dispute. Many had ended up in Alexander's own service, so he will have been familiar with tales of the injustices visited upon them by their fellow citizens. However, the edict elicited consternation from the city-states of southern Greece. Not only would the leading citizens have to live with neighbours who bore them serious grudges, but the restitution of land and property appropriated from the exiles by the local governments might have to be implemented.

It would seem that Alexander also let it be known in the Greek world that he would be amenable to accepting the award of divine honours should any city be disposed to approve them. In this he was implicitly emulating his hero and ancestor Achilles, who had similarly been voted such honours by the Epirotes.

The Marriages at Susa

In the early summer of 324BC Alexander married the Persian princesses Stateira and Parysatis, both daughters of former Persian Great Kings. Alexander's father had extensively exploited polygamy as an instrument for cementing alliances and coalitions. Now Alexander followed suit, but with the innovation of simultaneously marrying over ninety of his Friends and Companions to daughters of the Persian nobility. It would seem he was keen to forge a new Graeco-Persian ruling class destined to inherit and consolidate his empire. A gorgeous description of the nuptial festivities written by Alexander's chamberlain, Chares, still survives. The banqueting tent was sumptuously decorated with cloths of purple, scarlet and gold. Pillars plated with gold and silver and encrusted with jewels supported its canopy. It housed a hundred couches of solid silver and the curtains were embroidered with gold and depicted figures of animals.

Prizes and decorations were issued to Alexander's loyal lieutenants and he offered to discharge the debts of his Macedonian troops. These veterans were at first suspicious when they were asked to register their names and details of their debts with Alexander's officials. However, on learning of the controversy the king agreed to make the process anonymous and dispensed an enormous sum approaching fifty tonnes of gold to his grateful men.

The Mutiny at Opis

Alexander sailed down the river Eulaeus in the early autumn of 324BC and thence westwards along the Persian coast and 300 miles up the river Tigris to the city of Opis. Here Alexander announced his intention to send home to Macedonia those of his veterans who were too old or infirm to serve in future campaigns. However, the rank and file were distrustful of his motives, for he had recently received substantial reinforcements of Persian and other non-Greek troops into some of the senior regiments of his army. At Susa the veterans had been displeased to see an army of 30,000 youths of foreign or mixed birth parading with Macedonian arms and termed the "Epigoni", which means literally the "Afterborn" and was originally the term for the sons of the seven legendary heroes who went up against Thebes. During the mass meeting at Opis some of the veterans began hurling accusations of betrayal at Alexander: the very same "Barbarians" that they had risked their lives to conquer were supplanting them. Alexander responded with characteristic decisiveness. He leapt down among the mutinous throng and personally pointed out thirteen recalcitrants, whom he commanded his guards to arrest (Figure 1.15). Whilst they were being dragged away to execution, Alexander angrily reproached the subdued mob with a long list of his achievements on their behalf. If they wished, let them all abandon him and return to Macedon. He would make up numbers with foreign levies and continue his campaigns without them. The furious king withdrew to the palace and began to issue orders restructuring his forces to reduce reliance on his Macedonian veterans. After three days the veterans woke up to the fact that their position was being further undermined and that there was little they could do to prevent it. They marched en masse to the palace and tearfully begged the king to relent and reinstate them. Alexander tearfully complied. The veterans further complained that some Persian aristocrats had been granted the status of "kinsmen" to the king, entitling them to kiss him. Alexander spontaneously extended this institution to encompass all of his veterans and duly accepted slobbering kisses from many of them. At Opis Alexander effectively reversed the defeat inflicted at the hands of his veterans at the Hyphasis in India. Ten thousand elderly and invalided veterans were each given a valedictory present of 25 kilograms of silver and packed off home as planned under the command of Craterus, who was to take over the Regency of Macedon from Antipater.

Figure 1.15. Quelling the mutiny at Opis (by A. Castaigne 1899)

The Death of Hephaistion

In October of 324BC the court progressed at a leisurely pace to Ecbatana in the mountains. There was much feasting and merrymaking and Alexander organised athletic and artistic contests for entertainment. During November, whilst the courtiers were distracted by the festivities, Hephaistion, Alexander's closest friend and official deputy, fell gravely ill with a feverish disease resembling typhoid. After a week or so, he seemed to be over the worst and was beginning to recover his appetite. His doctor Glaucias complacently deserted his patient to attend the boys' athletics in the theatre. In his absence Hephaistion consumed a boiled chicken washed down with a flagon of wine. He promptly relapsed into agony and soon after died, even before Alexander could be summoned from the theatre. The king was devastated and ordered that the doctor be hanged. He plunged the court into a kind of orgy of mourning and ordered Perdiccas to convey the corpse to Babylon and to prepare an extravagant funeral.

Against the Cossaeans

Alexander distracted himself from an obsessive grief by leading a punitive expedition against a nearby tribe of mountain bandits known as the Cossaeans. In January and February of 323BC, despite wintry weather, the king destroyed or captured many Cossaean strongholds, thus compelling the submission of the whole nation. Those slain in combat with Alexander were considered sacrifices to the soul of Hephaistion.

Death in Babylon

In the spring of 323BC Alexander returned to lowland Mesopotamia, bound for the metropolis of Babylon, where Perdiccas had almost completed the preparations for Hephaistion's obsequies. Construction of a fleet of a thousand ships, with which the king intended to circumnavigate Arabia, was also well advanced. Alexander entered Babylon in early April after defying a warning by the Chaldean priests that the place was dangerous to him. He knew that they had failed to progress a project he had instigated to renovate the principal temple and suspected that they might still be seeking to thwart his plans. Envoys arrived in the metropolis from the Greek city-states offering Alexander divine honours and requesting his arbitration in various disputes.

The funeral of Hephaistion took place in early May. Diodorus has preserved for us a magnificent description of a pyre, which imitated the city's ziggurat in size and shape. Archaeologists have discovered a large brick foundation exhibiting signs of intense heat and scorching near the eastern wall of the city. In the aftermath Alexander sought to escape the morbid atmosphere and torpid heat of his capital. He embarked upon an engineering expedition up the Euphrates River designed to improve a canal system intended to divert the annual spate of the river into the marshes to the southwest. In returning to Babylon via these same marshes, some members of his flotilla went astray, so he lingered whilst they caught up.

At the end of May Alexander held a banquet in honour of Nearchus. He drank with his Friends at a late night party, but fell ill with stabbing pains in his back and limb joints. He was carried back to his suite of rooms within the ancient palace of Nebuchadnezzar, but he was already in a fever. Over the next few days the fever was intermittent with bouts in the evenings followed by remissions during daylight hours. Alexander was ferried across the river to the Hanging Gardens to lie beside the irrigation reservoir. But his fever grew worse and the remissions became briefer, then ceased altogether. Around 6th June the king's condition suddenly deteriorated and he was carried back to the palace.

Alexander's Lovers by Andrew Chugg

Senior officers were ordered to gather in the courtyard. Alexander could barely speak and was in a continuous raging fever. On the 9th June the rank and file demanded to see him, rumours having spread that he had already expired. The Friends allowed them to file past his bed whilst he greeted them with his eyes (Figure 1.16). He is widely stated to have handed his signet ring to Perdiccas, who was the most senior of his officers then present, but when asked to whom he left his kingdom, he said only, "To the strongest". When finally Perdiccas asked him at what times he wished his divine honours to be paid to him, he answered, "When you are happy." These were the last words of the king.

Figure 1.16. The death of Alexander (after Karl von Piloty, 1886)

A group of senior courtiers held an overnight vigil in the Temple of Marduk, but Alexander drank wine and became delirious. On the 10th June he sank into a coma and in the early evening his doctors pronounced him dead. An orgy of mourning broke out in the city engulfing Greeks and Persians alike. Nevertheless the king's body continued to appear curiously fresh and lifelike in the steamy heat, which may suggest that he continued to cling to life in a terminal coma for several more days.

Despite wild rumours of poisoning, which emerged some months after Alexander's death, all the known details of the case history of his fatal illness are highly consistent with a diagnosis of falciparum malaria contracted from a mosquito bite in the marshes. The full list of the symptoms and the case history are not entirely consistent with any other significantly probable diagnosis and are very difficult to reconcile with a poisoning scenario.

Last Plans

Perdiccas found memoranda among Alexander's papers which offer detailed insight into what might have been had the king lived longer. Alexander intended to embellish the Greek world with a series of fabulous temples that would have put the Parthenon in the shade and to build a tomb for his father that would have rivalled the pyramids. He meant to construct elegant and spacious new cities and to populate them with peoples transplanted from Europe into Asia and vice versa in order to weld his empire together through ties of intermarriage and kinship between the races and by this policy progressively to bring about a unity of mankind under his rule. He proposed to command the construction of a Mediterranean fleet of a thousand gargantuan vessels and to make a road along the northern coast of Africa as far as the pillars of Heracles. By these means he intended to march his army from Egypt to the Atlantic after completing the conquest of Arabia. Probably, he would have returned through Spain, France and Italy, where his uncle had already died during campaigning. Alexander's ambitions were virtually boundless and his power had become immense. It is unlikely that any human opposition could have stopped him. The conquest of the entire planet lay potentially within his grasp.

But when Perdiccas put Alexander's plans before the Assembly, they were hastily voted down as foolishly extravagant and impractical in the absence of Alexander's leadership. The Macedonians deemed it a nobler use of the king's treasure and resources to line their own pockets.

2. "A Philosopher in Arms"

In 1931 Wilcken[2] famously asserted that the study of history could offer no harder task than the definition of Alexander's personality. It is therefore with a giddy sense of the rashness of the pursuit that I have made this chimera the principal quarry of a fresh investigation. To underline the difficulties Wilcken made the further complaint that, even back then, so many personalities had been ascribed to the king that it was no exaggeration to say that every historian had his own Alexander. In 1954, Heuss suggested that the Alexander described by our sources is like a wineskin into which any vintage may be poured.[3] Unfortunately, perceptions can only be said to have deteriorated markedly in the meantime, with some historians even arguing that a definitive interpretation must linger forever tantalisingly beyond our grasp. Badian[4], for example, has confided that it has always seemed to him that any attempt to construct an all-embracing interpretation is inevitably worthless. But this is surely a council of unwarranted despair, which is effectively confuted by the enormous extent of the extant evidence. At least half a million words describing Alexander's life and career survive from the ancient world and most of this material is more or less traceable to around a dozen accounts by people who knew the king personally. This relative wealth of literary evidence is bolstered by hundreds of sculptures and paintings of Alexander, by his extensive numismatic legacy and by considerable and growing archaeological evidence and associated artefacts.

From this perspective, a better explanation of the proliferation of modern Alexanders would be that a combination of apologists, romantics and pursuers of various political and ideological agendas has plagued the study of the king. The latter approach is exemplified by treatments of Alexander from Mussolini's Italy or Hitler's Third Reich, whilst Tarn's breathtaking distortions sought to portray the king as a paragon of the English Country Gentleman or Scottish Laird, wickedly slandered by his ancient biographers insofar as they imputed any homosexual inclinations. Still others, whom Badian has reproached with the title of minimalists, insist on refuting absolutely every suggestion of emotion in Alexander's motives in favour of a relentless, calculating rationalism. This reductionism leads to such absurdly contradictory notions as that Alexander was secretly pleased to turn back at the Hyphasis and that he voyaged down the Indus and marched through the Gedrosian desert for want of politically viable

---

[2] Ulrich Wilcken, Alexander the Great, Leipzig, 1931, Preface.
[3] A. Heuss, Alexander der Grosse und die politische Ideologie des Altertums in Antike und Abendland 4, 1954, p.102.
[4] E Badian, Some Recent Interpretations of Alexander in Alexandre le Grand: Image et Réalité, Entretiens Tome XXII, Fondation Hardt, 1976, p.298.

alternatives.[5] This interpretation of Alexander seemingly owes much to the android character of Data in Star Trek: The New Generation.

Even superficially reasonable accounts tend sometimes with hypercritical pedantry to treat every slight perceived mismatch between the ancient sources as evidence of deliberate deceit, whereas in fact it is obvious that most of these discrepancies are accidental or illusory. Innocent derivations for such errors deserve more credence, considering that virtually all our ancient sources are secondary in nature and have suffered at least tens of transcriptions in their passage down the centuries. Consequently, we are too often confronted by the disturbing spectacle of historians actually playing either chief prosecutor or defence counsel, whilst professing that they are writing from the perspective of impartial judges. The effect has been to render Alexander's reputation a hapless victim of fashion. Most recently, the modern western distaste for warfare and the vilification of military might has encouraged a fierce assault upon his character. But this is doubly conceited. In the first place, it is the same sort of anachronism as condemning Socrates to purgatory for failing to embrace Christianity. In Alexander's world orthodox morality lauded the warrior and celebrated his conquests. Philosophical objections to violence had scarcely even been formulated. Secondly, it is anyway presumptuous to assume that modern attitudes to conflict are inherently more ethical.

As Arrian[6] says: "Anyone who reproaches Alexander should not do so solely on the evidence of what merits censure in him, but rather should found his critique on a comprehensive view of his life and career." To illustrate the point, it would seem that both Roosevelt and even more particularly Churchill, heroes of the struggle against Nazism, must have condoned and endorsed the policy of creating firestorms in German cities with thousand bomber raids. Hundreds of thousands of relatively innocent German civilians, mainly women, children and pensioners, perished horribly for the sake of scant military advantage for the Allies. Alexander never did anything quite so pointlessly terrible and the morality of even his most questionable actions is more equivocal. Yet by focussing on his few misdeeds, writers like Worthington have recently tried to make him out to be another Hitler. Moderate historians are starting to cringe: for example, Holt[7] has recently responded: "Mine may be called a moderate view: Alexander was not as noble and wholesome as Tarn believed, but also not as vile and deranged as some scholars have lately suggested."

In fact, Alexander generally sought to avoid unnecessary bloodshed and it is at least uncertain whether more people died as a result of his campaigns than should anyway have been killed in consequence of the continual localised warfare that was a ubiquitous feature of his age. Alexander's campaigns appear

---

[5] E.g. R. Andreotti, Die Weltmonarchie Alexanders des Grossen in Überlieferung und geschichtlicher Wirklichkeit, Saeculum 8 (1957), 120ff.
[6] Arrian, Anabasis 7.30.1.
[7] F. Holt, Alexander the Great and the Mystery of the Elephant Medallions, p.115.

in some regions to have left a measure of uncharacteristic peacefulness in their wake (at least for the duration of his reign) since he imposed a situation where local issues and disputes had to be referred to his authority for arbitration and settlement instead of being resolved by conflict.[8] Furthermore, Alexander was recognised by his contemporaries as a paragon of conscientiousness and fidelity in an era more generally characterised by brutality, callousness and treachery. Arrian was particularly concerned to draw this distinction to the attention of his readers: "But remorse for misdeeds was to my knowledge peculiar to Alexander among the kings of old times…"[9]

Plutarch has recorded an anecdote, which amply illustrates Arrian's point. When his allies voted to raze Thebes and enslave her citizens after she had twice revolted, Alexander failed to intervene to save her, but merely protected the priests, those who had voted against the rebellion and the house and descendants of the Theban poet Pindar.[10] Later in his career, wrote Plutarch:

When Greek mercenaries serving on the enemy's side came into Alexander's hands, he would order the Athenians among them to be kept in chains, because, while they might have lived at the expense of the Athenian city-state, they were yet serving as mercenaries, and so also the Thessalians, because, though they owned the finest land, they did not till it. But the Thebans he let go free, saying, 'These alone, because of us, have neither city nor land left to them.' [11]

In the first century AD the Roman rhetorician Publius Rutilius Lupus attributed the authorship of the following glowing epitaph to Aristotle:

Alexander of Macedon lacked no judgement in planning, nor valour in fighting, nor generosity in his favours, but only cruelty in punishment. When there was a dilemma, he showed himself the wisest; when there was fighting to be done against the enemy, he was the bravest; when a reward was to be given to those deserving it, he was most generous; and when punishment had to be inflicted on anyone, he was most merciful.[12]

The debate about Alexander has continually ricocheted from one extreme to another. Much that was aired in the twentieth century seems to tell us more about its authors' personalities than Alexander's. A different approach is indicated, if genuine progress is to be fostered. I propose, therefore, to engage with the problem of Alexander's character through an investigation of his personal life and most particularly through his relationships with those individuals identified in our sources as his sexual partners. These accounts will also extend to cover the entire biographies of Alexander's lovers. Even after his demise, their continuing life stories offer important insights into the context of Alexander's achievements, a perspective neglected elsewhere. In particular, the

---

[8] We hear of envoys coming before Alexander for this purpose, e.g. Diodorus 17.113.3.
[9] Arrian, Anabasis 7.29.1.
[10] Arrian, Anabasis 1.9.9-10; Diodorus 17.14; Plutarch 11.5-6.
[11] Plutarch, Moralia 181A-B (Sayings of Kings and Commanders, Alexander 22).
[12] Jacoby, FGrH 153F.5.

extent to which the tragedy of Alexander's early death swelled to engulf almost all of his family, friends and lovers will be revealed in all its remorselessness.

But firstly there are some basic foundation courses to the edifice of Alexander's character, which must underpin any architectural masonry. For these things the evidence remains mainly uncontroversial, despite the fact that some aspects have rarely been given the prominence that they merit in biographies of the king.

The common cliché is for Alexander to be represented as an inspirational species of war leader in most modern works. It is of course indisputable that he was a truly brilliant strategist and tactician and many would rank him in the top echelon of the all-time list of military geniuses, perhaps even placing him at its head. It may therefore come as something of a surprise to a modern audience that Alexander was to an equal extent seen by his contemporaries as something of an intellectual and even - in the broadest possible sense – as a philosopher. Furthermore, the evidence hints that the king himself was to a degree complicit in the presentation and dissemination of this image of himself.

In the first place, it is clear that Alexander's educational credentials were unambiguously first rate. The core of his learning was famously instilled at the Temple of the Nymphs near Mieza by Aristotle[13] (Figure 2.1), who later founded the Lyceum at Athens and is independently recognised as the leading scholar of Alexander's epoch. The philosopher's tutelage of the prince began in 343-2BC when Alexander was thirteen and lasted around 3 or 4 years. During this period Aristotle is believed to have composed treatises on Monarchy and on Colonies specifically for the edification of his royal pupil,[14] but the curriculum was evidently wide-ranging and included, for example, herbal medicine and the works of Homer.[15] According to Strabo, who probably took the anecdote from Callisthenes, Alexander personally annotated a copy of the Iliad provided by Aristotle and later enshrined it in a fabulously beautiful casket captured from Darius.[16] Alexander subsequently corresponded frequently with his former tutor: though now lost, a book of letters to Alexander is listed among Aristotle's works by Diogenes Laertius and various matters of their correspondence are mentioned elsewhere in the ancient literature. Indeed, one long letter concerning the wonders of India, purportedly penned by Alexander for Aristotle's benefit, survives in a late manuscript tradition that is badly contaminated with mythical elements. It is virtually certain that Alexander visited the Academy in Athens, when he was sent to the city as his father's emissary aged 18 after the victory at Chaeronea.[17] Much later, following his conquest of Persia, he tried to make a present of 50 Talents (a huge sum equal

---

[13] Plutarch, Life of Alexander 7.
[14] WD Ross, Aristotle, London 1923, p.4.
[15] Plutarch, Life of Alexander 8.
[16] Strabo, Geography 13.1.27.
[17] Justin 9.4.

to around a hundred kilograms of gold) to Xenocrates, the Head of the Academy and a regular correspondent of his friend Hephaistion.[18] However, the philosopher refused to accept all but half a talent, which he declared to be sufficient to meet his needs.

Figure 2.1. Aristotle teaching Alexander (J. L. G. Ferris, c.1895)

Alexander exhibited a fond appreciation of philosophy, poetry, theatre and medicine throughout his career and he took trouble to sponsor the philosophers, actors and poets whom he met. Many were engaged in his retinue. Plutarch states that Alexander himself played the lyre with charm and skill in his youth, though his father thought that the display of such artistry was beneath a

---

[18] Diogenes Laertius, Xenocrates.

"A Philosopher in Arms"

king.[19] We have a letter addressed to the fourteen-year-old Alexander by the Athenian orator Isocrates, in which he refers to Alexander studying the philosophical debating technique known as eristics, presumably under the tutelage of Aristotle.[20] Furthermore, Alexander went out of his way to visit Diogenes the Cynic in Corinth to enquire whether he might perform any service for him.[21] When Diogenes merely asked him to stand aside, so as not to block his sun (Figures 2.2 and 2.3), the king reproved those of his companions who ridiculed the Cynic by declaring that were he not Alexander, he would be Diogenes. It is tempting to dismiss this as an idle quip, but Diogenes literally means Zeus-born in Greek, which is an interesting double-meaning in the light of Alexander's later posturing as the son of Zeus-Ammon (see Appendix A). Furthermore, some consider the rayed disc that was the device of Alexander's family to be a sunburst, rather than a starburst, in which case Diogenes' remark might also have been double-edged. Others have suggested that this anecdote was fabricated,[22] perhaps by Onesicritus, Alexander's helmsman, who was himself a pupil of the infamous Cynic. However, Hammond[23] has pointed out that the mention by Arrian of two particular sets of guards (hypaspists and pezhetairoi) accompanying Alexander on this occasion is an extraordinarily authentic detail. In the light of Alexander's behaviour in other contexts, it is likely that the king was sincere in expressing his respect for philosophy. Diogenes Laertius cites another exchange from the meeting:

Alexander: *Do you not fear me?*
Diogenes: *No, for what are you, a good or evil thing?*
Alexander: *Good.*
Diogenes: *Who, then, would fear the good?*

Both Plutarch and Diogenes Laertius give the site of the meeting as the Craneion and the latter tells us that this was a gymnasium at the gates of Corinth, where too Diogenes later died.

At the time of the meeting Diogenes is said to have been scantily attired in a loincloth and to have inhabited some kind of wooden tub in order to wallow in the austerity of his ascetic creed. The episode is therefore closely paralleled by Alexander's encounters with the Gymnosophists (i.e. naked philosophers) in India. Indeed, Arrian[24] considers the comparison so significant that he abandons his usual chronological evolution of events in juxtaposing the two situations.[25] Onesicritus is undoubtedly our ultimate source for the details of

---

[19] Plutarch, Pericles 1.5; cf. Plutarch, Moralia 334C-D.
[20] Isocrates, Letter 5, To Alexander.
[21] Plutarch, Life of Alexander 14.1-3; Arrian, Anabasis Alexandrou 7.2.1 & Discourses of Epictetus 2.13.24; Diogenes Laertius, Diogenes 6; Dio Chrysostom, 4th Discourse on Kingship.
[22] E.g. JR Hamilton, Plutarch – Alexander: a Commentary (Oxford, 1969), p.34.
[23] NGL Hammond, Sources for Alexander the Great (1993), p.28.
[24] Arrian, Anabasis 7.1.5-7.3.6.
[25] See also Appendix XX in PA Brunt's Loeb edition of Arrian.

Alexander's encounters with the group of Indian philosophers led by Dandamis. He is the stated source for Strabo,[26] who writes that, "Mandanis [elsewhere Dandamis], the eldest and wisest of the group… commended the king because, while administering so great an empire, he felt a desire for wisdom and that [Alexander] was the sole example he had seen of a man pursuing philosophy in arms." The episode is also recounted by Plutarch[27] and in a late and embroidered form by Palladius.[28] There also survive accounts of a purported dialogue between Alexander and another group of ten Gymnosophists, most notably in Plutarch's Life of Alexander and the Metz Epitome,[29] but also in the Alexander Romance.[30] Hammond[31] thinks that this is originally from Megasthenes, though his arguments are not conclusive. However, Plutarch seems to be using a different source than Onesicritus for his version of the dialogue and matching material in the Metz Epitome shows that the source was Cleitarchus. This may mean that the reports of Alexander's philosophical debates in India do not rely entirely upon Onesicritus, but the matter is clouded by evidence that Cleitarchus in turn used both Onesicritus and Megasthenes.

Nevertheless, the specifics of the dialogue itself may well have been concocted to suit the known circumstances, as was probably the case for most parts of the speeches of Alexander reported by Arrian, Curtius and others. It is intriguing that one of the questions put to the Gymnosophists by Alexander, that concerning whether day or night came first, had famously been put to Thales according to Diogenes Laertius and Thales' answer was very similar to that given by the Gymnosophists.[32] Plutarch also quotes Alexander saying, "It is kingly to do well and be ill spoken of," whilst Diogenes Laertius attributes the coining of this aphorism to Antisthenes, the founder of the Cynical school of philosophy.[33] Either Alexander was so familiar with the teachings of these philosophers that he frequently paraphrased them or else some early writer has put their words into his mouth. Whichever is the true explanation, it is revealing of Alexander's philosophical affiliations in the early sources.

---

[26] Strabo, Geography 15.1.63-66.
[27] Plutarch, Life of Alexander 65; Metz Epitome 78-83.
[28] Palladius, On the Life of the Brahmans in Legends of Alexander the Great, trans. Richard Stoneman, Everyman 1994.
[29] Plutarch, Life of Alexander 64.
[30] E.g. AM Wolohojian, The Romance of Alexander the Great by Pseudo-Callisthenes (Armenian version), 223.
[31] NGL Hammond, Sources for Alexander the Great, pp.121-124.
[32] Diogenes Laertius, Thales 9.
[33] Plutarch, Moralia 181F; Diogenes Laertius, Antisthenes 4.

"A Philosopher in Arms"

Figure 2.2. Alexander visiting Diogenes at Corinth (Louis Loeb, 1899)

That Onesicritus provided a relatively philosophical portrait of Alexander is also suggested by the quotation of Alexander given by Lucian:-

I should like, Onesicritus, to come back to life for a little while after my death to see how men read these present events then. If now they praise and welcome them, do not be surprised, for they think, every one of them, that this is a fine bait to catch my goodwill.

Lucian, Essay on How to Write History

"These present events" could also mean "these things before us", so Pearson[34] has argued that Alexander was reading a draft of part of Onesicritus' book. He reasoned that the king's comment therefore denigrates Onesicritus and must have been quoted to damage him by a third party. However, it is pure supposition that Alexander was referring to any written account rather than to events happening around him. In particular, the Greek verb translated here as "read" means also to know again. It has a similar generality in Greek as the English verb "to read", which may be used to mean interpret or know, as in the case of the reading of minds. In truth, Onesicritus is far more likely to have quoted philosophical conversations between himself and Alexander than any

---

[34] L Pearson, The Lost Histories of Alexander The Great, p. 87.

other contemporaneous historian. As I have noted, Onesicritus was a keen student of cynical philosophy and this is an excellent example of Alexander embracing the same ethos. Furthermore, Alexander's words cannot denigrate Onesicritus, unless you already believe for other reasons that Onesicritus wrote lies and distortions. Since Pearson's interpretation still does not make the words intrinsically derogatory of Onesicritus, he does not in fact have any good reason to suppose that they do not come from Onesicritus' book. Why, anyway, should Alexander have been so profoundly fascinated by people's reactions to mere fabrications as to wish to return from the dead to observe them? Surely such an intense expression of interest would only be justified by knowledge of posterity's judgement of Alexander's *actual* behaviour or achievements? It is a recognised fact that Alexander exhibited considerable concern to secure the adulation of posterity throughout his career: for instance, Arrian quotes him as saying, "Toil and risk are the price of glory, but it is a lovely thing to live with courage and to die leaving an everlasting fame."

Our impression of Onesicritus as the most biographical of the lost primary sources is reinforced by his having recorded and listed some of the books that Alexander had sent out to him in Asia by Harpalus.[35] The identities of their authors attest to an impeccable literary taste, with the inclusion of all three of the great tragic playwrights, Aeschylus, Sophocles and Euripides. Furthermore, it is from Onesicritus (as well as Callisthenes), that we hear the revealing story of the recension of the Iliad prepared by Aristotle and kept beneath Alexander's pillow; Dio Chrysostom (4th Discourse on Kingship, 39) says Alexander knew the Iliad by heart. He was virtually a bookworm by ancient standards, as well as a connoisseur of theatre and poetry.

This side of the king's character also beams forth from his penchant for quoting Euripides, who was especially highly regarded and fondly remembered in Macedon, where he had written the Bacchae whilst residing at the court of King Archelaus a year or so before his death in 406BC. Numerous of our sources quote Alexander reciting the playwright. These instances clearly emanate from more than one primary source, so there is no doubt that they represent authentic reports of one of Alexander's traits. They also span the king's career, for Plutarch[36] reveals that Alexander quoted an equivocal line from the Medeia to Pausanias, before the latter assassinated his father, whilst Nicobule[37] has the king recite an entire scene of Andromeda during the banquet that saw the onset of his fatal illness. Plutarch[38] also records Alexander quoting from the Bacchae and another, unidentified play of Euripides in criticism of Callisthenes. Arrian[39] cites Alexander reciting Euripides to express cynicism to the Chaldean priests,

---

[35] Plutarch, Life of Alexander 8.
[36] Plutarch, Life of Alexander 10.4.
[37] Athenaeus 12.537d.
[38] Plutarch, Life of Alexander 53.2-3.
[39] Arrian 7.16.6; the quote is from an unknown play by Euripides, which is now lost.

"A Philosopher in Arms"

who were warning him against entering Babylon. It is intriguing that both Plutarch and Curtius[40] mention the incendiary quotation from Euripides' Andromache pronounced by Cleitus in his confrontation with Alexander, which resulted in his death at the king's hands. Was Cleitus adding insult to injury by parodying Alexander's habit of quoting Euripides?

Figure 2.3. Alexander blocks Diogenes' sun (1696)

The other literary masterpiece that was ever on Alexander's lips was his beloved Iliad. This he certainly knew well enough that he sometimes resorted to paraphrasing passages in his everyday conversations. As will be shown, some examples of this, though faithfully recorded by our sources, seem previously to have escaped the notice of scholarship.

---

[40] Plutarch, Life of Alexander 51.5; Curtius 8.1.28-29.

Alexander's Lovers by Andrew Chugg

We know that Alexander actively sought to recruit philosophers into his retinue. The most prominent in the extant sources are Aristotle's great-nephew, Callisthenes of Olynthus, Anaxarchus of Abdera and the gymnosophist Calanus, who accompanied the king during his return from India, only to immolate himself in purifying fire when the expedition reached Persia. This was said to have been his response to suffering from some kind of intestinal disorder,[41] which certainly underlines the sincerity with which the gymnosophists practiced what they preached.

Anaxarchus is stated to have consoled Alexander with a rather obsequious argument that the king stood above the law, when Alexander was stricken with remorse after his killing of Cleitus.[42] This recalls the idealistic concept of a virtuous and excellent philosopher-king supposed to stand above the law and emulate godhead as expressed by Aristotle in his Politics and Nicomachian Ethics.[43] Aristotle seemingly dedicated his philosophical treatise on the Cosmos to Alexander, an act that hints at his philosophical aspirations for his pupil.

The evidence suggests that Alexander maintained a genuine interest in philosophical issues, probably stimulated by the inculcation of Aristotle's curriculum. However, he was far from being an uncritical practitioner of philosophical ideals. Despite his professed admiration for the abstemiousness and asceticism practiced by Diogenes and the gymnosophists, his own behaviour was notably extravagant in the exploitation of material wealth: the Susa weddings and the funeral of Hephaistion are excellent examples. It is perhaps especially admirable, perhaps almost scientific in its empiricism, that he was quite capable of rejecting philosophical notions, which he considered to have been refuted by his personal observations and experiences. Plutarch[44] says he fell out with Aristotle, because he found the latter's conviction that barbarians (i.e. non-Greeks) should be treated as sub-humans to be false and counterproductive. In general, Alexander always exhibited a keen intellectual curiosity in philosophical matters, but it is difficult to recognise any sign of the fervour of a disciple. Though the expedition against Persia began as a crusade to liberate fellow Greeks from the barbarian yoke, it ended with Persians inducted into the army, appointed to the rule of provinces and married into the royal family. In matters of policy, Alexander preferred pragmatism to ideology.

Plutarch expends great literary energy in forging a case that Alexander behaved and operated as a kind of philosopher-king. He alludes to this point of view in his Life of Alexander, for example saying of the king:

He was by nature a lover of learning and a lover of reading… that eager yearning for philosophy, which was embedded in his nature and which ever grew with his growth, did not

---

[41] Arrian 7.3; Plutarch 69.3.
[42] Arrian, 4.9.7; Plutarch, Life of Alexander 52.3.
[43] A. B. Bosworth, Alexander and the East: The Tragedy of Triumph, Oxford 1998, pp.104-107.
[44] Plutarch, Life of Alexander 8.3 & Moralia 329B.

"A Philosopher in Arms"

subside from his soul, as is testified by the honour in which he held Anaxarchus, by his gift of fifty talents to Xenocrates, and by the attentions which he so lavishly bestowed upon Dandamis and Calanus.

Plutarch, Life of Alexander 8

However, Plutarch invested the main thrust of his argument in his less widely read essays "On the Fortune or Virtue of Alexander", wherein he repeatedly described Alexander as behaving "like a philosopher".[45] Plutarch's views in this respect have been dismissed as rhetorical exercises by Bosworth,[46] but they actually deserve some attention and even respect. Plutarch was vastly familiar with the lost primary sources, written by men who knew Alexander personally and shared in his campaigns. Hammond[47] has found evidence for at least twenty-three sources for Plutarch's Life of Alexander. Conversely, Hammond argues that the other surviving histories are mainly based on two or three sources each. Consequently, it is probable that Plutarch's account of Alexander is not only the most biographical to come down to us, but also the most representative of the very wide range of perspectives that existed in the lost primary sources. Furthermore, it is unlikely that Plutarch originated the philosophical Alexander. Rather he is probably preserving an otherwise lost tradition from a subset of the primary sources, including, for example, Onesicritus.

It is also pertinent to recall that Alexander's era was the age of the ideal of the philosopher-king, as famously conceived and promulgated in the Republic of Plato, who had been the mentor of Aristotle at the Academy. Clearly, it would be surprising if this novel and demanding model of kingship was not impressed upon the youthful Alexander. When we recall Plato's ill-fated attempts to realise this ideal with Dionysius and Dion in Syracuse,[48] we can better appreciate the allure of the opportunity dangled before Aristotle to succeed where his preceptor had failed: to achieve a kind of realisation of the dream that societies should be ruled by well-meaning philosophers rather than by tyrants, oligarchs or even democrats. For it is a strange distortion of history, when we see the Socratic School portrayed as the Philosophy Department of the Athenian Democracy. In reality the political thrust of Socrates and his followers was stimulated by a keenly felt revulsion for the horrors perpetrated in Athens and her colonies by the democratic state: the ravaging of Melos, the execution of the admirals and the general misconduct of the Peloponnesian War. After all, was it not a worse thing that evil should be perpetrated in the name of all the citizens, rather than just a few? Basically, this was why the young, oligarchic noblemen of the eupatrid classes embraced the Socratic elenchus with especial warmth.

---

[45] Plutarch, Moralia, especially 327-333.
[46] A. B. Bosworth, Alexander and the East: The Tragedy of Triumph, Oxford 1998, pp.2-3.
[47] NGL Hammond, Three Historians of Alexander the Great (1983) and Sources for Alexander the Great (1993), CUP.
[48] Plato, Letters VII and VIII.

Fundamentally, this was why the restored Democracy elected to execute Socrates, when even the tyrannous Thirty had tolerated him as a merely irritant gadfly.

Where Socrates failed with Alcibiades and Critias and Plato failed with Dionysius and Dion, can Aristotle be said to have succeeded with Alexander? Did Alexander see himself as an incarnation of the Philosopher-King? It would seem that there is an unrecognised element of the truth in this perspective on Alexander's career, but it is far from being the entire truth. Confronted by the dramatic vastness and infinite complexity of Asia, Alexander gradually invented his own pragmatic philosophy of power. Ironically too, the most readily discernible influence of the Socratic School upon Alexander's behaviour appears to derive from its most prodigal exponent, the mercenary Xenophon. If Alexander consciously pursued any Socratic ideal of kingship, it was Xenophon's version as defined in the Cyropaidia, a work of political philosophy, which masquerades as a biography of the founder of the Persian Empire. Numerous of Alexander's reported idiosyncrasies have striking parallels in Xenophon's idealised conception of Cyrus. Here are a few of the innumerable instances of Alexander's emulation of Cyrus: as Cyrus adopted the Median dress,[49] so Alexander adopted Persian attire[50]; Cyrus stayed with the wounded rather than go off to dinner[51] and Alexander also kept company with his casualties after battles[52]; Cyrus gave gifts of food and drink to those he wished to honour[53] and Alexander, we are told, when the rarest fruits or fish were brought to him from the sea-coast, would distribute them to each of his companions until he was the only one for whom none remained.[54]

Arrian[55] notes that Alexander is said to have recalled Xenophon and the Ten Thousand in his address to his troops before the battle of Issus. If he had therefore read Xenophon's Anabasis, it is overwhelmingly likely he also knew the same author's Cyropaidia. In short, anyone who wishes to understand Alexander's perspective on his world needs to examine the Cyropaidia and the Iliad with just as much care and attention as Plutarch, Arrian, Curtius and the other conventional sources that specifically address Alexander's career.

My own investigations on the subject of Alexander's tomb have contributed one new strand to the evidence for the intellectual Alexander. I have shown that there are good reasons to suppose that the semicircle of life-size statues of Greek poets and philosophers at the Memphite Serapeum in North Saqqara were among the adornments of the first tomb of the king, fashioned by

---

[49] Xenophon, Cyropaidia 8.1.40.
[50] Plutarch, Life of Alexander 45.
[51] Cyropaidia 5.4.18.
[52] E.g. Arrian 2.12.1.
[53] Cyropaidia 8.2.4.
[54] Plutarch, Life of Alexander 23.5.
[55] Arrian, Anabasis 2.7.8.

"A Philosopher in Arms"

command of his general, friend and putative half-brother Ptolemy Soter.[56] These early-Hellenistic sculptures are located so as to guard the entrance to a temple constructed by the pharaoh Nectanebo II, which is the likely site of Alexander's initial sepulchre. Homer presides over the group at its centre, just as his works lay at the heart of the king's literary tastes.

Another Alexander has grown to dominate the modern conception of the king: this is Alexander the soldier, a strategist of genius and an inspirational leader of men. The truth of these things is indisputable. They are a quintessential aspect of the history of the king. But equally and assuredly they constitute an incomplete version of the truth, sufficiently restrictive in its perspective and limited in its focus as to render Alexander an incomprehensible megalomaniac in the diatribes of his modern detractors. It is not enough to know the king's mind or to list his victories. We must pierce through innumerable layers of obfuscation and propaganda to reach his heart and feel his tragedy. It is, therefore, ultimately essential to see Alexander through the eyes of those he loved and who loved him in return.

---

[56] AM Chugg, The Sarcophagus of Alexander the Great? Greece & Rome, April 2002 and The Sarcophagus of Alexander the Great, Minerva Sept-Oct 2002.

3. Hephaistion, The Chiliarch

"Fire walk with me..." David Lynch, Twin Peaks

Introduction

The kingdom of Macedon in the mid 340's BC was a land still steeped in Homeric tradition, yet also permeated and entranced by the scintillating cultural revolution of the classical age instigated by Periclean Athens. Such was the context in which one of the most significant yet controversial romances in history took flame. This was the ardent friendship of Alexander, Crown Prince of Macedon, and Hephaistion Amyntoros, which was to endure until the latter's death among the mountains of distant Persia almost two decades later. Their relationship took as its exemplar the Homeric tradition of the heroic friendship of Achilles and Patroclus. From Athens came Aristotle to catalyse their dreams with the philosophy of the Platonic Academy. With such passionate precepts to inspire them, how could they fail to demonstrate the peculiar ability of love to conquer all?

At The Court of King Philip

In the second quarter of the 4th century BC the city-state of Thebes took over the role of the dominant military power in Greece from Sparta. A regiment entirely comprising pairs of homosexual lovers called the Sacred Band, which had been founded by her leading general, Epaminondas, spearheaded her army. The concept was that members of the Band would be ashamed to exhibit any sign of cowardice in front of their lovers, so the regiment would prove exceptionally brave and unyielding in battle. Following a Theban military intervention in Macedon in 368BC, Philip the son of Amyntas, future king of Macedon and father of Alexander, was the most prominent member of a large group of hostages held to guarantee Macedon's support for the Theban hegemony. He was lodged for three years in the house of Epaminondas' father and the experience would seem to have imbued him with the chivalric model for gay romance, which was epitomised by the Sacred Band.[57] Certainly, Philip's court was subsequently famous for its same-sex affairs:-

> Did [the Friends and Companions of Philip] not in some cases, grown men though they were, go shaved and depilated, in other cases even go so far as to have anal intercourse with each another, though they were bearded? In fact each had in his train two or three sex-minions, and they themselves granted to others the same favours. Hence one might rightly assume that they

---

[57] Diodorus 16.2; Justin 6.9.7 & 7.5.2-3; Plutarch, Pelopidas 26.

were not Companions, but companionesses [i.e. courtesans], and might rightly call them not soldiers, but catamites; for they were man-killers by nature, man-whores by habit.

Theopompus, Histories 49 (Athenaeus 6.260e-f & Polybius VIII 9.9-12)

Onomarchus gave a laurel wreath of gold, votive offering of the Ephesians, to Physcidas, the son of Lycolas of Trichoneium, a beautiful boy. This boy was taken to Philip by his father and was there prostituted, and afterwards dismissed without reward.

Theopompus quoted by Athenaeus 13.605b

Nevertheless, Philip as king achieved still greater renown as the lover of innumerable women, at least seven of whom he made his brides. Athenaeus (13.557b-e) comments that it was axiomatic that "Philip always married a new wife with war in mind", often that is for purposes of policy and diplomacy as much as for love. Athenaeus has also provided us with comprehensive list:-

i) Audata of Illyria whose daughter was Cynane

ii) Phila, sister of Derdas and Machatas

iii) Nicesipolis of Pherae in Thessaly, mother of the princess Thessalonike

iv) Philinna of Larissa, whose imbecilic son was named Arrhidaeus

v) Olympias of Molossia, mother of Alexander and Cleopatra

vi) Meda, daughter of Cothelas

vii) Cleopatra, niece of Attalus, whose daughter was Europa

Hammond thinks one other, a daughter of Atheas, is a possibility.[58]

Justin notes that Philip had many sons,[59] though we know that only two legitimate sons survived him: these were Alexander and the mentally impaired Arrhidaeus. Additionally, Ptolemy Soter is strongly rumoured to have been his illegitimate offspring by Arsinoë.[60] If so, he was probably fathered when Philip was 14, between his stints as a hostage in Illyria and at Thebes.

However, Philip's love life was ultimately overshadowed by the disastrous scandal, which erupted from his relationship with the young Orestid aristocrat, Pausanias. The king had appointed this handsome youth to be one of his bodyguards, whilst also conducting an affair with him. However, the king's ardour eventually became distracted by a second youth, also (confusingly) called Pausanias. The first Pausanias was moved by jealousy to insult the second with accusations of effeminacy and promiscuity. The second Pausanias took the first's bitter invective very much to heart. Tragically, within days he virtually committed suicide by insinuating himself between the king and his assailants in

---

[58] N. G. L. Hammond, Philip of Macedon (London, 1994) 42.
[59] Justin 9.8.
[60] Pausanias 1.6.2; Curtius 9.8.22; Armenian Alexander Romance 269; Aelian in the Suda s.v. Lagos confirms that Ptolemy was a bastard and only the adoptive son of Lagos.

the turmoil of a battle against the Illyrians, having previously confided to his friend Attalus that he intended to put his bravery and fidelity well beyond the reproach of his vanquished rival.

Attalus subsequently revenged his friend's untimely demise by getting the first Pausanias drunk at a party and consigning him whilst senseless to be raped by Attalus' muleteers. An incensed Pausanias brought the matter of his maltreatment before the king, who offered his condolences together with compensation in the form of a higher rank among his bodyguards. However, Philip conspicuously failed to impose any actual punishment upon Attalus, whose niece he was in the process of wooing. And so Pausanias began to nurse a festering grudge against his monarch, whose ostensible kindness seemed to mask a private contempt for his bodyguard. When, some time after, Attalus was appointed as one of Philip's generals, Pausanias, feeling his betrayal to be complete, stabbed the king to death at a celebration of the wedding of Alexander's sister, Cleopatra, to Alexander of Epirus in the theatre at Aegae.[61]

From these circumstances it can be appreciated that the Macedonian court in which Alexander and Hephaistion grew up was likely to have been not merely sympathetic but positively encouraging to same-sex affairs between young men. In the light of the tradition set by Thebes and Sparta, it was probably considered beneficial to the maintenance of morale on the battlefield. In this context it would have been relatively abnormal for handsome youths such as Alexander and Hephaistion to spend their teenage years devoid of homosexual experiences.

Yet, equally, the Macedonian court would have expected a parallel and active interest in the opposite sex from its princes and aristocratic youths. Among the clannish and continually feuding leading families of Macedon, the production of numerous potential heirs and marriageable daughters was an urgent social imperative. This was especially true of the royal family, among whom assassinations, murders and deaths in battle were particularly commonplace. The begetting of offspring was a duty for which Alexander would have been expected to practice frequently.

Adolescence

We know from Arrian that Hephaistion was the son of a certain Amyntor and a native of Pella in Macedon.[62] The name Hephaistion alludes to the Greek god of fire, Hephaistos, but it was not particularly common in Macedon at the time. Conversely, the name Amyntor may be a Hellenisation of the name Amyntas,

---

[61] The principal sources are Diodorus 16.93-94 and Justin 9.6; Aristotle Pol. 1311b2-4 provides unimpeachable contemporary corroboration of the story by stating that, "the attack on Philip by Pausanias [occurred] because Philip allowed him to be outrageously treated by Attalus and his company."
[62] Arrian, Indica 18.3.

which was in widespread use within the Macedonian aristocracy and the royal family. We are told by Curtius that Hephaistion was the same age as Alexander (*sicut aetate par erat regi*) and that he was reared and educated with the prince (*cum ipso pariter eductus*).[63] This tends to suggest that he was among the companions of the prince during his studies with Aristotle at the Precinct of the Nymphs near Mieza, whilst Alexander was in his mid-teens.[64] This inference is further corroborated by the fact that a book of letters to Hephaistion, though now lost, is listed among the works of Aristotle by Diogenes Laertius.[65]

There is also a reference to Hephaistion's friendship with Alexander at the age of 15 in the semi-legendary version of the king's career known as the Alexander Romance, which appears to have been edited together from older tales in Alexandria in the 3rd century AD. This mention occurs in the context of an apocryphal story concerning Alexander's participation in the Olympic chariot race at Pisa:-

And one day when Alexander was 15 years old… sailing with Hephaistion, his friend, he easily reached Pisa… and he went off to stroll with Hephaistion.[66]

The significance of this is that it explicitly mentions Alexander's friendship with Hephaistion fully five years before they first appear together in the more authoritative ancient sources. It is also interesting that the Olympic Games really were held in 340BC when Alexander was 15, so perhaps there is an element of truth in this story.

One further hint of an early association between the pair is the fact that another set of letters to Hephaistion from Xenocrates, the Head of the Academy in Athens between 339/8 and 314/3BC, is also recorded by Diogenes Laertius.[67] The most likely occasion for Hephaistion to have made the acquaintance of Xenocrates is Alexander's visit to Athens as Philip's envoy following the battle of Chaeronea in 338BC.[68] We know that Alexander himself was personally on good terms with Xenocrates, since Plutarch records that he sent the philosopher a gift of 50 talents, although Xenocrates declined to accept all but half a talent of it on the grounds that he had no need of such wealth.[69]

Some have sought to refute an early beginning for the relationship of Alexander and Hephaistion by virtue of the latter's absence from a group of five "companions" of the prince, namely Harpalus, Nearchus, Ptolemy, Erigyius and

---

[63] Curtius 3.12.16.
[64] Plutarch, Life of Alexander 7.
[65] Diogenes Laertius, Lives of Eminent Philosophers, Aristoteles.
[66] The Romance of Alexander the Great by Pseudo-Callisthenes, Sections 49-50, Armenian version, translated by A M Wolohojian, Columbia University Press, 1969; see also Richard Stoneman (trans.), The Greek Alexander Romance, Book I.18, 1991.
[67] Diogenes Laertius, Lives of Eminent Philosophers, Xenocrates.
[68] Justin, Epitome of the Philippic History of Pompeius Trogus 9.4.
[69] Plutarch, Life of Alexander 8.4.

Laomedon, who were exiled by Philip in 337/6BC.[70] He did this to punish Alexander for his abortive attempt to marry the daughter of Pixodarus, Satrap of Caria, because Philip had himself been negotiating the marriage of his imbecile son, Arrhidaeus, to this girl. However, these "companions" all seem to have been significantly older than the prince and were probably merely leading members of Alexander's clique at the Macedonian court.[71] Philip probably picked out the most politically dangerous of the prince's supporters, rather than his most intimate friends.

There is also some circumstantial evidence that is consistent with an amorous sexual relationship between Alexander and Hephaistion during their teenage years. This takes the form of several anecdotes concerning Alexander's indifference to women in this period. The most controversial of these is related by Athenaeus:-

So Hieronymus, in his Epistles, quotes Theophrastus as saying that Alexander was not well-disposed to sexual love (aphrodisia). *Olympias, at any rate, and Philip were aware of this, and actually caused the Thessalian courtesan Callixeina, who was a very beautiful woman, to lie with him; for they feared he might prove to be a womanish man* (gynnis), *and Olympias often begged him to have intercourse with Callixeina.*

Athenaeus, Deipnosophistae 10.435a

Hieronymus of Cardia was a protégé of Eumenes, Alexander's Secretary. He wrote what is generally considered to be the most reliable history of the Wars of the Successors following Alexander's death. Similarly, Theophrastus was a protégé of Aristotle and his successor as head of the Lyceum at Athens. He died in ~287BC at an advanced age. He probably knew Olympias and Alexander. To him also are attributed a number of other hostile (and possibly slanderous) stories about the Macedonian King and Queen.

In this quotation *gynnis* is a sort of masculine gender version of the Greek word for a woman. Especially in the context of this passage there is an unambiguous imputation that Alexander was the passive partner in a relationship with another man. Nevertheless, some have instead interpreted the story as an indication of impotence, partly because Athenaeus also speculates that Alexander's reputation for sexual restraint might be attributable to too much drinking. Thus he quotes Aristotle to the effect that the semen of drunkards becomes watery immediately before the Callixeina story. However, Alexander was known to have fathered at least two children when Theophrastus wrote and the term *gynnis* would hardly seem apposite for a case of impotence or infertility.

The truth of Theophrastus' tale has been doubted on the entirely reasonable grounds of his known antipathy to Alexander and Olympias. However, Plutarch has a story, which seems to come from a favourable source, but which suggests the same pattern of women being thrust upon the reluctant youth:-

---

[70] Plutarch, Life of Alexander 10.4; Arrian, Anabasis 3.6.5.
[71] W Heckel, The Marshals of Alexander's Empire, London, 1992, section iv.

Hephaistion, The Chiliarch

A girl was brought to him [Alexander] late in the evening with the intent that she should spend the night with him, and he asked her, 'Why at this time?' She replied, 'I had to wait to get my husband to go to bed'; whereupon Alexander bitterly rebuked his servants, since, owing to them, he had so narrowly escaped becoming an adulterer.

Plutarch, Moralia 179E

This is told among the Sayings of Alexander that relate to his later teenage years, for Plutarch presents all of these quotations in approximately their chronological order. It makes it much more difficult to dismiss Theophrastus. Even if there is an element of exaggeration, it is nevertheless an old aphorism that the most effective propaganda is founded in truth. Plutarch has also written that Alexander did not sleep with any woman before Barsine,[72] which appears to mean after the Battle of Issus in 333BC, when he was 23. Maybe this will not be deemed so astounding relative to modern abstemious sexual standards, but it was rather remarkable, if true, for a prince in 4th century BC Macedonia.

Finally on this point, Aelian reports that Apelles, the painter, fell in love with Alexander's mistress, Campaspe (a.k.a. Pankaste or Pakate), who came from Larissa in Thessaly and was "said to have been the first woman Alexander slept with."[73] Pliny wrote that Alexander casually gave "Pankaspe" to the painter, demonstrating that his own feelings for her were rather slight (see Frontispiece). This woman may be identical with Callixeina, who was also described as a Thessalian courtesan by Theophrastus. It would not be unusual for an hetaira to have both a given and a professional name: Callixeina, meaning "beautiful guest-woman", reads like the latter.

Assuming these accounts from early sources are not entirely fictional, the alternative explanations of Alexander's behaviour would appear to be:-

a) Impotence or similar sexual dysfunction
b) A genuine dislike of the active role in sex
c) Moral objections
d) A passionate ongoing affair (with Hephaistion)

The first may readily be discounted by virtue of his subsequent fatherhood and his affair with the eunuch Bagoas. The second is dubious on the same grounds, although Plutarch quotes Alexander as saying that sleep and sex above all else made him conscious of his mortality.[74] Yet it is ambiguous whether this was a sincere complaint or an ironic rebuke to his flatterers, since he also once used the blood flow from a wound in his leg as witness to his mortality.[75]

---

[72] Plutarch, Life of Alexander 21.4.
[73] Aelian, Varia Historia 12.34; Pliny, Natural History 35.86-7; Pankaste is called Pakate by Lucian, Imagines 7; the manuscripts of Pliny mostly have Campaspe, but the Codex Bambergensis of Pliny NH has Pancaspe, which harmonizes better with Lucian and Aelian.
[74] Plutarch, Life of Alexander 22.3.
[75] Plutarch, Moralia 180E.

Alexander's Lovers by Andrew Chugg

On the issue of sexual morality, Alexander does seem to have held strong views against rape, the sexual abuse of slaves, stealing of other men's partners or any kind of sexual aggression. Numerous anecdotes illustrate his moderation and restraint relative, for example, to the occasionally disreputable behaviour of his father:-

Moreover, when Philoxenus, the commander of his forces on the sea-board, wrote that there was with him a certain Theodorus, of Tarentum, who had two boys of surpassing beauty to sell, and enquired whether Alexander would buy them, Alexander was incensed, and cried out many times to his friends, asking them what shameful thing Philoxenus had ever seen in him that he should spend his time making such disgraceful proposals. And on Philoxenus himself he heaped much reproach in a letter, bidding him to send Theodorus to perdition, merchandise and all.[76] He severely rebuked Hagnon also for writing to him that he wanted to buy Crobylus, whose beauty was famous in Corinth, as a present for him. Furthermore, on learning that Damon and Timotheus, two Macedonian soldiers under Parmenio's command, had raped the wives of certain mercenaries, he wrote to Parmenio ordering him, in case the men were convicted, to punish them and put them to death as wild beasts born for the destruction of mankind.

Plutarch, Life of Alexander 22.1-2

A story is told that Alexander wrote to Theodorus, the brother of Proteas, "If you are not in love with your music-girl, please send her to me for ten talents." Another of Alexander's Companions, Antipatrides, brought a beautiful lyre-player to a drinking party. Alexander, stirred to love at the sight of her, asked Antipatrides whether he happened to be at all in love with the girl; and when he admitted that he was, Alexander said, "You abominable wretch! Please take her away from here at once." Alexander restrained himself and did not touch the woman...On another occasion Cassander forced Python, beloved by Evius the flute-player, to kiss him, and Alexander, seeing that Evius was vexed, leapt up in anger against Cassander, exclaiming, "It isn't permissible even to fall in love with anybody, because of you and people like you."

Plutarch, Moralia 760C & Sayings of Alexander 19 & 20, Moralia 180F

But Carystius in his Historical Notes says: "Charon of Chalcis had a beautiful boy who was dear to him. But when Alexander, at a drinking party in the house of Craterus, praised the boy, Charon bade him kiss Alexander; and Alexander said, 'Not so! For that will not delight me so much as it will pain you.' For, passionate as this king was, he was in like measure self-controlled when it came to the observance of decency and the best form. When, for example, he had taken captive the daughters of Darius and his wife as well, a woman of very distinguished beauty, he not only kept his hands off them, but he even refrained from letting them know that they were captives, and ordered that everything be done for them just as if Darius were still king. Therefore Darius, on learning this, raised his arms and prayed to the Sun that either he or Alexander might be king."

Athenaeus 13.603b-c.

---

[76] Cf. Plutarch, Moralia 333A & 1099D.

However, these moral stances did not exclude relationships with either men or indeed women, as Alexander's later practice confirmed. Apart from his three wives, his mistress Barsine and reputed liaisons with Cleophis and Thalestris, we have scandalised comments from the Latin historians about the harem he inherited from Darius[77]:-

The royal quarters had a complement of 365 concubines, the number Darius had possessed, and along with them were herds of eunuchs also accustomed to prostitute themselves.

Curtius 6.6.8

To copy the Persians in their excesses as well as their dress, [Alexander] divided his nights among the troops of royal concubines, women of superlative beauty and noble birth.

Justin 12.3.10

Among the Greek sources, Diodorus tells essentially the same story, confirming that the common source must have been Cleitarchus, whose lost History Concerning Alexander was used by the authors of all these surviving texts:

Alexander, following Darius, retained in his retinue concubines as numerous as the days of the year, women of such superlative loveliness as selection from all the lands of Asia could gather in. Nightly they processed around the king's bower, so he could choose which he wished to deflower. In fact Alexander rarely employed their services and generally stuck to his established practices, for fear of offending his fellow Macedonians.

Diodorus 17.77.6-7

Even whilst still the Crown Prince of Macedon, Alexander would have experienced no shortage of unattached and willing girls, so it is hardly surprising that his apparent abstinence in the face of such plenty should have perplexed Olympias.

In the final analysis, it is his affair with Hephaistion which provides the most satisfying and cogent explanation of his indifference to women in his youth and which is most consistent with the entire body of evidence. We can easily understand why Alexander would not have welcomed distractions, if his affections were fully committed elsewhere. In direct support of this view, it is relevant to note that Lucian makes Philip complain about Alexander's *excessive affection for Hephaistion (Hephaistiona hyperagapon)* in his Dialogues of the Dead.[78]

Appearance & Demeanour

The ancient writers provide some limited information on Hephaistion's appearance in the context of an incident following the battle of Issus when the

---

[77] These comments of Curtius and Justin relate to the time just after the death of Darius, at which point the former Great King's harem fell into Alexander's hands: *for Darius, though engaged in war in which his entire empire was at stake, took round with him 360 concubines, according to the account given by Dicaearchus in the 3rd book of his History of Greece.* Athenaeus, Deipnosophistae 13.557b.
[78] Lucian, Dialogues of the Dead 12.

captured Persian queens mistook Hephaistion for the king. Arrian states that Hephaistion and Alexander were dressed identically,[79] but that the former was taller. Curtius also notes Hephaistion's superior stature,[80] whilst Diodorus adds that he was more handsome than the king.[81] Justin[82] introduces Hephaistion as:-

A favourite (percarus) of Alexander's firstly because of his good looks and boyish charms, then for his complete compliance with the King's wishes.

The reference to Hephaistion's good looks and boyish charms is an undisguised allusion to the ancient supposition that the relationship was sexual and the reference to Hephaistion's compliancy could also be seen as a sexual allusion.

However, Hephaistion was not considered effeminate, as another passage from Curtius makes clear:-

Therefore [Alexander] welcomed the emissaries from the Sacae and gave them Euxenippus as their escort. He was as yet a mere youth and beloved by [conciliatum] *the king for his cuteness of those years, but, although he was equally as handsome as Hephaistion, he could not match his masculine charm* [lepore], *being barely manly at all it appears.*[83]

The word *conciliatum* is rather allusive, but the context implies that it is the homoerotic attractions of Hephaistion and Euxenippus in Alexander's eyes that are being compared. The implication is that Hephaistion triumphed over his rival for Alexander's affection by virtue of his virility. The word for charm in the original Latin is *lepore*, which is the same as the word for a hare (in the ablative case). A hare was a traditional gift from the homosexual lover to the beloved. This subtle piece of innuendo is probably the closest any of our ancient sources comes to insinuating that Hephaistion might have been the active partner in the relationship.

There is an even more fascinating aspect of this passage. It is likely that "Euxenippus" is in fact an obscure reference to Bagoas the Eunuch. He was in Alexander's service at this time and is stated by Athenaeus and Plutarch as well as Curtius himself to have had a sexual relationship with the king. The wording "flower of his youth" (*aetatis flore*) recalls "flower of boyhood" (*flore pueritiae*) with which Curtius had earlier introduced Bagoas.[84] The name "Euxenippus" is actually a modern revision by Hedicke and nobody of this name is found elsewhere in the ancient sources on Alexander. The manuscripts read *excipinon* or *escipinon*. It is possible that this is some kind attempt to transliterate a Greek title meaning "Welcomer" or "Greeter" using the Latin verb *excipio*. This would fit well with the task of looking after the delegation and is consistent with the kind of duties that might fall upon a eunuch. Furthermore, the significant stress

---

[79] Arrian, Anabasis 2.12.6.
[80] Curtius 3.12.16.
[81] Diodorus 17.37.5.
[82] Justin, Epitome 12.12.11.
[83] Curtius 7.9.19.
[84] Curtius 6.5.23.

placed on *excipinon* being *"not at all manly"* begs some kind of explanation. It is not very likely terminology for one of Alexander's teenage pages, for they were fiercely virile sons of the Macedonian nobility. Especially in the light of the manuscript difficulties, we should not allow Hedicke to invent a new unmanly man in the flower of his youth with whom Alexander had a sexual relationship, when we already know of an individual who fits the circumstances perfectly.

Apart from the sketchy literary vignettes at least ten ancient sculptures survive, which have more or less tentatively been identified as depictions of Hephaistion. However, it is appropriate to introduce and head a review of the set with the single surviving Hephaistion portrait with a near certain attribution.

Figure 3.1. Votive relief inscribed "To the Hero Hephaistion" (sketch by the author)

Thessalonike Relief (Figure 3.1): The identifications of several other prominent images of Hephaistion rely principally upon close association with representations of Alexander. However, this votive relief now in the Macedonian city of Thessalonike (but found at ancient Pella) is more definitely attributable, by virtue of its inscribed dedication by a certain Diogenes, *To the Hero Hephaistion* [ΔΙΟΓΕΝΗΣΗΦΑΙΣΤΙΩΝΙΗΡΩΙ or DIOGENES

HEPHAISTIONI HEROI in Latin characters]. It was sculpted in the last quarter of the fourth century BC.[85] The young man holding the reins of a horse should almost certainly be identified as a depiction of the deceased hero. Whilst this is the most securely identified of all the representations of Hephaistion, it is unfortunately particularly bland in its characterisation of the hero and lacks those subtle idiosyncrasies in which a critic might recognise realistic portraiture. Its date (323 - c.300BC) shows that the decision delivered to Alexander in May of 323BC by the Oracle of Ammon, that Hephaistion be worshipped as a hero, had some enduring influence after the king's death.[86] It has been assumed that Diogenes was the name of an ordinary individual, who had some reason to wish to honour the memory of Alexander's Chiliarch by commissioning this votive piece. However, I have recently realized that there is a strong case to be made that Diogenes, meaning literally "the Zeus-born" in Greek, refers to Alexander himself. It seems this was the official epithet adopted by the king to reflect his salutation as the son of Zeus-Ammon by the Oracle at Siwa, so it was appropriate that it be used in a context where Hephaistion is designated as a hero in accordance with a pronouncement by the same oracle. I give a detailed account of the complex matter of Alexander's deification and the evidence for his adoption of the epithet *Diogenes* in Appendix A. (Probability that this sculpture depicts Alexander's Hephaistion >95%)

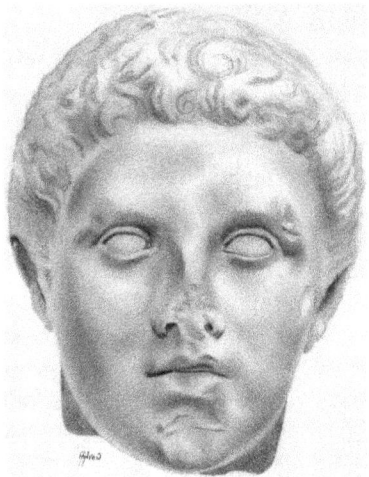

Figure 3.2. The Getty Hephaistion (sketch by the author)

The Getty Head (Figure 3.2): This head of Hephaistion is now in the Getty Museum at Malibu together with the Getty head of Alexander and other fragments in an Attic style. They are said to derive from Megara and date to around 325 - 320BC. Just over life size, this sculpture relies for its identification

---

[85] Andrew Stewart, Faces of Power: Alexander's Image and Hellenistic Politics, California (1993), p.453 & fig. 72.
[86] Plutarch, Life of Alexander 75; Arrian, Anabasis 7.23.6.

on its association with the head of Alexander from the same fragmentary composition and its passing resemblance to the hero of the Diogenes relief at Thessalonike. The composition was sufficiently highly regarded as to have been repaired in ancient times following damage by some earthquake or tumult. However, doubts remain on whether the Getty fragments even come from the same composition, which makes this identification relatively problematical. (Probability 40%)

Figure 3.3. Hephaistion on the Alexander Sarcophagus (sketch by the author)

Alexander Sarcophagus (Figure 3.3): The central rider in the long battle scene on the Alexander Sarcophagus (and also the right-most horseman in the hunting scene on the opposite face) is often said to be Hephaistion. This magnificent tomb was found in the royal cemetery of Sidon in 1887 along with over a dozen less significant sarcophagi. Stylistically, it dates to the last quarter of the 4th century BC. The long battle scene includes Alexander himself on the left and is clearly a highly authentic but idealised representation of a fight between the Macedonian and Persian forces: most probably the battle of Issus. Abdalonymus of Sidon must be the favourite candidate for its original occupant in view of the dating and subject matter. Central prominence in the long battle scene panel of this stunningly fine sarcophagus is given to a Macedonian cavalryman who may well be Hephaistion. Alexander himself has literally been sidelined in the composition in favour of this individual. The most plausible explanation seems to be that Abdalonymus was acknowledging his debt to Hephaistion, who had been responsible for his appointment as king of Sidon.[87] Nevertheless, this remains conjectural and it is also feasible, if less likely, that Abdalonymus was instead honouring one of the Diadochi, such as Antigonus or Ptolemy. (Probability 60%)

---

[87] Curtius 4.1.16-26; Diodorus Siculus 17.47; Justin 11.10.8-9.

Figure 3.4. The Demetrio Hephaistion from Egypt (sketch by the author)

Demetrio Hephaistion (Figure 3.4): This Hephaistion was formerly in the Demetrio collection, but is now in the National Archaeological Museum at Athens. This statuette is a full-length portrayal and is believed to derive from Ptolemaic Egypt, most probably Alexandria. It was most likely sculpted in the 1st century BC and forms a pair with the Demetrio Alexander. Their stances are near mirror images and Alexander's pose matches that of the Alexander Aigiochos, also from Alexandria and now in the British Museum. The clothing of both Demetrio statuettes is identical and relatively correct, comprising a chiton-tunic, a chlamys-cloak, a zona-belt and open-toed lace-up boots with flaps (piloi) at their upper rims. Regarding the tunic, the cloak and the belt, we have contemporaneous references for Alexander's adoption of just such a costume.[88] However, arguments have been put forward that the open-toed style of the boots is unlikely to be earlier than the second century BC and this seems to be the principal basis for suggesting the relatively late date.[89] The clarity of its association with a fairly certain depiction of Alexander makes this a particularly good candidate for a representation of Hephaistion. (Probability 75%)

---

[88] E.g. Ephippus of Olynthus, quoted by Athenaeus, 12.537e-538b; Diodorus Siculus 17.77.5.
[89] Andrew Stewart, Faces of Power, p.339.

Hephaistion, The Chiliarch

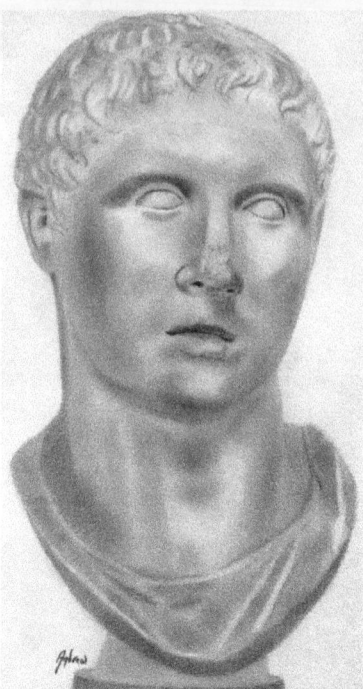

Figure 3.5. The Kyme Hephaistion (sketch by the author)

Kyme Hephaistion (Figure 3.5): From Kyme in Aeolis (NW Turkey), it was found among a group of fragments that included an Alexander-Helios, which seems closely related in style. Each was designed to slot into a full size armoured statue. The pair and some, but not all, elements of the associated group have features that suggest a late Hellenistic date (c.125-75 BC). In particular, these pieces have been tentatively linked with Mithridates VI Eupator of Pontos in the context of his struggle against Rome (89-84BC). It is now in the Archaeological Museum at Istanbul. (Probability 50%)

Figure 3.6. Hephaistion at Alexander's shoulder - the Alsdorf Relief (sketch by the author)

Alsdorf Relief (Figure 3.6): In the Alsdorf Relief, which is a Roman period sarcophagus panel (c.AD200–AD250) held in the Alsdorf collection in Chicago,[90] Hephaistion is supposed to be the hero standing behind the shoulder of a nude Alexander with a seated Heracles. Perhaps Alexander is cast in the role of Meleager, whose ghost Heracles encountered in the underworld. The horse at the right may be Bucephalus. This panel comes from the Antioch area and dates from the Severan period, when Caracalla instigated a major revival of Alexander's cult. The rather prominent chin of this Hephaistion is slightly reminiscent of Ptolemy, but it might also reflect the relatively crude quality standard of this sculpture. (Probability 50%)

Figure 3.7. The Prado head: a possible Hephaistion (sketch by the author)

Prado Head (Figure 3.7): A possible head of Hephaistion in the form of a damaged bronze; now in the Prado, but formerly in the Odeschalchi Collection at Rome. This is the head from a twice-life-size bronze statue originally from the Greek world, which seems on grounds of style and workmanship to be an original from the generation after Alexander's death. It may be a hero or a god, but is most usually seen as one of Alexander's Successors (the Diadochi) with Demetrius Poliorketes or Lysimachus as favourite candidates.[91] However, the date and provenance would also suit a cult statue of Hephaistion, and this identification has been advocated by some,[92] though it should probably be regarded as a possibility rather than a probability. (Probability 25%)

---

[90] The Search for Alexander: An Exhibition, Andronikos et al., New York Graphic Society, Boston (1981), Item 40.
[91] The Search for Alexander: An Exhibition, New York Graphic Society, Boston (1981), Item 12; Stephan F Schröder, Katalog der antiken Skulpturen des Museo del Prado in Madrid, Band 1, Mainz am Rhein (1993), Item 9.
[92] Michael Wood, In the Footsteps of Alexander the Great, BBC (1997), p.221; Andrew Stewart, Faces of Power: Alexander's Image and Hellenistic Politics, California (1993), p.453.

Hephaistion, The Chiliarch

Figure 3.8. Pebble mosaic with a possible Hephaistion on the left (sketch by the author)

Pebble mosaic of a stag hunted by two men and a dog (Figure 3.8): This was found in ancient Pella, Macedonia. It is argued that the figure on the right is Alexander by virtue of the upsweep from the forehead and central parting of his hair (anastole) and the dating of the composition to the late 4th century BC. The taller but coeval figure on the left wields a double-headed axe, which is an attribute of the god Hephaistos, thus he may be Hephaistion.[93] However, this is still a somewhat tenuous basis for the attribution. (Probability 35%)

Youth wielding a double-head axe in the frieze above the entrance to Tomb II at Vergina: If this frieze depicts Philip II hunting in the company of his Royal Pages and Alexander, as would seem likely, then the youth wielding a double-headed axe against the lion is quite possibly Hephaistion, since this implement was symbolic of Hephaistos, after whom he was named. (Probability 30%)

In addition to these, Andrew Stewart also mentions three other Roman copies and an original Greek head wearing a Corinthian helmet from Kos.[94] However,

---

[93] See, for example, Paolo Moreno, Apelles: The Alexander Mosaic, Skira Editore, Milan (2001), pp. 102-4; the dog could be Peritas, cf. Plutarch, Alexander 61 & Theopompus Hist., Fragmenta, 340, line 2 from Julius Pollux, Onomastikon V.42.

[94] Andrew Stewart, Faces of Power: Alexander's Image and Hellenistic Politics, California (1993), Appendix 6: Hephaistion, p.453-455.

the identification of the latter owes much to the supposed association of Alexander with the helmet worn by Athena on his gold staters, which in turn may derive from the mistaken 16th century belief that this Athena was a portrait of Alexander himself. As for the Roman works, a basalt head in Venice may depict the same person as the Prado bronze and it has been postulated that a helmeted Macedonian figure at Naples and a head in the Munich Antiquarium might represent Alexander's Chiliarch. The probabilities of each one of these candidates being genuine are all less than about 25%.

Do any of these representations reveal the real Hephaistion? Stewart argues that attempts to identify Hephaistion on physiognomic grounds among the extensive corpus of Hellenistic portrait heads are doomed by the lack of an established tradition. There is some truth in this, for the most probable Hephaistions differ sufficiently from one another that they would not readily be recognised as the same person without reference to their contexts. Nevertheless, there is a degree of pattern in the repetition of regular, boyish, clean-shaven features with short curly hair, all of which points also agree with the literary tradition, where Hephaistion is stated to have been boyishly good-looking. Yet the portrayal of regular features is more liable to engender bland results that lack distinctive traits, for it requires more accomplished artistry to distinguish much character in a notably handsome face. It is possible that the differences between the appearances of the more probable Hephaistions are due more to lack of subtlety in artistic technique, rather than to the absence of a clear ancient tradition for portraits of Alexander's Chiliarch as suggested by Stewart.

There is also some literary evidence on the subject of ancient portraits of Hephaistion. It is interesting to note a comment by Pliny[95] concerning a lost work:-

[Alexander's sculptor Lysippus] also made a Hephaistion, Alexander the Great's friend, a statue that many attributed to Polyclitus, even though he lived a century beforehand...

However, the most famous lost depiction of Hephaistion is probably that in Aetion's painting of the Marriage of Alexander and Roxane. This was probably painted in Alexander's lifetime during the mid 320's BC and exhibited at the Olympic Games in 324BC.[96] We know it mainly from a detailed description by Lucian:-

But why need I mention those old Sophists, historians and chroniclers, when there is the recent story of Aetion the painter? They say that when he took his picture The Marriage of Roxane and Alexander to Olympia and exhibited it there, Proxenides, one of the Olympic judges there at that time, was delighted with his talent and made Aetion his son-in-law. And what was so wonderful about this painting of his, you may ask, that a judge of the games should give his

---

[95] Pliny, Natural History 34.64.
[96] See the discussion by Andrew Stewart, Faces of Power: Alexander's Image and Hellenistic Politics, University of California, 1993, p.182.

daughter in marriage to an outsider like Aetion? The picture is actually in Italy; I've seen it myself and can describe it to you.

The scene is a very beautiful chamber, and in it there is a bridal couch with Roxane, a maiden of extraordinary beauty, sitting upon it; her eyes are cast down in modesty for Alexander is standing there. There are also some smiling cupids: one, standing behind Roxane, removes the veil from her head showing her to the bridegroom; another takes the sandal off her foot like a true slave, already preparing her for bed; and a third has grabbed Alexander's cloak and is pulling him with all his might towards Roxane. The King himself holds out a crown to the girl, and their best man and helper, Hephaistion, stands by with a blazing torch in his hand, leaning on a very handsome youth. His name is not inscribed, but I think he is Hymenaios. On the other side of the picture are more cupids playing among Alexander's armour; two of them are carrying his spear, represented like labourers staggering under the weight of a beam; two more are dragging a third who reclines on his shield – their king, no doubt – holding it by the handgrips; and another has sneaked inside the breastplate, which is lying face up on the ground – he seems to be waiting in ambush, in order to scare the rest when they drag the shield past him.

All this is not needless triviality and a waste of labour. Aetion is calling attention to Alexander's other love – War – and implying that in his love for Roxane he did not forget his weapons. A further point about the picture is that it had a real matrimonial significance of quite a different sort – it courted Proxenides' daughter for Aetion! So as a by-product of Alexander's Wedding he came away with a wife for himself and the King for best man. His reward for his marriage of the imagination was a real-life marriage of his own.[97]

Lucian's description has inspired a number of reproductions of Aetion's masterpiece from the renaissance onwards, some by famous artists such as Botticelli (elements of his Venus and Mars seem inspired by it) and Giovanni Antonio Bazzi, who is known as Sodoma. The latter based a fresco in the Villa Farnesina in Rome on Lucian's words (see the cover). A rather less accomplished but even more literal interpretation was produced by Johan Erdmann Hümmel in the 19th century.[98]

Lucian's identification of the *very handsome youth* with Hymenaios does not really gel very well with the rest of his description of the work. Hymenaios is the Greek god of marriage, who was traditionally depicted as a winged cupid-like figure bearing a torch and bringing a man together with his future wife. Why, therefore, does Hephaistion bear the torch in the painting and why does he lean on the youth, thus making the latter a mere onlooker? The cupid dragging Alexander towards Roxane would seem to have a better claim to be Hymenaios than the handsome youth. Furthermore, it is anomalous that the fourth of the principal figures should be a god, when the other three are all real historical characters, especially since Lucian did not observe any divine attributes for the youth.

---

[97] Lucian, Herodotus sive Aetion 4-7.
[98] Reproduced in Alexander the Great, The Heroic Ideal, Pierre Briant (1996) p. 139.

If we wish to solve the mystery of the youth's identity, then we should be looking for a suitable contemporaneous character from Alexander's court and we need to seek a thread which links all four principal figures. Actually Lucian has already found the likeliest unifying theme, when he suggests that the armour refers to Alexander's love of war. By extension the entire composition might be interpreted as a study of Alexander's various loves and passions. In this light the true identity of the youth is unambiguous: it must be Bagoas the eunuch that Hephaistion leans upon rather than Hymenaios. In the context of the painting Bagoas is being supplanted by Roxane in Alexander's affections and Hephaistion leans on him to restrain him from jealous intervention and perhaps to comfort him.

This interpretation also explains why the youth was not named by the artist. Bagoas was probably the most scandalous of Alexander's loves among his contemporaries and Arrian even seems to have tried, though without complete success, to edit him out of his histories. To have named him would have made the fact that the painting was a study of Alexander's loves, rather than a simple celebration of his marriage, quite explicit and would have made a daring work positively dangerous for its artist at a time when Alexander still reigned. For example, Antipater might have felt obliged to censure Aetion had he been even less discreet. Of course, a secondary possibility is that somebody had later arranged for Bagoas' name to be erased in the cause of sanitizing Alexander's reputation.

It is fairly certain that Alexander's relations with both Roxane and Bagoas were sexual, so the revised interpretation of Aetion's painting should be taken to provide a broad hint from a contemporaneous source that the relationship with Hephaistion also had a sexual element, a matter that has proven controversial.

The Nature of the Affair

The first appearance of Hephaistion in the more authoritative ancient sources occurs in the context of Alexander's visit to Troy shortly after the main body of the Greek expeditionary force had crossed into Ionia during May 334BC (Figure 3.9).

When Alexander reached Troy…some say he crowned the tomb of Achilles, while Hephaistion, others say, placed a wreath on Patroclus' tomb; and Alexander, so the story goes, blessed Achilles for having Homer to proclaim his fame to posterity. Arrian 1.12.1

Then, going up to Troy, he sacrificed to Athena and poured libations to the heroes. Furthermore, the gravestone of Achilles he anointed with oil, ran a race by it with his companions, naked, as is the custom, and then crowned it with garlands, pronouncing the hero happy in having, while he lived, a faithful friend, and after death a great herald of his fame.
Plutarch 15.4

Hephaistion, The Chiliarch

He also conducted sacrifices at Troy, before the tombs of the heroes who had died in the Trojan war.

Justin 11.5.12

Figure 3.9. Alexander and Hephaistion sacrifice at Troy (by A. Castaigne 1898)

Dicaearchus, a contemporary of Alexander, wrote an entire lost book *On the Sacrifice at Troy*.[99] A fragment of this treatise, preserved by Athenaeus, discusses Alexander's erotic relationship with the eunuch Bagoas, so it is evident that it must have dealt specifically with the amorous aspects of Alexander's friendship with Hephaistion through the circumstances of the ceremony at Troy. The significance of this public ritual was the effective public proclamation of a parallel between the relationship of Achilles with Patroclus and that of Alexander with Hephaistion. The meaning of this avowal has been spelt out by Aelian:-

Note that Alexander laid a wreath on Achilles' tomb and Hephaistion on Patroclus', hinting that he was Alexander's eromenos, as Patroclus was of Achilles.

Aelian, Varia Historia 12.7

In Alexander's era it was axiomatic that the relationship between Achilles and Patroclus had been sexual. This is evident in a discussion of a sexual relationship between a lover (*erastes* = older active partner) and his beloved (*eromenos* = younger passive partner) in Plato's Symposium:-

---

[99] Athenaeus, Deipnosophistae 13.603a-b.

Alexander's Lovers by Andrew Chugg

Very different was the reward of the true love of Achilles towards his lover Patroclus – his lover and not his beloved (the notion that Patroclus was the beloved one is a foolish error into which Aeschylus has fallen, for Achilles was surely the fairer of the two, fairer also than all the other heroes; and, as Homer informs us, he was still beardless, and younger by far.)

Plato, Symposium 179e-180a

The mention of Aeschylus refers to his lost play, The Myrmidons, in which Achilles would seem to have been represented as the *erastes* with Patroclus as his *eromenos*. Conveniently, some fragments of the Myrmidons have survived to provide even more explicit evidence of the way in which Alexander's contemporaries interpreted the friendship of Achilles and Patroclus:-

Antilochus, weep for me [Achilles] the living, rather than for him [Patroclus], the dead; for I have lost my all...No care did you [Patroclus] have for the chaste consecration of our thighs; O thou most ungrateful for my many kisses... and the devout union of our thighs! ...and yet, since I [Achilles] love him, they are not repulsive to my sight.

Aeschylus, Fragments 64-66 of The Myrmidons

The repeated reference to "thighs" in the fragments of The Myrmidons would appear to be an allusion to intercourse. It has an interesting echo in a comment attributed to the Cynic philosopher Diogenes in a letter addressed to Alexander:-

If you wish to be beautiful and good, throw away the rag you have on your head and come to us. Yet you will not be able to do so, for you are held fast by Hephaistion's thighs.

Diogenes of Sinope, Letters 24

The "rag" is presumably the diadem, which was the symbol of Hellenistic monarchy. It is argued by some that this letter is an ancient forgery, but it does seem anyway to be early, certainly Hellenistic rather than Roman in date.[100] It has, however, not been clearly established that it is not authentic. It should certainly be cited whenever anyone asserts the oft-repeated misconception that no contemporaneous voice is explicit about the erotic nature of the relationship between Alexander and Hephaistion. It is also clearly stated that Hephaistion was Alexander's "eromenos" in the Discourses of Epictetus:-

Alexander ordered the temples of Asclepius to be burned, when his eromenos died.[101]

Although Hephaistion is not actually named by Epictetus, it is clear that he is the *eromenos* of Alexander who had died, because Arrian in his Anabasis mentions the same story of the temple of Asclepius being razed in the context of Hephaistion's death.[102] It should also be recalled that the Discourses were actually written-up by Arrian, so Epictetus' words effectively carry the weight of Arrian's authority as the most highly regarded ancient historian of Alexander.

---

[100] Abraham J. Malherbe, The Cynic Epistles, Society of Biblical Literature, No. 12, 1977, pp.14-18.
[101] Epictetus, Discourses 2.22.17.
[102] Arrian, Anabasis 7.14.5.

Hephaistion, The Chiliarch

Curiously, Heckel has recently urged that credence be given to the 19th century opinion of Perrin that Alexander and Hephaistion first compared themselves to Achilles and Patroclus after the battle of Gaugamela. He suggests that the story of the Trojan sacrifices was invented by later writers to fit the comparison between the two couples and that Alexander merely showed respect for Achilles as his putative maternal ancestor. However, Aeschines gave the following outline of some of the anti-Macedonian antics of Demosthenes in a speech in 330BC:-

But when Philip was dead and Alexander had come to the throne, Demosthenes again put on prodigious airs and caused a shrine to be dedicated to Pausanias and involved the [Athenian] senate in the charge of having offered sacrifice of thanksgiving as for good news. And he nicknamed Alexander "Margites"; and he had the effrontery to say that Alexander would never stir out of Macedonia, for he was content, he said, to saunter around[103] in Pella...

Aeschines, Against Ctesiphon 160

Demosthenes' use of the nickname "Margites" for Alexander was stated by Harpocration to have been corroborated by Alexander's contemporary, Marsyas of Pella.[104] Margites was the name of a caricature of Achilles in a poem attributed to Homer, which parodied his Iliad. Rufus B. Richardson (Against Ctesiphon, Boston & London, 1889, p. 167) has explained, "Demosthenes asserted, then, that Alexander, in his aspiration to be the second Achilles, would never get farther than to become a caricature of him".[105] We therefore have it on the authority of Demosthenes that it was widely known in Greece that Alexander sought to emulate Achilles as early as 336BC, before he had even stirred out of Macedonia.[106] We also have Arrian's incidental comment that "Alexander had a rivalry with Achilles from boyhood".[107] Alexander's lobbying of the Greeks for divine honours also fits within the context of his emulation of Achilles, since the latter was awarded such honours by the people of Epirus according to Plutarch.[108] Furthermore, one of Achilles' epithets in the Iliad is *dios*, which is often translated as "shining", but which also means "divine".[109]

---

[103] This sauntering may have been a play on the fact that Alexander's tutor, Aristotle, was a member of the peripatetic school of philosophers.
[104] Jacoby, FrGrH 135 F 3; see Plato, Alcibiades II, 147 for the account of Margites by Homer; see also Aristotle, Poetics 13.92, who writes of Homer, "His Margites indeed provides an analogy: as are the Iliad and the Odyssey to our tragedies, so is the Margites to our comedies."
[105] See also Plato, *Alcibiades* II.147c on Margites and Achilles.
[106] It would be wrong, however, to imagine that Alexander himself was obsessively keen to be compared with his hero: when Choirilos sought to flatter the King with a poetical version of just such a comparison, Alexander remarked that he would rather be Homer's Thersites than Choirilos' Achilles: Porphyrion ad Hor. Ars P.357 (FrGrH 153 F 10a).
[107] Arrian, Anabasis 7.14.4
[108] Plutarch, Life of Pyrrhus 1
[109] Divine honours did not imply omniscience, omnipotence or immortality, but resembled a type of sainthood, except that they were awarded for superhuman achievement rather than for piousness, holiness and humility. Alexander could legitimately claim descent from Zeus, since Achilles' father, Peleus, was said to have been the grandson of Zeus. Furthermore, Heracles,

Alexander's Lovers by Andrew Chugg

We know from Plutarch and Pliny that Aristotle had edited a recension of the Iliad for Alexander, which he eventually kept by his bed or beneath his pillow in a fabulously beautiful casket captured from Darius.[110] Strabo (13.1.27), probably following the account of Callisthenes, the son of Aristotle's niece, explicitly attributes Alexander's behaviour at Troy to his infatuation with Homer's Iliad and with his supposed descent from Achilles and Andromache via his Molossian mother, Olympias:

For Alexander wanted to take [Troy] under his protection, as a way of renewing his tie of blood, and he was also a lover of Homer. At least there is supposed to be a recension of the Homeric poems (the so-called Recension of the Casket), which Alexander, along with Callisthenes and Anaxarchus, perused and to some extent annotated and which he subsequently stored in an elaborately ornamented casket that he found among the Persian treasure. Alexander's kindness towards the Trojans, then, was prompted both by his interest in the poet and by his kinship, which he claimed by descent from the Aeacid kings of the Molossians, among whom they say that Andromache, Hector's widow, was once queen.[111]

Also from Plutarch we have the story that Alexander's tutor, Lysimachus, ingratiated himself with the prince by calling Alexander, Achilles; Philip, Peleus and himself, Phoinix, the instructor of Achilles. It is therefore verging on the incredible that the comparison of Hephaistion with Patroclus had not occurred to Alexander by the time he became king.

Arrian ultimately reprises the comparison with Achilles and Patroclus for his epitaph on the relationship between the two friends:-

In fact the death of Hephaistion had proved a great misfortune to Alexander himself, and Alexander, I believe, would have preferred to have gone first himself rather than experience it during his lifetime, just as I think Achilles would have preferred to die before Patroclus rather than to have been the avenger of his death.

Arrian 7.16.8

It is clear from the ancient accounts that Alexander himself represented his relationship with Hephaistion as comparable with that between Achilles and Patroclus. It is also evident that in Alexander's time the partnership of Achilles and Patroclus was seen as unambiguously erotic and was described using the explicitly sexual terms, *eromenos* and *erastes*. The syllogism is straightforward and was anciently stated by Aelian: Alexander's relationship with Hephaistion was sexual and Alexander himself publicly advertised it in such terms. In the ancient sources this was axiomatic and to my knowledge none says otherwise. The

---

Alexander's putative ancestor on his father's side, was attributed a kind of dual divine-human paternity by Zeus and Amphitryon, and Alexander may have emulated this precedent in claiming both Zeus-Ammon and Philip as his fathers: see A. B. Bosworth, Alexander and Ammon, pp.51-75 in Greece and the Eastern Mediterranean in Ancient History and Prehistory, ed. K. H. Kinzl, Berlin 1977.

[110] Plutarch, Life of Alexander 8, 26 and Moralia 327F; Pliny, Natural History 7.29.108.
[111] Strabo, Geography 13.1.27.

suggestion that they might just have been good friends is an entirely modern interpretation, which relies on astonishingly disingenuous and tendentious reasoning.[112]

* * * * * * * *

There is a gap of 18 months between Troy and Hephaistion's next appearance in surviving ancient literature in November of 333BC:-

Just before the Battle of Issus, as Eumenes of Cardia says in his letter to Antipater, Hephaistion came early into Alexander's tent. He blundered or was confused (as I was) or was driven to it by some god when he gave my greeting: 'Health to you, king,' he said, 'it is already time to set the battle-line.' The others present were upset by the strange address, and Hephaistion almost died for shame. But Alexander said, 'I accept the omen. It has been promised us a safe return from the battle.'

Lucian, Pro Lapsu 8

Apparently, Hephaistion gave a Greek valediction when he appeared to those present only just to have arrived in the tent and this caused him extreme embarrassment. Lucian presents it as a mere slip of the tongue, but why should anything so trivial give rise to such acute discomfort? And why should Eumenes, who was Hephaistion's personal enemy, have enjoyed recalling the incident in a letter probably written after Alexander's death? It has been pointed out[113] that these circumstances would make more sense, if we were to suppose Hephaistion surreptitiously to have been with Alexander throughout the night. This would seem therefore to provide a further hint of a romantic basis for the relationship. Probably, Eumenes wished to imply that Hephaistion had been the king's minion.

On the following day, with the battle safely won, there transpired one of the great chivalric episodes in Alexander's life, when Alexander and Hephaistion went to visit the captured women of Darius' family:-

So at daybreak, the King took with him the most valued of his Friends, Hephaistion, and came to the women. They both were dressed alike, but Hephaistion was taller and more handsome. Sisyngambris [Darius' mother] took him for the King and did him obeisance. As the others present made signs to her and pointed to Alexander with their hands she was embarrassed by her mistake, but made a new start and did obeisance to Alexander, He, however, cut in and said, 'Never mind, Mother. For actually he too is Alexander.'

Diodorus 17.37.5-6

There is, however, a story that the next day Alexander himself visited the tent with Hephaistion and no other Companion; and Darius' mother, not knowing which of the two was the king, as both were dressed alike, approached Hephaistion and did him obeisance, since he appeared the taller. Hephaistion drew back, and one of her attendants pointed to

---

[112] E.g. the essay on Alexander's Attitude to Sex in W.W. Tarn, Alexander the Great II, Sources and Studies, Cambridge 1948, pp. 319-326.
[113] Jeanne Reames-Zimmerman

Alexander's Lovers by Andrew Chugg

Alexander and said he was the king; she drew back in confusion at her mistake, but Alexander remarked that she had made no mistake, for Hephaistion was also an Alexander.

Arrian, Anabasis 2.12.6-7

And now, after the proper rites had been performed for the bodies of the dead, Alexander sent a messenger to the captive women that he himself was coming to them, and, denying admission to his throng of attendants, he entered the tent with Hephaistion. He was by far the dearest to the king of all his Friends; brought up with him, and the confidant of all his secrets, he also had more freedom than anyone else in admonishing him, a privilege which he nevertheless used in such a manner that it seemed rather to be allowed by the King than claimed by himself: and though Hephaistion was of the same age as the King, he nevertheless excelled him in bodily stature. Hence the queens, thinking that he was the King, did obeisance to him in their native fashion. Thereupon some of the captive eunuchs pointed out which was Alexander, and Sisigambis fell at his feet, begging pardon for not recognising the King, whom she had never seen before. The King, taking her hand and raising her to her feet, said, 'You were not mistaken, mother; for this man too is Alexander.'

Curtius 3.7.15-17

Hammond has indulged in some special pleading in seeking to explain away Alexander's comment as a pun on the king's name, since the Greek roughly translates as 'keeper of men'.[114] He fails, however, to explain why it should be appropriate for the Persian ladies to make obeisance to Hephaistion instead of the king simply because he was also a 'keeper of men'. Hammond also finds himself at odds with the interpretation of the event by ancient writers, who have inferred from this story that:-

In utroque enim esse Alexandrum salutatum.

"To salute either was to salute Alexander."

Itinerarium Alexandri, Müller-XXXVII or Volkmann-XV (c.AD340)

Furthermore, Curtius obviously regarded this story as an ideal opportunity to comment on the closeness of the relationship between Hephaistion and Alexander, which makes no sense if he thought Alexander was merely quipping.

Complex and illogical puns being laid aside, it is the literal sense of Alexander's comment that he regarded Hephaistion as a second manifestation of himself, a sort of *alter ego* in fact. This, as it happens, is perfectly consistent with a recognised and well-referenced Greek definition of personal friendships:-

And by friendship they mean a common use of all that has to do with life, wherein we treat our friends as we should ourselves.

Diogenes Laertius, Zeno 7.124

In the first place, then, let us begin at the hearthstone, as the saying is, with the story of men's lives which history has left us regarding steadfast friends, and let us take as witness and counsellor in our discussion the long and distant ages in which are mentioned, as paired in the

---

[114] NGL Hammond, Three Historians of Alexander the Great, Cambridge, 1983.

Hephaistion, The Chiliarch

bond of friendship, Theseus and Peirithoüs, Achilles and Patroclus, Orestes and Pylades, Phintias and Damon, Epaminondas and Pelopidas. For friendship is a creature that seeks a companion; it is not like cattle and crows that flock and herd together, and to look upon one's friend as another self and to call him 'brother' as though to suggest 'th'other', is nothing but a way of using duality as a measure of friendship.

Plutarch, de amicorum multitudine, 2.93E

In fact there is a more poignant example of Alexander treating Hephaistion as his alter ego as a sort of epitaph on their relationship:-

As part of the preparations for the funeral [of Hephaistion, Alexander]... proclaimed to all the peoples of Asia that they should sedulously quench what the Persians call the sacred fire, until such time as the funeral should be ended. This was the custom of the Persians when their kings died, and people thought that the order was an ill omen, and that heaven was foretelling the King's own death.

Diodorus 17.114.4

*   *   *   *   *   *   *   *

Plutarch mentions various day-to-day familiarities between Alexander and Hephaistion, such as a present of small fish and a letter about a hunting accident.[115] However, one anecdote particularly testifies to an extraordinary level of trust between the friends:-

Olympias often wrote [to Alexander with complaints], but Alexander kept her writings secret, except once when Hephaistion, as was his habit, read with him a letter, which had been opened; the King did not prevent him, but took the ring from his own finger and applied its seal to Hephaistion's lips.

Plutarch, Life 39.5

Among the Sayings of Kings in his Moralia, Plutarch adds that this letter contained "secret slanders against Antipater", the Regent in Macedon, which was absolutely the most sensitive of matters of state. A hostile recipient could have used such information to foment a rebellion in Macedon.

Olympias even seems to have attacked Hephaistion personally in these poisonous epistles, for Diodorus[116] records Hephaistion's reproachful response, incorporating an ostensibly haughty use of the royal we:-

Stop quarrelling with us... You know that Alexander means more to us than anything.

It is likely, however, that this adoption of the *pluralis majestatis* was tongue in cheek, since it may well constitute Hephaistion's reply to the following letter from Olympias expressing particular vexation with Alexander's royal generosity to his closest friends:-

[Olympias wrote to Alexander]: I beg thee to find other ways of conferring favours on those thou lovest and holdest in honour; as it is thou makest them all the equals of kings...

---

[115] Plutarch, Life of Alexander, 28.3 (fish) & 41.3 (letter).
[116] Diodorus 17.114.3.

Alexander's Lovers by Andrew Chugg

Plutarch, Life 39.5

It is indeed the case that Alexander went to some lengths to establish Hephaistion as a member of the royal family in the context of the marriage ceremonies between prominent Macedonians and the ladies of the Persian nobility held at Susa in 324BC:-

To Hephaistion [Alexander] gave Drypetis, another daughter of Darius, sister of his own wife (for he desired Hephaistion's children to be cousins of his own).

Arrian 7.4.5

[Alexander] proceeded to Susa, where he married Stateira, the elder daughter of Darius, and gave her younger sister Drypetis as wife to Hephaistion.

Diodorus 17.107.6

Curtius notes in passing that Drypetis was thoroughly lovelorn in her mourning for her dead husband.[117]

*   *   *   *   *   *   *   *

By the time of the invasion of India Hephaistion and Craterus had become Alexander's immediate deputies with clear seniority over his other commanders. In this context Alexander is quoted as stating that Craterus loved the king (*philobasileus*), whereas Hephaistion loved Alexander (*philalexandros*).[118] During this period these two men became the figureheads of the two rival factions within the army. The integrationists, who believed that the future of the Empire lay in achieving concord and unity among its nations, supported Hephaistion. Conversely, the traditionalists, who expected Macedonian supremacy in all things, backed Craterus. Their rivalry led to escalating tension and on one occasion the feud broke out into open conflict when the two commanders drew their swords on each other. Alexander was forced to intervene to prevent a fierce and potentially fatal dual. The usual source is Plutarch's Life of Alexander:-

[Alexander] saw that among his closest friends Hephaistion approved his course and joined him in changing his mode of life, while Craterus clung fast to his native ways. He employed the former in his business with the Barbarians, the latter in that with the Greeks and Macedonians. And in general he showed most affection for Hephaistion, but most esteem for Craterus, thinking and constantly saying, that Hephaistion loved Alexander, but Craterus loved the King. For this reason, too, the men cherished a secret grudge against one another and often came into open collision. And once, on the Indian expedition, they actually drew their swords and closed with one another, and as the friends of each were coming to his aid, Alexander rode up and abused Hephaistion publicly, calling him a fool and a madman for not knowing that without Alexander's favour he was nothing; and in private he also sharply rebuked Craterus. Then he brought them together and reconciled them, taking an oath by

---

[117] Curtius 10.5.20.
[118] The same terms are used by Diodorus 17.114.2 and by Plutarch, Life of Alexander 47 and Moralia 181D.

Ammon and the rest of the gods that he loved them most of all men; but that if he heard of their quarrelling again, he would kill them both, or at least the one who began the quarrel. On which account they subsequently neither did nor said anything to harm one another, not even in jest.

Plutarch, Life of Alexander 47.5-7

However, there is a second version of the same incident in the essay "On the Fortune or Virtue of Alexander" in Plutarch's Moralia. In this account, Plutarch gives a direct quote of Alexander's words, which may have been copied verbatim from the writings of an eyewitness. Hammond[119] has suggested this source could be Aristobulus, but Onesicritus may be a better candidate, since he was Alexander's helmsman in India and therefore frequently in his company:-

Even so Alexander's forces, having lost him, maintained a gasping, agitated, and feverish existence through men like Perdiccas, Meleager, Seleucus and Antigonus, who, as it were, provided still a warm breath of life and blood that still pulsed and circulated. But at length the host wasted away and perished, generating about itself maggots, as it were, of ignoble kings and rulers in their last death-struggle. This, then, it is likely that Alexander himself meant when he rebuked Hephaistion for quarrelling with Craterus: 'What,' said he, 'will be your power and your accomplishments, if someone bereave you of your Alexander?'

Plutarch, Moralia 337A

That the quotation is not Plutarch's invention is suggested by the fact that it is not entirely congruent with his interpretation of Alexander's intervention. This becomes obvious when we ask, what is the relevance of someone depriving Hephaistion of Alexander in this context? The logical answer is that Hephaistion has got himself into a situation where Alexander may be bereaved of him. Alexander is therefore asking him to consider what his feelings would be, if Alexander managed to get himself killed in a frivolous dual. He seems to be suggesting that power and fame would be no compensation for the personal tragedy. This interpretation makes sense of the incident and explains Alexander's particular choice of words, whereas Plutarch's gloss, that Alexander was publicly belittling his dearest friend, makes Alexander's words merely a random castigation, unrelated to the specifics of this clash.

Commander and Diplomat

Hephaistion's career in Alexander's service was filled with spectacular and demanding missions, which were generally performed with consummate success. His record is especially impressive, because, despite the fact that most of the early historians seem to have been at best neutral in their sentiments towards Alexander's alter ego, none appears to have found any significant grounds to criticise Hephaistion's conduct of military or diplomatic operations.

---

[119] N. G. L. Hammond, Sources for Alexander the Great, Cambridge (1993) p. 83.

We have to wait until the aftermath of the Battle of Issus at the end of 333BC for the first report of one of Hephaistion's special assignments. This was nothing less than the selection of a new king for Sidon: an illustrious beginning to a glittering career, which must have been viewed by contemporaries as setting Hephaistion well above the rank of provincial royalty:-

Then Alexander marched down into Phoenicia and received the town of Byblos in surrender. Thence he came to Sidon, a city renowned for its antiquity and the fame of its founders. In it Straton was ruling, supported by the power of Darius; but because he had surrendered rather at the desire of the people than of his own accord, he was deemed unworthy to rule and Hephaistion was allowed to choose as king from among the Sidonians the one whom he thought most worthy of that high station. Hephaistion was the guest of two young men distinguished among their countrymen; when they were offered the privilege of ruling, they said that according to the custom of their country no one was admitted to that eminence unless born of royal stock. Hephaistion, admiring the lofty spirit that declined what others sought by fire and sword, said "Accept my congratulations, since you have been the first to appreciate how much greater it is to disdain royal power than to receive it. But name someone of royal descent, who will remember that he is holding a sovereignty that was conferred by you." And they, though they were aware that many, eager for so great a prospect, were already courting various friends of Alexander from excessive longing for the throne, decided that no one was preferable to a certain Abdalonymus, a man who had, it is true, a distant connexion with the royal family, but who, because of narrow means, was cultivating a garden in the suburbs at scanty profit.

Curtius 4.1.15-20[120]

As we have seen, Abdalonymus seems to have prospered in his new role and the gratitude of the new king of Sidon seems to have been manifested in the wonderful sculptural celebration of Hephaistion's role in the Battle of Issus, which lies at the centre of one of the long panels of the 'Alexander Sarcophagus' (Figure 3.3).

When Alexander had taken Tyre after a protracted and bitter siege, he moved south along the coast in the late summer of 332BC to tackle what was to prove the last foothold of Persian resistance on the Mediterranean coast at Gaza. In this context, Hephaistion's first recorded military mission was the command of the fleet on the voyage from Tyre to Gaza.

Alexander, after ordering Hephaistion to coast along the shore of Phoenicia with the fleet, came with all his forces to the city of Gaza.

Curtius 4.5.10

---

[120] Cf. Justin 11.10.8 who corroborates Curtius; Diodorus 17.46-47, who writes of "Ballonymus" being made king of Tyre by Hephaistion (but Curtius does say that additional territories were brought under the crown of Sidon and it is not impossible that these included Tyre); Plutarch, On the Fortune or Virtue of Alexander 340C-E, seems (erroneously) to have translated these events to Paphos.

Hephaistion, The Chiliarch

Heckel calls this 'a relatively minor task now that Alexander controlled the seas',[121] but the fleet remained a key component of the as yet unfulfilled plan to dominate the entire eastern Mediterranean coast. It was also a formidable naval force comprising hundreds of vessels and no mean command irrespective of the circumstances. The fleet actually arrived in Egypt ahead of the army, perhaps still under Hephaistion's command. Alexander himself boarded at Pelusium and sailed up the Nile, taking over the territory without Persian opposition.[122]

During the sojourn in Egypt Hephaistion seems to have engaged in a fresh diplomatic initiative to arrange a *rapprochement* between Alexander and Demosthenes of Athens. Harpocration quotes Marsyas of Pella as stating that Demosthenes sent Aristion to Hephaistion to seek a reconciliation with Alexander:-

Aristion... a Samian or a Plataean, according to Diyllus and a companion of Demosthenes from boyhood. He was sent by him to Hephaistion for the purpose of a reconciliation, as Marsyas records in the fifth book of his work "On Alexander".[123]

This account is strongly corroborated by Aeschines in his speech Against Ctesiphon given in Athens in 330BC:-

For, as the people of the Paralus[124] *say, and those who have been ambassadors to Alexander (and the story is sufficiently credible) there is one Aristion, a man of Plataean status,*[125] *son of Aristobulus the Apothecary, known perhaps to some of you. This young man, distinguished for extraordinary beauty of person, once lived a long time in Demosthenes' house (what he used to do there or what was done to him is a scandal that is in dispute, and the story is one that it would be quite improper for me to repeat). Now I am told that this Aristion, his origin and personal history being unknown to the King, is worming himself into favour with Alexander and getting access to him. Through him Demosthenes has sent a letter to Alexander, and has secured a certain degree of immunity for himself, and reconciliation; and he has carried his flattery to great lengths.*

Aeschines, Against Ctesiphon, 162

The Paralus, an Athenian state galley, reached Alexander upon his return to Tyre in the Summer of 331BC and found Demosthenes' envoy well-ensconced.[126] It would therefore seem probable that Aristion's lobbying of Hephaistion took place whilst the army was in Egypt, which would fit with Arrian's comment that many embassies reached Alexander at Memphis.[127]

---

[121] W Heckel, The Marshals of Alexander's Empire, London, 1992, section ii.2, p.69.
[122] Arrian, Anabasis 3.1.1-3; Curtius 4.7.1-3.
[123] Jacoby, FrGrH 135 F 2.
[124] The citizen crew of the state dispatch ship Paralus.
[125] Plataean status was special class of Athenian citizens of foreign extraction who had received their citizenship in return for services to the city-state. Aristion's family were presumably of Samian descent, but he at least had been awarded the citizenship of Athens; see also the entry in the Suda under "Aristaios".
[126] Arrian, Anabasis 3.6.2.
[127] Arrian, Anabasis 3.5.1.

Aeschines is obviously insinuating that Demosthenes' erstwhile boyfriend deployed his personal charms to good effect in this mission. Subsequent events suggest that the understanding that was reached proved beneficial to both parties. It helps to explain Athenian neutrality in the rebellion of Agis, the Spartan king, against Macedon, which reached its climax shortly afterwards at the Battle of Megalopolis, where Antipater decisively suppressed the revolt.

There is an intriguing possible explanation for Demosthenes' personal envoy to have approached Hephaistion in the first instance. An inscription has survived which records the award of Athenian citizenship to Amyntor son of Demetrius and his descendants in 334BC.[128] There is a reasonable chance that this Amyntor was identical with Hephaistion's father, in which case Hephaistion himself would have been an honorary Athenian at the time of Demosthenes' diplomacy. As has already been noted, Hephaistion is known to have corresponded with Xenocrates, who was head of the Academy in Athens at this time.

If Hephaistion did persuade Alexander to reach an accommodation with Demosthenes at this crucial juncture, as would seem likely from the circumstances, then he was significantly responsible for saving the situation for Macedon in Greece by preventing the revolt of Agis spreading to Athens and her allies.

Plutarch[129] mentions that Alexander wrote to Hephaistion about an ichneumon hunt, when the latter "was away on some business". The ichneumon is a mongoose that hunts out crocodile eggs and would most likely have been encountered by Alexander in North Africa. Therefore, Hephaistion probably spent some time away from camp on some special mission in Egypt. It is possible that this was either connected with the Athenian diplomacy or with his command of the fleet.

* * * * * * * *

As Alexander marched back northwards from Egypt into Syria in order to resume the contest with Darius, he projected a strong vanguard forward to the crossing of the Euphrates at Thapsacus, where they were to construct bridges suitable for the main body of the army. Hephaistion is *rumoured* to have commanded this vanguard, which found itself confronted by Mazaeus, the Persian Satrap of Babylon, with several thousand Persian cavalry on the opposite bank of the river (however, this story may be apocryphal).[130] Robin Lane Fox has speculated that Hephaistion may have entered into covert

---

[128] IG ii² 405.
[129] Plutarch, Life of Alexander 41.3.
[130] Robin Lane Fox, Alexander the Great (London, 1973), Chapter 15, p. 226; R. D. Milns, Alexander the Great (London, 1968), p. 112; however, W. Heckel, The Marshals of Alexander's Empire (London, 1992), p.77, note 87, suggests that Hephaistion's role in bridging the Euphrates is not recorded in the ancient sources, so the story may be a modern figment.

Hephaistion, The Chiliarch

negotiations with Mazaeus on this occasion, on the grounds that some features of the Satrap's subsequent behaviour seem to have favoured the Macedonian cause: for example, he failed to oppose Alexander's crossing of the Euphrates, subsequently withdrew from the battle of Gaugamela at a point when his troops were experiencing some success against Alexander's left wing and eventually surrendered Babylon to Alexander without a fight and was immediately reappointed to its governorship. Although this is basically guesswork, it would be consistent with a subsequent pattern in Hephaistion's behaviour, where he seems to have encouraged policies of reconciliation and integration with the senior Persians. It would also provide a second instance of his suborning a leading member of the opposition to add to his negotiations with Demosthenes.

Having played a major role in the build-up to the climactic clash of the war, Hephaistion duly appears in our sources as the "commander of the bodyguards" in the actual battle of Gaugamela, where he received a spear wound to his arm.

Of the most prominent group of commanders [at Gaugamela], Hephaistion, commander of the bodyguards [ton somatophylakon hegoumenos], *was wounded with a spear thrust in the arm...*

Diodorus 17.61.3

[At Gaugamela] Hephaistion was struck in the arm by a spear; Perdiccas, Coenus and Menidas were all but slain with arrows.

Curtius 4.16.32

At this juncture [of the battle of Gaugamela], since at first the Macedonians were between two fires, Parmenio sent a despatch rider to Alexander to report with all haste that his troops were in distress and needed help. On receiving this message, Alexander turned back from further pursuit, and wheeling round with the Companion cavalry, came galloping down on the Persian right and charged first the enemy cavalry in flight, the Parthyaeans, some Indians and the Persians, the most numerous and best of the enemy forces. This proved the fiercest cavalry engagement of the whole action... There about sixty of the Companions of Alexander fell, and Hephaistion himself, Coenus and Menidas were wounded.

Arrian 3.15.1-2

Hephaistion is thus specified to have commanded the actual cavalry bodyguard of Alexander at Gaugamela and to have been in the thick of the fiercest cavalry engagement of that battle and probably the toughest and most glorious action of the entire war. He also seems to have come close enough to the enemy to be wounded by a spear thrust, whilst it is notable that the other senior casualties were caused by arrows, presumably therefore at a distance from the enemy.

Heckel's suggestion[131] that command of the bodyguards meant that Hephaistion led the *agema* of the hypaspists is curious, since, firstly, the hypaspists were an elite infantry corps, whilst Arrian speaks specifically of a cavalry engagement. Secondly, it was normal practice in this period for lovers to fight side by side, so

---

[131] W Heckel, The Marshals of Alexander's Empire, London, 1992, p.70.

the position of commander of Alexander's personal escort would have been an ideal role for Hephaistion.

Heckel's interpretation was inspired by the paradox that the 200-strong Royal Squadron of the Companion Cavalry, which is believed to have had the particular function of defending the Macedonian king in mounted engagements, is known to have been commanded by Cleitus the Black at Gaugamela.[132] Heckel has therefore inferred that Hephaistion must have commanded the infantry equivalent of the Royal Squadron of the cavalry, which was a section of the hypaspists called the agema (corps). Heckel believes that these hypaspists are also occasionally referred to as bodyguards by our sources, although I have argued in detail that there are no instances in our sources where the precise term *somatophylax* (i.e. literally body-guard in Greek) does not refer to the seven (later eight) senior bodyguards of the king (or else occasionally equivalent elite bodyguards of other members of the royal family) in *The Death of Alexander the Great*.[133] As noted, Heckel's hypothesis particularly embroils him in having to explain how Hephaistion was wounded in the company of a cavalry unit that had just previously almost galloped right beyond the field of the battle in a hot pursuit, when Heckel supposes him to be in command of an infantry unit.

We should therefore take Diodorus literally, and conclude that he actually means what he wrote: that Hephaistion led the group of seven high-ranking Macedonians who constituted the elite unit dedicated to the protection of the king's person, who are formally designated as Bodyguards (Somatophylakes).[134] Later in Alexander's reign this group included many of the top-ranking regimental commanders and cavalry officers (Hipparchs) and their role as the king's personal escorts had become rather honorary in nature. Nevertheless, Bosworth[135] has commented on the dramatically contrasting situation prior to Gaugamela, when there is no known instance of a Bodyguard being cited as the commander of an army unit. Indeed, in the first half of the reign there are instances of Bodyguards being replaced when the incumbents were appointed to command army units or to govern Satrapies.[136] Even as late as the Mallian campaign (early 325BC) the Somatophylakes Leonnatus and Aristonous appear to have been acting as Alexander's personal bodyguards.[137] The logical conclusion is that the Bodyguards retained their traditional role as the sovereign's personal escort during battles at least up to Gaugamela. Hephaistion

---

[132] Diodorus Siculus 17.57.1; Arrian, Anabasis 3.11.8.
[133] A M Chugg, The Death of Alexander the Great: A Reconstruction of Cleitarchus, 2009, pp. 14-18 on *The Palace Regiment of the Hypaspists and the Somatophylakes*.
[134] Note that there are some other Greek terms, such as *doryphoros* (literally spear-bearer) that the reader will find translated as guard or bodyguard, but this discussion is confined to the literal term *somatophylax*.
[135] A B Bosworth, Conquest & Empire, Appendix C, Section IV, The Structure of Command.
[136] Heckel, The Marshals of Alexander's Empire, Section V, The Somatophylakes; Arrian, Anab. 1.24.1, 2.8.4, 2.10.7, 2.12.2 (Ptolemaeus son of Seleucus), also 2.12.2 (Balakros) & 3.16.9 (Menes).
[137] Curtius 9.5.15-18; Arrian, Anabasis 6.10.1.

Hephaistion, The Chiliarch

is believed to have been a Bodyguard from early in Alexander's reign and it would not be surprising if he had become the most senior Bodyguard at the time of Gaugamela. Some historians think he may have replaced a certain Ptolemaios, who died at Halicarnassus in 334BC,[138] but an even earlier appointment is just as likely. Certainly, Hephaistion is prominent in Arrian's list of the Bodyguards in 325BC.[139]

This is an attractive hypothesis, because it explains just why, despite being given a number of very senior missions, Hephaistion is never specified as commander of any particular military unit prior to Gaugamela. It resolves an awkward silence construed by those who have wrongly supposed Hephaistion to have been gradually promoted up the army ranks by Alexander. Instead the king appointed Hephaistion directly into an elite post that lay outside the normal army command structure but within his closest personal retinue. Reading the sources literally in this respect (without complex and unnecessary prevarications) also has the effect of duly placing Hephaistion at Alexander's side at Gaugamela and probably also in the earlier battles, which is exactly where our understanding of his relationship with the king should incline us to place him. Furthermore, there is no contradiction if Alexander's immediate escort at Gaugamela were the Bodyguards, whilst the far more numerous Royal Squadron of the Companion Cavalry provided for the broader scale protection of the king.

* * * * * * * *

In the aftermath of Gaugamela Alexander marched in triumph to Babylon, then advanced towards the ancient heart of the empire in Persis. The satrap Ariobarzanes sought to defend the narrow pass called either the Persian or Susian Gates, but Alexander led a force up a narrow mountain path by night and attacked the satrap's force from the rear. Polyaenus uniquely claims that Hephaistion and Philotas led a simultaneous frontal assault on the Persian positions, whereas Arrian and Curtius assign this particular command to Craterus.[140] Nonetheless, both Arrian and Curtius also mention a third Macedonian force led by Philotas and Amyntas, though there is some ambiguity and disagreement concerning its function. It is probably this third column to which Polyaenus refers. It has usually been considered that Polyaenus was in error in mentioning Hephaistion in this context, since his anecdotal treatment of Alexander's stratagems is frequently garbled.[141] However, it is suspicious that *Amyntas* is substituted for Hephaistion the son of *Amyntor* by Arrian and

---

[138] Arrian, Anabasis 1.22.7.
[139] Arrian, Anabasis 6.28.4; Diodorus 16.93.9 states that Philip advanced Pausanias among the Bodyguards, implying a gradation of rank among the seven Somatophylakes.
[140] Polyaenus 4.3.27; Curtius 5.4; Arrian, Anabasis 3.18.3-9; Plutarch, Alexander 37.1-2; Diodorus 17.68.
[141] E.g. Heckel, The Marshals of Alexander's Empire, Section II, The New Men, Hephaistion, p. 71, note 64.

Curtius, because it is easy to see how the latter might have been corrupted to the former in some early manuscript, whereas the converse is less straightforward to conceive. For this reason, it remains possible that Polyaenus is actually correct in attributing a key role to Hephaistion in this action.

* * * * * * * *

Hephaistion next figures in the sources shortly after the death of Darius, at which time, according to Curtius,[142] Alexander had his friend bring the Persian captives before him for an examination of their cases. It was considered that the war against the Persians had in a sense reached its conclusion with the death of the former Great King.[143] Consequently, in a spirit of reconciliation, it was deemed appropriate to free many of the prisoners and even to appoint some of them, such as Darius' brother Oxathres, to positions within Alexander's own administration and entourage. It is likely that Hephaistion's role in this process was central, because it turns out to be the first definite instance of a recurrent pattern or theme in his activities. By championing collaboration with the conquered peoples Hephaistion was to emerge as the leading light of the integrationist party among Alexander's senior officers.[144] This faction sought to reconcile the conquered peoples with their new masters through such measures as integrating their leaders into senior positions in the new regime and encouraging inter-racial marriages and religious and cultural tolerance. It was opposed by a vociferous group of traditionalist officers, who believed in Macedonian supremacy and the uninhibited exploitation of the conquered lands. Although the integrationists were pre-eminent whilst Alexander lived, for the king's own sympathies lay with them, the traditionalists were nevertheless destined to exert a baleful influence on events after Alexander's death.

* * * * * * * *

The accounts of Curtius and Plutarch suggest that Hephaistion played a prominent role in the downfall of Philotas and his father Parmenion. At the time of their ruin Philotas was the commander of the Companion Cavalry, which was the most senior appointment in the army, whilst his father had been left in Media as its governor with an army group and custody of a great deal of treasure at his disposal to secure Alexander's lines of supply and communications. Alexander had, it seems, long harboured suspicions against the boastful and brash Philotas. Ptolemy and Aristobulus confided that the infidelity of Philotas had already been reported to Alexander in Egypt and Plutarch mentions that Philotas' mistress, Antigona, had recited to the king various of his private remarks that were derogatory of Alexander.[145] However,

---

[142] Curtius, 6.2.9.
[143] Diodorus, 17.74.3.
[144] Plutarch, Life of Alexander 47.3-5.
[145] E.g. Arrian, Anabasis 3.26.1; Plutarch, Moralia 339E-F, where Plutarch claimed that Alexander did not reveal his suspicion of Philotas even to Hephaistion, but it is in fact impossible that he or his source could know with certainty what Alexander discussed in confidence with Hephaistion.

Hephaistion, The Chiliarch

matters were brought to a head when a certain Dymnus, who is said to have been one of Alexander's Friends, became involved in organising a plot against the king's life. Dymnus disclosed the plot and the names of various co-conspirators, including Demetrius, who was one of the seven Bodyguards, to a youth called Nicomachus, whom he had taken as his eromenos. Nicomachus was appalled and in his turn divulged the matter to his elder brother Cebalinus, who promptly sought to alert the king. However, being of modest station, Cebalinus could not gain direct access, but instead had to petition one of Alexander's Friends to bring the matter before the king. He happened to choose Philotas as his intermediary, but the cavalry commander twice failed to raise the matter with Alexander on successive days. In desperation, the frustrated Cebalinus waylaid Metron, one of the Royal Pages, who promptly conveyed the gist of the plot to the king. Dymnus dramatically confirmed the truth of the accusations by mortally stabbing himself, when men were sent to arrest him. Alexander then confronted Philotas, who admitted to some degree of negligence in having suppressed Cebalinus' information for the two days, but vehemently denied any actual involvement in the conspiracy. Alexander seems to have been inclined to forgive Philotas this indiscretion, perhaps with an eye to the strategic position of his father athwart his lines of communication. However, a private council of the king's most senior Friends was unanimously of the opinion that Philotas should be arrested, tried and tortured upon conviction to determine whether a more extensive conspiracy, perhaps implicating Parmenion, were being concealed. The arrest was organised in the dead of night by a coterie of Alexander's most loyal supporters, who are most likely identical with the attendees at the earlier meeting:-

Then in the second watch, when the lights had been put out, there came to the King's tent with a few others Hephaistion, Craterus, Coenus and Erigyios, these from the number of his Friends, and from the Bodyguard Perdiccas and Leonnatus.

Curtius 6.8.17

That Curtius should have listed Hephaistion first among this group, when he had previously made Craterus the leading spokesman against Philotas,[146] is a strong indication that Hephaistion had also swung his considerable influence decisively against the commander of the Companion Cavalry. Philotas was condemned to death by a vote of the Assembly of the Macedonians. Afterwards, the king's Friends decided that a more rigorous inquisition of the prisoner was called for:-

Hephaistion and Craterus and Coenus said that the truth ought to be forced from him by torments; and those who had recommended the other course [of immediate stoning] went over to their opinion. Therefore the council was dismissed and Hephaistion with Craterus and Coenus arose to put Philotas to the question.

Curtius 6.11.10-11

---

[146] Curtius 6.8.2-10.

Alexander's Lovers by Andrew Chugg

And Plutarch has:-

Consequently [Philotas] was arrested and put to the question, the companions of the King standing by at the torture, while Alexander himself listened behind a stretch of tapestry. Here, as we are told, on hearing Philotas beset Hephaistion with abject and pitiful cries and supplications, he said, "Ah, Philotas, if you are so weak and unmanly as this, how could you involve yourself in such a dangerous business?"

Plutarch, Life of Alexander 49.6

It therefore appears probable that Hephaistion not only endorsed the arrest, torture and execution of Philotas, but that it was actually he, rather than Craterus or Alexander, who led the process. In the first place, this tends to suggest that Hephaistion, as commander of the Bodyguards and the first of Alexander's Friends, already outranked Craterus at this stage of the expedition. It also reveals Hephaistion as a ruthless defender of Alexander's personal safety and security. He was seemingly sufficient of a realist to recognise the necessity of extracting the secrets of any plots to which Philotas might have been privy.

Against this interpretation, it might possibly be argued that some early historian was seeking to besmirch Hephaistion's reputation by subtly raising his profile in the context of this unpleasant episode. However, this runs into immediate difficulty in that Hephaistion is specified as leading the torture session in both Curtius and Plutarch, but these authors gave different sets of details and were most probably using different primary sources for these events.

It is clear that the trial and torture of Philotas was a distasteful business, for which Hephaistion bore a large part of the responsibility. The question, however, is whether this action was justified by the circumstances? Assuming that the information given by our sources is accurate, it is unlikely that Philotas was directly involved in Dymnus' plot. Had he been, then he would surely have triggered an immediate attempt on Alexander's life or have had Cebalinus and Nicomachus killed once he discovered that they were striving to betray the conspiracy, which had been divulged to them. Conversely, had he been completely loyal to Alexander, it is difficult to explain his protracted inaction, especially if Cebalinus had implicated such senior figures as Dymnus and Demetrius, men who would have enjoyed direct access to the king. Instead, his behaviour seems most consistent with a deliberate decision to stand aloof and allow the plot a chance to succeed. Had Alexander been assassinated, then Philotas and his father would have been in a strong position to seize control of the empire, perhaps through the medium of a puppet king. Philotas may have miscalculated that he would be able to excuse his silence as having arisen from incredulity, in the event of the plot failing or being discovered. He had previously been successful in deflecting such vague charges on at least one occasion. In practice, his judgement on this point turned out to be only slightly flawed, for it does indeed seem that Alexander's initial instinct was to pardon him once again. In view of his subsequent prominence in this matter, we might reasonably speculate that it was Hephaistion, who persuaded Alexander to consult the council of his Friends, which then advised that a much harsher line should be taken. Nevertheless, on a moral level, Philotas was virtually as guilty in his failure to act to forestall the plot as the conspirators themselves and there was significant prior evidence of his disloyalty (and for what it may be worth, further evidence was extracted during the torture.) Hephaistion was therefore probably justified in advocating the arrest and trial of Philotas before the Assembly of the Macedonians.

But why did Hephaistion go on to insist that Philotas should be tortured, once he had been convicted and condemned and had even offered a confession before the torture began? Should we add viciousness and spite to our conception of Hephaistion's character? In fact the evidence cannot really support such an inference, because there were overwhelming security imperatives that demanded that Philotas be put to the question. Firstly, there remained a strong possibility that Philotas may have been concealing some more extensive plot and that some of the conspirators had evaded Alexander's net. Secondly, evidence was needed against Parmenion, because, whether or not he was actually guilty, his downfall was made inevitable by the strategic position he occupied across Alexander's supply lines. Had he not been neutralised, he might have posed an enormous threat to the expedition, for he could not possibly have been trusted to forgive Alexander for executing his last surviving son. Finally, Hephaistion's instinctive reaction would probably have been that Philotas should be treated harshly, so as to deter further attempts against Alexander's life. From this point of view, the severity of Hephaistion's treatment of Philotas could be interpreted as further evidence for the intensity of his relationship with Alexander.

Philotas and the convicted conspirators were ultimately stoned to death according to Curtius (Figure 3.10) or shot down with javelins according to Arrian.

In the immediate wake of the Philotas affair, Hephaistion was appointed joint commander of the Companion Cavalry together with Black Cleitus.[147] Was Alexander now reluctant to place this command under a single officer, for fear of the arrogance and ostentation of the previous incumbent being emulated? Arrian suggests that Alexander was prepared to trust not even Hephaistion with sole command of so powerful a section of the army. Yet Hephaistion probably did become overall commander following the killing of Cleitus less than two years later.[148] More likely, therefore, the parallel appointment of Cleitus was part of a strategy to appease the traditionalist faction in the army, which had recently been critical of Alexander's overtures to his Persian subjects. There was evidently a feeling in some quarters that the Macedonians had merely succeeded

---

[147] Arrian, Anabasis 3.27.4.
[148] Hephaistion is named as the commander of one among four to eight regiments/hipparchies of the Companion Cavalry by Arrian (5.12.2) in Northern India, but he was probably also its overall commander: Diodorus (18.3.4) states this explicitly.

in replacing one Great King with another. Philotas specifically alleged under torture that this viewpoint had been expressed by an officer called Hegelochus.[149] Such dawning suspicions had probably motivated the conspiracy of Dymnus in the first place.

Figure 3.10. The trial and stoning of Philotas and the conspirators (1696)

It may have been the appointment of Hephaistion as joint-commander of the Companion Cavalry, which inaugurated the dramatic change in the status of the seven Bodyguards from this time. In retaining his status as a Bodyguard, whilst commanding a large contingent of cavalry, Hephaistion set a new pattern, which was to be followed by Perdiccas and others in the ensuing years.

* * * * * * * *

In the Bactrian and Sogdian campaigns from late 330BC to mid 327BC there are only a few scattered references to Hephaistion as a military commander, but sufficient nevertheless to indicate his continuous prominence at the forefront of events. Firstly, Alexander formed an *ad hoc* Council of War comprising

---

[149] Curtius 6.9.23-25.

Hephaistion, The Chiliarch

Hephaistion, Craterus and Erigyius together with the other Bodyguards at the River Jaxartes (a.k.a. Tanais) prior to the ill-fated attack on the Scythians, who were slinging rude insults from its further bank in the late summer of 329BC.[150] Then Arrian states that Hephaistion was the commander of one of the five columns with which Alexander launched an invasion of Sogdiana in the spring of 328BC, but Curtius makes Hephaistion, Coenus and Alexander himself the commanders of just three columns in his account of the same operation.[151] Possibly, the columns attributed to Perdiccas and Ptolemy were rather smaller than the other three. In the context of this invasion, it would seem possible that Hephaistion was responsible for the foundation of the important Hellenistic city (Alexandria-Oxiana?), which has been excavated at Ai Khanoum close by the strategic confluence of the Oxus and Kochba rivers.[152] Finally, in the aftermath of the killing of Cleitus at Samarkand in the Autumn of 328BC, Hephaistion led a foraging expedition with a section of the army towards the territory of Bactriana.[153]

The exact date and venue are uncertain, but sometime in late 328BC or early 327BC in Bactria or Sogdiana there was an attempt further to extend the policy of integration through the medium of an experiment in the Persian custom that the Greeks referred to as "proskynesis". Both Arrian and Curtius exploit this occasion for elaborate, set-piece speeches on the issue of the propriety of treating men as gods, which spectacularly miss the point and are of doubtful historicity. However, Plutarch cites an excellent source in the person of Chares, Alexander's Chamberlain, who was undoubtedly an eyewitness of the events and whose other fragments seem to be reliable. The authenticity of this particular extract is supported by its partial repetition in Arrian's Anabasis, but the sentence indicating the prominence of Hephaistion in this event is uniquely preserved at the end of the following quotation from Plutarch:-

Chares of Mytilene says that on one occasion at a banquet Alexander, after he had drunk, passed the cup to one of his friends, who took it and rose so as to face the shrine of the household; next he drank in his turn, then made obeisance (proskynesis) to Alexander, kissed him and resumed his place on the couch. All the guests did the same in succession, until the cup came to Callisthenes. The King was talking to Hephaistion and paying no attention to Callisthenes, and the philosopher, after he had drunk, came forward to kiss him. At this Demetrius, whose surname was Pheidon, called out, "Sire, do not kiss him; he is the only one who has not made obeisance to you." Alexander therefore refused to kiss him, and Callisthenes exclaimed in a loud voice, "Very well then, I shall go away the poorer by a kiss." Once this rift between them had occurred, it was easy for Hephaistion to be believed when he

---

[150] Curtius 7.7.9.
[151] Arrian, Anabasis 4.16.2; Curtius 8.1.1.
[152] See F L Holt, Alexander the Great and Bactria, Supplement to Mnemosyne, E J Brill, 1988, pp. 62-3.
[153] Curtius 8.2.13.

said that the philosopher had promised him to make obeisance to Alexander and had then broken his word.

Plutarch, Life of Alexander, 54.3-55.1

Alexander sent round a loving cup of gold, first to those with whom he had made an agreement about obeisance; the first who drank from it rose, did obeisance, and received a kiss from Alexander, and this went round all in turn. But when the pledge came to Callisthenes, he rose, drank from the cup, went up to Alexander and made to kiss him without having done obeisance. At that moment Alexander was talking to Hephaistion, and therefore was not attending to see whether the ceremony of obeisance had been carried out by Callisthenes. But as Callisthenes approached to kiss Alexander, Demetrius son of Pythonax, one of the Companions, remarked that he was coming without having done obeisance. Alexander did not permit Callisthenes to kiss him; and Callisthenes remarked, "I shall go away short of a kiss."

Arrian, Anabasis 4.12.3-5

It is important to note that Arrian confirms that Alexander had secured prior agreement to proskynesis from many of the attendees at this banquet and he does so specifically in the context of relating Chares' version of the event.[154] Although Arrian fails to name Hephaistion as the agent of these negotiations, the fact that Chares evidently recorded Hephaistion as having claimed such a role in the case of Callisthenes makes it seem highly likely that Hephaistion was the organiser of the event and possibly even its instigator. Given also that Arrian mentions the prior agreements without expressing any doubts about their authenticity, it is probable that Chares also merely reported the fact of their existence and Hephaistion's role in securing them. The implication in Plutarch's account that Hephaistion was lying looks like Plutarch's own gloss on the situation, which is certainly understandable, since Plutarch probably felt a particular affinity with Callisthenes as a fellow scholar and philosopher. It is of course impossible for Plutarch actually to have known what transpired in a private conversation between Hephaistion and Callisthenes: at best he is preferring some lost report of Callisthenes' denial over Chares' account of Hephaistion's accusation. In fact it is difficult to see how Hephaistion could possibly have failed to discuss the matter of the obeisance with Callisthenes beforehand, in view of the fact that it evidently was raised with a range of less opinionated courtiers. Equally, it would seem unlikely that Callisthenes would ever have been invited to the banquet, if he had not tacitly agreed to support the proskynesis experiment in advance.

If Aristotle's terse judgement on his great-nephew is accurate, then reneging on such an agreement might well have been second nature to him:-

Aristotle seems to have come near the truth when he said that Callisthenes possessed great eloquence, but lacked common sense.

Plutarch, Life of Alexander, 54.1

---

[154] Arrian, Anabasis 4.12.3.

Hephaistion, The Chiliarch

Various other anecdotes concerning Callisthenes confirm that he was a personage of considerable self-importance, who was singularly deficient in tact. Amongst other indiscretions, he is quoted as claiming that Alexander's fame was contingent upon Callisthenes' history of his campaigns.[155] Furthermore, various highly seditious remarks, which are likely to have reached Alexander's ears at the time, are attributed to Callisthenes by our sources. When the leader of a plot among a group of Alexander's Royal Pages to assassinate their liege lord and monarch, Hermolaus, asked Callisthenes how he might become an illustrious man, the sophist replied, "By killing the most illustrious."[156] Arrian reports a similar conversation between Callisthenes and Philotas.[157] When the Pages' Conspiracy failed, Callisthenes was arrested and kept in fetters for seven months, eventually dying of disease, when infested by lice at the time Alexander received a chest wound in India. At least such was the account of Chares, who was corroborated by Aristobulus.[158] Ptolemy wrote that Callisthenes was hanged right away, but he is surely whitewashing the high-command (including himself) of their neglect of the prisoner during Alexander's illness.[159]

The exact nature of *proskynesis* is uncertain, but it most probably involved genuflection accompanied by a gesture, which resembled the blowing of a kiss.[160] Greeks normally reserved such supplicatory behaviour for images of their gods, but to Persians proskynesis was merely an expression of respect for their king and was specifically devoid of religious connotations. Alexander's problem was that his Asian subjects were persisting in offering him proskynesis, whilst the Macedonians and the Greeks continued to greet him with the same casual familiarity as ever. Clearly, this dichotomy will have been a growing source of embarrassment and friction in Alexander's court, for some of the Persians will by 328BC have outranked many of the Greeks and Macedonians in Alexander's service. The proskynesis experiment is therefore properly seen as an attempt to remove these discrepancies in court formalities in line with the policies of the integrationist party. However, both Arrian and Plutarch state that Alexander abandoned the attempt to persuade the Macedonians and Greeks to offer him proskynesis due to Callisthenes' recalcitrance and the evident hostility of the traditionalist Macedonian faction towards the policy. The willingness of Alexander to back down on this point tends to suggest that he had always been lukewarm on the idea of obeisance and had perhaps been persuaded to attempt its introduction by some prominent courtier of the integrationist faction. In view of his probable responsibility for the organisation of the banquet, Hephaistion is the most obvious culprit.

---

[155] Arrian, Anabasis 4.10.1-2.
[156] Plutarch, Life of Alexander 55.2.
[157] Arrian, Anabasis 4.10.3-4.
[158] Plutarch, Life of Alexander 55.5.
[159] Arrian, Anabasis 4.14.3.
[160] Cf. P A Brunt, Arrian's History of Alexander, Appendix XIV, Section 8.

Alexander's Lovers by Andrew Chugg

* * * * * * * *

In the context of Alexander's invasion of India in the second half of 327BC, Hephaistion emerges clearly as the king's preferred deputy in the military leadership of the expedition. Initially, he was appointed commander of the main body of the army entering India, responsible for bridging the Indus, whilst Alexander was preoccupied by roving campaigns in the territories adjacent to the line of march. Subsequently, between the Indus and the Ganges the roles seem to have been reversed, when Hephaistion led a task force in a separate campaign to subdue an Indian kingdom. In all these missions, the ancient sources report unqualified success for Alexander's general.

[On reaching the river Cophen/Kabul in northern India Alexander] divided his army and sent Hephaistion and Perdiccas to the territory of Peucelaotis towards the river Indus...with instructions to take by storm or receive in surrender all towns on their march; when they had reached the Indus, they were to make preparations for crossing the river...They arrived at the Indus and performed Alexander's instructions. But Astis, the hyparch of the district of Peucelaotis, attempted revolt, and perished himself, besides involving in ruin the city to which he had fled for refuge; for Hephaistion and his troops captured it after a siege of thirty days... Hephaistion, Perdiccas and their men fortified another city, called Orobatis, for [Alexander], and leaving a garrison there went on towards the river Indus; on arrival they were engaged in following all Alexander's instructions for bridging the Indus... [Alexander] also found a wood good for felling near the river, and had it cut down by his troops, and ships built, which went down the river Indus to the bridge Hephaistion and Perdiccas had built for Alexander long before... On arriving at the river Indus, Alexander found a bridge made over it by Hephaistion.

Arrian, Anabasis 4.22.7-8 & 4.28.5 & 4.30. & 5.3.5

When no one else came to meet him [Alexander] sent Hephaistion and Perdiccas ahead with a section of his troops to crush any opposition to his power, giving them orders to advance to the river Indus and construct boats to ferry the army to the far banks. Because a number of rivers had to be crossed, they put the boats together in such a way that they could be dismantled, transported by wagon and then reassembled... [Alexander] reached the river Indus, where he found that all the preparations he had ordered for the crossing had been made by Hephaistion.

Curtius 8.10.2-3 & 8.12.4

The Metz Epitome 48 clarifies that Hephaistion had also aggregated large stocks of provisions for the march that lay ahead.

Curtius also mentions Hephaistion's role in attacking the Indian left wing with his regiment of the Companion Cavalry in the victorious battle against Porus at the river Hydaspes [Jhelum].[161] This was part of the main onslaught led by Alexander himself. During the ensuing advance across northern India, Hephaistion led a large independent task force in the subjugation of a substantial Indian kingdom.

---

[161] Curtius 8.14.15.

Hephaistion, The Chiliarch

In his pursuit Alexander arrived at the river Hydraotes... Here he despatched Hephaistion, giving him part of the army, two phalanxes of foot and his own and Demetrius' hipparchies of cavalry with half the archers, to the country of the rebellious Porus, with orders to hand it over to the other Porus, together with any independent Indian tribes dwelling by the banks of the Hydaspes; these too he was to win over and entrust them to Porus to govern.

Arrian, Anabasis 5.21.4-5

Arrian also indicates that Hephaistion's responsibilities included the fortification of an Indian city on the river Acesines.[162] His account is broadly echoed by Diodorus and Hephaistion's campaign is mentioned in passing by Curtius.[163] The former adds that Hephaistion thereby "conquered a big piece of India" and that Alexander "commended him for his successes", so this would appear to have been a significant and highly successful campaign in a populous region, which was nevertheless almost ignored by the ancient historians, whose focus remained fixated upon Alexander himself.

Nearchus listed Hephaistion first among the honorary trierarchs of the ships for the protracted river voyage down first the Hydaspes, then the Acesines and finally the Indus.[164] This is unlikely to have been by chance and more probably indicates his established primacy among Alexander's Friends at that juncture. His principal responsibility during this phase was the command of the main body of the army, which marched down the eastern bank of the river, whilst Craterus commanded a smaller force on the western side and Alexander himself led the fleet aboard his flagship.[165] In the land of the Mallians, Hephaistion again led a task force five days' march ahead of the main body of the troops as far as the confluence of the Acesines with the Hydraotes.[166] Whilst Hephaistion was absent on this mission, Alexander suffered a terrible arrow wound to his chest in a Mallian stronghold. As soon as he was able to travel, though still dreadfully weak, the King sailed downriver to Hephaistion's camp and a highly emotional reunion; the more so since rumours of Alexander's death had preceded him.[167]

Thereafter Alexander made a speedy recovery and Hephaistion next achieves prominence in our sources at Patala near the apex of the Indus Delta, where he is once again stated to have commanded a large part of the army and to have been responsible for the fortification of the city and the construction of extensive port facilities to support the fleet.[168] Subsequently, he continued to command the bulk of the troops and undertook the foundation of a city at Rhambacia, whilst Alexander ranged about conducting operations to quell local

---

[162] Arrian, Anabasis 5.29.3.
[163] Diodorus 17.91.1 & 17.93.1; Curtius 9.1.35.
[164] Arrian, Indica 18.
[165] Arrian, Anabasis 6.2.2 & 6.4.1; Diodorus 17.96.1.
[166] Arrian, Anabasis 6.5.6.
[167] Arrian, Anabasis 6.13.
[168] Arrian, Anabasis 6.17.4 & 6.18.1 & 6.20.1.

resistance in the land of the Oreitae on the way to Gedrosia.[169] Eventually, Hephaistion rejoined Alexander for the searing march across the relentlessly arid Gedrosian desert.[170]

In the light of this succession of triumphant and unblemished military commands during the Bactrian and Indian campaigns up to the threshold of the Gedrosian wilderness, it may well come as a shock to realise that Hephaistion's modern detractors argue that he was an ineffective or incompetent military officer. Heckel does so on the basis of the supposed absence of evidence of his military successes and argues that this shows that he owed his ever-increasing power entirely to Alexander's patronage.[171] However, in the first place, absence of evidence is not the same as evidence of absence. Secondly, most of the primary sources (Ptolemy, Aristobulus, Cleitarchus, Nearchus, Onesicritus, Chares) had scant motivation for dwelling upon Hephaistion's achievements in their works. Thirdly, as we have seen, it is simply untrue to claim that there is no evidence of Hephaistion's military successes, when in fact the sources repeatedly indicate favourable outcomes, albeit in an understated fashion. Finally, there seems to be no evidence whatsoever which could be deemed to suggest that Hephaistion was responsible for any military debacles, disasters or even setbacks. On the contrary, he was among those decorated for bravery by Alexander at the time of the Susa marriages in 324BC.[172]

Heckel's response to these points is to claim that Perdiccas acted as Hephaistion's "minder" in the Indus bridging campaign, despite the fact that there is no hint of this in the sources, for there are other instances where Arrian names several commanders for a single mission.[173] Actually there is a more straightforward motive for Arrian and Curtius to have mentioned Perdiccas in the context of this mission: Ptolemy, who was Arrian's source, made strenuous efforts to indicate which military units were deployed in which operations during Alexander's campaigns and noting Perdiccas' presence would have been a means of pointing out that his regiment of the Companion Cavalry also accompanied Hephaistion. Arrian goes on to state: "all the Companion Cavalry not assigned to Hephaistion" stayed with Alexander, which is a clear indication that Hephaistion actually commanded the mission.[174]

Heckel further suggests that Hephaistion's other campaigns were either minor or non-military. For example, he dismisses Diodorus' statement that Hephaistion conquered by warfare (*katapepolemekos*) a large part of India and declares that this was a mere diplomatic endeavour, notwithstanding the fact

---

[169] Arrian, Anabasis 6.21.3 & 6.21.5; Curtius 9.10.6.
[170] Arrian, Anabasis 6.22.3.
[171] W. Heckel, The Marshals of Alexander's Empire, London (1992) pp.76-78.
[172] Arrian, Anabasis 7.5.6.
[173] E.g. Arrian, Anabasis 3.18.6, where Amyntas, Philotas and Coenus are jointly instructed to march part of the army into a plain and to bridge a river.
[174] Arrian, Anabasis 4.23.1.

that this was hostile territory and Arrian records that Hephaistion was given a major section of the army to perform this mission.

* * * * * * * *

Regarding Hephaistion's formal status within Alexander's expedition, Arrian notes that he was among the seven Bodyguards (*Somatophylakes*) when Peucestas was enrolled to make their number up to eight in Carmania in 325BC.[175] In all probability, Hephaistion had long been a key member of this elite group of the most senior of Alexander's staff officers. As we have noted, the only sensible interpretation of Diodorus' assertion that Hephaistion commanded the *Somatophylakes* at Gaugamela would be that he was then already the most senior member of this illustrious band.

The Chief Minister of the Persian Great King was known as the *Hazarapatis* (or *Hazarapatish*), which roughly translates from the Persian as "commander of a thousand". The Greeks in turn rendered this title fairly literally as *Chiliarch* on translating it into their own language. The incumbent was second only to the Great King himself in rank and prestige. Indeed, a decade before Alexander's conquest, a eunuch called Bagoas had for a while virtually ruled the empire, whilst bearing the title of Chiliarch. It is quite certain that Alexander appointed Hephaistion to this exalted rank, probably sometime after Gaugamela, though the exact date is uncertain. Arrian gives Hephaistion the title of Chiliarch in his Anabasis, but he associates it with Hephaistion's command of the senior regiment of the Companion Cavalry, which is odd, since the proper title for such an appointment was Hipparch.[176] It is likely that Arrian is mistakenly conflating Hephaistion's separate offices of Chiliarch and Hipparch of the senior regiment of the Companion Cavalry (the latter seems also to have entailed overall command of the Companion Cavalry, for Hephaistion is so described by Appian, Syrian Wars 57.)[177] However, Photius has provided an epitome of Arrian's lost History of the Successors of Alexander, which states that, after Alexander's death, Perdiccas was appointed "to command the Chiliarchy which Hephaistion had originally held" and that this "entrusted him with the entire kingdom" in the context of the joint-kingship of Alexander's infant son and imbecilic half-brother, who were of necessity mere puppets.[178] It looks as though Arrian knew that Hephaistion had commanded the senior regiment of the Companion Cavalry *and* had acted as Alexander's Chief Minister

---

[175] Arrian, Anabasis 6.28.4.
[176] Arrian, Anabasis 7.14.10.
[177] NGL Hammond, Sources for Alexander the Great, Cambridge 1993, pp296-7 reaches this conclusion and is supported by Jeanne Reames in her treatise on Hephaistion; James Romm notes in the Landmark Arrian in respect of Arrian, Anabasis 7.14.10 that, "It seems possible that Arrian has confused this newly created Chiliarchy with a separate office, command over the Companion cavalry…"; PA Brunt reaches the same conclusions in App. XXIV.4 of the Loeb Arrian, II p.511.
[178] This is Photius 92, Epitome of Arrian's Events after Alexander; Photius 82, Summary of Dexippus' Events after Alexander also mentions this (it is likely that Dexippus used Arrian's work or that they had a common source).

by virtue of his title of Chiliarch, but that he failed to distinguish clearly between the two roles, perhaps because he did not understand the Persian origins of the title and consequently thought that "lord of a thousand" had to refer to Hephaistion's military command in some way.

Happily Diodorus removes any possible ambiguity by stating that Perdiccas, when he became Chiliarch, relinquished command of the Companion Cavalry in favour of Seleucus[179] and also by noting:-

Antipater also made his own son Cassander Chiliarch and second in authority. The position and rank of Chiliarch had first been brought to fame and honour by the Persian kings, and afterwards under Alexander it gained great power and glory at the time when he became an admirer of this and all other Persian customs. Diodorus 18.48.5[180]

Obviously, Alexander's Chiliarch can only have been Hephaistion. Furthermore, Diodorus' statement that Alexander revived this title at the same time as he embraced other Persian customs makes it difficult to date Hephaistion's appointment later than the time of the proskynesis experiment (i.e. 328BC). This would also help to explain why it was Hephaistion who organised this experiment. It might further be argued that Hephaistion seemed already to be acting with the authority of a Chiliarch in the case of the Philotas affair. The common source of Diodorus 17.77.4 and Curtius 6.6.1-8 was Cleitarchus and it is clear from their accounts that Cleitarchus placed Alexander's main phase of "Persianisation" in the immediate aftermath of the death of Darius in ~August 330BC. This was also the period in which the previous Chiliarch, Nabarzanes, surrendered to Alexander in Hyrcania, so this is the occasion for the appointment of Hephaistion to which Diodorus would appear to be referring.

* * * * * * * *

Following Alexander's triumphant return to Persia and Mesopotamia in early 324BC, Hephaistion's personal triumph over his competitors in the Macedonian hierarchy was manifest. Craterus, his only significant rival in the military command structure, was packed off back to Macedonia with the army veterans to take over the Regency of Macedon from Antipater. A serious quarrel with Eumenes, Alexander's Secretary and a Hipparch of the Companions after Hephaistion's death, seems to have been settled in Hephaistion's favour. At Susa in the summer Alexander virtually adopted Hephaistion into the Royal Family by granting him the hand of Darius' younger daughter in marriage at the same time as Alexander himself married the elder princess:-

[Alexander] also held weddings at Susa for himself and the Companions. He himself married Darius' eldest daughter, Barsine, and, as Aristobulus says, another wife as well, Parysatis, the youngest daughter of Ochus. He had already taken to wife Roxane, the daughter of

---

[179] Diodorus 18.3.4.
[180] See also Arrian, Events After Alexander, F1.38 epitomised by Photius 92 [72a or 9.38], where Cassander is also granted the title of Chiliarch "of the cavalry".

Hephaistion, The Chiliarch

Oxyartes the Bactrian. To Hephaistion he gave Drypetis, another daughter of Darius, sister to his own wife, for he desired Hephaistion's children to be cousins of his own.

Arrian, Anabasis 7.4.4-5[181]

Hephaistion had reached an exalted pinnacle of power and influence. He had become Alexander's acknowledged partner in government and in all things. Yet the Chiliarch of the empire had only months to live.

Personality

In addition to the persistent antagonism between Hephaistion and Olympias and the feud with Craterus in India, in the last year or so of his life the Chiliarch became embroiled in a serious quarrel with Eumenes the Secretary.

[Eumenes] frequently incurred Alexander's displeasure and put himself in some danger through Hephaistion. The quarters that had been taken up for Eumenes, Hephaistion assigned to Evius, the flute-player. Upon which, in great anger, Eumenes and Mentor came to Alexander and loudly complained, saying that the way to be regarded was to throw away their arms and turn flute-players or tragedians; so much so that Alexander chided Hephaistion; but soon after changed his mind again, and was angry with Eumenes, and accounted the freedom he had taken to be rather an affront to the King than a reflection upon Hephaistion.

Plutarch, Life of Eumenes 2.1[182]

That Hephaistion's several quarrels with Craterus, Eumenes and Olympias figure so prominently among the written evidence for his career has led many historians to ascribe an aggressive and irascible personality to the Chiliarch.[183] If his adversaries had been random individuals from Alexander's entourage, then it might be possible to agree that Hephaistion was exhibiting a quarrelsome nature. However, these eminent antagonists were in fact Hephaistion's immediate and direct rivals for Alexander's affections, favour and patronage and they undoubtedly saw themselves as such. In the case of Craterus the truth of this is explicit in the "Alexander-loving" Hephaistion and "King-loving" Craterus epithets, the assignment of which is attributed to Alexander himself by Plutarch and Diodorus. As for Olympias, she surely felt that the depth of Alexander's relationship with Hephaistion tended to undermine her own influence with her son and she may especially have seen him as an obstacle to Alexander's begetting of heirs to his throne. Finally, the arguments between Hephaistion and Eumenes seem to have blown up after Hephaistion had been appointed Chiliarch by Alexander. It is likely that Eumenes will have seen Hephaistion's promotion as a threat to his own position as Alexander's Secretary, particularly because the title of Chiliarch had traditionally been accorded to the chief administrative officer of the Persian Empire. At the least

---

[181] Cf. Diodorus 17.107.6; Curtius 10.5.20.
[182] Plutarch is corroborated by a comment about a reconciliation in Arrian 7.13.1 (& 7.14.9).
[183] E.g. W Heckel, The Marshals of Alexander's Empire, London, 1992, p.83.

Eumenes will probably have felt sidelined and it is even possible that he had been requested to report to Alexander though the Chiliarch.

A potentiality for the emergence of antipathy between Hephaistion and these three individuals was therefore inherent in the political structure of Alexander's court. Given the nature of Hephaistion's relationship with the king, his enemies' most obvious and cutting jibe must have been to attribute his elevation to his performance in Alexander's bed rather than to his skills as a warrior, a commander and a diplomat. Plutarch's account of the quarrel with Eumenes actually mentions some such ill-judged and provocative accusations having been addressed to the Chiliarch by the Secretary.

Death, Obsequies and Worship

For sure we were the sunniest of men, but with my tears the shining years are gone,
For I shall never love my life again, though yet and yet my broken heart beats on.
So it's from time to time I drowse and dream the lost content of ages most benign:
In the dregs of my glass I glimpsed the Moon gleam as I toasted my Friends with the last of the wine.

By virtue of Alexander's remarkable reaction Hephaistion receives his greatest coverage in the ancient sources in the context of his untimely death at Ecbatana some time around the end of November 324BC. This event unleashed a torrent of lamentation from Alexander that shocked his contemporaries and astonished the ancient commentators. It remains today probably the most spectacular outpouring of untrammelled grief in recorded history.

Yet it has also remained largely misunderstood and misrepresented as indicative of incipient irrationality or "melancholy madness"[184] on the part of the king. In reality Alexander's response to his bereavement followed an unambiguously rational pattern and might reasonably be seen as both proportionate to the magnitude of his personal loss and concordant with Homeric tradition, once the leverage supplied by the enormity of Alexander's wealth and power at this time is factored into the evaluation.

The ancient sources presaged events, as was their wont, with dire auguries of Hephaistion's demise. Arrian repeated a story originally recorded by Alexander's engineering officer, Aristobulus:

Apollodorus of Amphipolis… wrote to Pythagoras his brother, as he was one of those seers who prophesy from the flesh of victims, to prophesy about his own welfare. Pythagoras wrote in answer asking who it was that he chiefly feared that he wanted the help of prophesy, and he replied that it was the King himself and Hephaistion. Pythagoras then sacrificed first in regard to Hephaistion and, as the lobe could not be seen on the liver of the victim, he reported this,

---

[184] So said Alexander's hostile contemporary, Ephippus of Olynthus, quoted by Athenaeus, Deipnosophistae 12.538a.

Hephaistion, The Chiliarch

and sealing his letter sent it to Apollodorus from Babylon to Ecbatana, showing that he had nothing to fear from Hephaistion, as in a short time he would be out of their way.

Arrian 7.18[185]

The principal surviving accounts of Hephaistion's fatal illness are the summaries by Plutarch and Arrian:-

When [Alexander] came to Ecbatana... he was once more occupied with theatres and festivals..., but during this time it chanced that Hephaistion had a fever; and since, young man and soldier that he was, he could not submit to a strict regimen, as soon as Glaucus (a.k.a Glaucias), his physician, had gone off to the theatre, he sat down to breakfast, ate a boiled fowl, drank a huge cooler of wine, fell sick, and in a little while died.

Plutarch, Alexander 72.1

At Ecbatana Alexander... held athletic and musical games and drinking bouts with the Companions. At this time Hephaistion fell ill, and his illness had run seven days, they say, when the stadium was filled with people, as there were athletic sports that day for boys; but when Alexander heard that Hephaistion was seriously ill, he left the stadium and hurried to him, but found him no longer living.

Arrian 7.14.1

Diodorus confines himself to the less helpful observation that:-

In the course of [parties at Ecbatana], Hephaistion drank very much, fell ill, and died.

Diodorus 17.110.8

Apart from the implicit allegation in each case that the illness was caused or was compounded by heavy alcohol consumption,[186] several diagnostically significant facts emerge:-

a) Hephaistion had a fever (and perhaps other symptoms) for at least around a week prior to his death and this fever was sufficiently severe for him to be subject to the care of a doctor (Glaucias).

b) After a week he would appear to have been improving, since Glaucias felt free to leave his patient to attend the boys' games in the theatre and since Hephaistion appears to have recovered his appetite. Against his doctors orders he consumed a heavy meal washed down with wine.

c) Following the meal Hephaistion collapsed and died within hours, too quickly even for Alexander to receive word and reach his bedside.

If it is assumed, as would seem reasonable, that his fever, his meal and his sudden death are all connected, then it is difficult to explain the case history in

---

[185] See also Plutarch 73.2 (although he does not mention Hephaistion).
[186] The persistence of this view owes something to the fact that there really was a tradition of heavy drinking at Macedonian parties and something more to the contemporary propagandist account of Ephippus concerning the deaths of Alexander and Hephaistion.

terms of alcohol poisoning. Alcoholism leads almost invariably to chronic and lingering sickness rather than acute symptoms with a sudden crisis. Only rarely and in exceptional circumstances does drinking entail prompt mortality. Even such rare cases usually involve spirits, since wine is not strong enough for it normally to be physically feasible to imbibe poisonous quantities of alcohol. Whereas the wine may well have exacerbated another source of illness, it is very unlikely to constitute the sole cause of Hephaistion's shockingly rapid expiry.

However, there is one very common medical scenario that provides a good fit to Hephaistion's case history. Serious bowel infections, and typhoid in particular, will normally produce a severe and protracted episode of fever, in the course of which the intestine frequently becomes ulcerated. The patient is therefore highly susceptible to perforations of the bowels in the earlier part of recovery from the disease before the damage has healed. In practice, this is one of the principal causes of mortality, especially in untreated cases. A serious perforation might particularly be stimulated by a heavy meal and would be expected to produce a prompt collapse of the patient. Death from internal bleeding and medical shock might well ensue on a timescale as short as hours.[187]

Although this scenario provides the most probable explanation of Hephaistion's death, it is not completely without problems. Most notably, seven days is a rather short period in the case of typhoid for a patient to recover sufficient appetite to stomach a solid meal. However, in the first place it is not necessary to insist that the disease was specifically typhoid and in the second it should be recognised that typhoid exhibits marked variations among its sufferers. Furthermore, the timescale of seven days probably merely refers to the term of the illness after which it had become generally known in the court that Hephaistion was seriously ill. The overall period of sickness would probably have been longer, since Hephaistion would not have wished to give Alexander cause for concern or his enemies cause for satisfaction until the severity of his illness was beyond concealment.

An alternative view would be the conspiracy theory, that one of Hephaistion's enemies, among whom we can count such powerful figures as Craterus and Eumenes, took advantage of the Chiliarch's bout of fever to mask a poisoning attack. But this implies an almost incredibly sophisticated and risky plot involving the suborning of Hephaistion's servants and probably also of his doctor. In fact, Arrian (Anabasis 7.14.4) does quote some earlier source as suggesting that Alexander hanged Hephaistion's doctor, Glaucias, "for a drug wrongly given or alternatively because Glaucias had seen Hephaistion drinking most immoderately and had not stopped him." But these sound more like accusations of medical negligence, than of deliberate plots. It is anyway difficult to see why a more straightforward poisoning attempt should not have been

---

[187] However peritonitis from a burst appendix would have been unlikely to kill Hephaistion sufficiently swiftly as to explain the reported suddenness of his demise.

preferable. Furthermore, there does not seem to have been any suspicion of foul play at the time, which militates strongly against poisoning in view of Alexander's attested medical and herbal knowledge.

* * * * * * * *

Extensive accounts of Alexander's reactions to his sudden and dramatic bereavement are given by Arrian, Plutarch and Diodorus among the principal ancient accounts of Alexander's career. Additionally, Plutarch provides tangential supplements in his Lives of Eumenes and Pelopidas. Even Justin's epitome of Trogus preserves a single sentence on the matter, but the relevant section of Curtius' history is unfortunately lost. These versions are augmented by important material in an item from Aelian's *Varia Historia* and an extended anecdote in Lucian's essay on Slander. One primary source even speaks directly to us via Egyptian papyri in the form of comments in a speech dating from 322BC by the Athenian orator Hypereides, which appear to refer to Hephaistion's posthumous worship as a hero. Finally, there is some archaeological evidence for Hephaistion's pyre from excavations at Babylon and it is sometimes suggested that a much-weathered lion monument (Figure 3.11) at Ecbatana (modern Hamadan), the site of the Chiliarch's demise, commemorates his career.[188]

Figure 3.11. The Lion of Hamadan: a monument to Hephaistion? (Sketch by the author)

In order to gain a true insight into the ways in which Alexander came to terms with his bereavement, it is necessary carefully to examine all of these testimonies. They exhibit a fair degree of unanimity on the vast magnitude of Alexander's grief, yet there is considerable complementarity in the details they

---

[188] See especially Robin Lane Fox, Alexander the Great; the evidence seems merely to be circumstantial, based on similar lion monuments having commonly been used to commemorate senior Macedonians (see Monumental Tombs of the Hellenistic Age, Janos Fedak, Toronto 1990, p.100). Hephaistion was the most famous Macedonian to die at Ecbatana/Hamadan.

choose to highlight. Nevertheless they also appear to differ in some specifics, such as the degree of deification that Alexander accorded to his dead lover. It is appropriate to begin with Arrian, since he provides a substantial critique of the treatment of this subject by a range of primary sources, which were familiar to him, but are otherwise lost to us.

Some say that he threw himself on his companion's body and lay there for the greater part of that day, bewailing him and refusing to depart from him, until he was forcibly carried away by his Companions. Others that he lay upon the body the whole day and night. Others again say that he hanged the physician Glaucias, for having wrongly given a drug; others say because he had not stopped Hephaistion, when he had seen him drinking excessively. That Alexander should have cut off his hair in honour of the dead man, I do not think improbable, both for other reasons and especially from a desire to emulate Achilles, whom from his boyhood he had an ambition to rival. Others also say that Alexander himself at one time drove the chariot on which the body was borne; but this statement I by no means believe. Others again affirm that he ordered the shrine of Asclepius in Ecbatana to be razed to the ground;[189] which would have been an act of barbarism, and by no means in harmony with Alexander's general behaviour... But the following statement, which has been recorded, does not seem to me entirely beyond the range of probability: that when Alexander was marching to Babylon, he was met on the road by many embassies from Greece, among which were some Epidaurian envoys, who obtained from him their requests. He also gave them an offering to be conveyed to Asclepius, adding this remark: "Although Asclepius has not treated me fairly, in not saving for me my Companion, whom I valued as much as my life." It has been stated by most writers that he ordered honours to be always paid to Hephaistion as a hero; and some say that he even sent men to Ammon's oracle to ask the god if it were permissible to offer sacrifice to Hephaistion as a god; but Ammon replied that it was not allowable. All the authorities, however, agree as to the following facts: that until the third day after Hephaistion's death, Alexander neither tasted food nor paid any attention to his personal appearance, but lay on the ground either bewailing or silently mourning; that he also ordered a funeral pyre to be prepared for him in Babylon at an expense of 10,000 talents (some say more) and that a decree was published throughout all the barbarian territory for the observance of public mourning. Many of Alexander's Companions dedicated themselves and their arms to the dead Hephaistion in order to show their respect to him; and the first to adopt this expedient was Eumenes, whom we mentioned as having been at variance with him. This he did that Alexander might not think he was pleased at Hephaistion's death. Alexander did not appoint anyone else to be Chiliarch of the Companion cavalry in the place of Hephaistion, so that the name of that general might not perish from the brigade; but that chiliarchy of cavalry was still called Hephaistion's and Hephaistion's standard, made by his command, went before it.[190] He also resolved to celebrate a gymnastic and musical contest, much more magnificent than any of the preceding, both in the multitude of competitors and in the amount of money expended upon it. For he provided 3,000 competitors in all; and it is said that these men a short time after also competed in the

---

[189] The story that Alexander ordered the temples of Asclepius to be burned is also recorded in Arrian's Discourses of Epictetus 2.22.17.
[190] The Greek is slightly ambiguous, leaving open a possibility that the standard was an image of Hephaistion.

Hephaistion, The Chiliarch

games held at Alexander's own funeral... Now arrived [at Babylon] the special envoys whom he had dispatched to Ammon to inquire how it was lawful for him to honour Hephaistion. They told him that Ammon said it was lawful to offer sacrifice to him as to a hero. Rejoicing at the response of the oracle, he paid respect to him as a hero from that time. He also dispatched a letter to Cleomenes, who was a bad man and had committed many acts of injustice in Egypt. For my own part I do not blame him for his friendship to Hephaistion, even when dead, and for his recollection of him; but I do blame him for many other acts. For the letter commanded Cleomenes to prepare a shrine for the hero Hephaistion in the Egyptian Alexandria, not just in the city itself but actually upon the island of Pharos, where the tower is situated. The shrine was to be huge and to be built at lavish expense. The letter also directed that Cleomenes should take care that it should customarily be named after Hephaistion; and moreover that his name should be engraved on all the legal documents with which the merchants entered into bargains. These things I cannot censure, except that he made so much ado about matters of trifling moment. But the following I must censure severely: "If I find," said the letter, "the sacred rites and temples of the hero Hephaistion in Egypt well completed, I will not only pardon you any crimes you have committed in the past, but in the future you shall suffer no ill treatment from me, however great may be the crimes you may commit." I cannot commend this message sent from a great king to a man who was ruling a large and populous country, especially as the man was a wicked one.

Arrian, 7.14.3-10 & 7.23.6-8

Arrian's account is particularly helpful, not merely for the facts he records, but also because he illustrates the degree of variation and contradiction, which he found displayed in the lost primary sources. For example, there was agreement that the doctor was executed for negligence, but some dissension regarding the precise nature of his mistakes. Nevertheless, Arrian's judgement on the reliability of the various anecdotes is sometimes suspect, because he appears to deploy Roman notions of propriety in royal conduct in formulating his opinions. In particular, Arrian's view that it was incredible that Alexander should have driven Hephaistion's funeral car is dubious and anachronistic. As has already been revealed, Alexander treated Homer's Iliad as a kind of manual for life: a viaticum. Since Homer describes Achilles bearing the head of Patroclus' corpse in his funeral procession, it is likely that Alexander would have considered his active participation in Hephaistion's funeral cortège to be entirely proper. A second flaw in Arrian's approach is his somewhat naïve belief that the best way of discerning the truth is to seek unanimity between the sources. Apart from the fact that it is far from impossible for all the sources to be wrong on some points, this approach potentially dismisses accurate accounts of events, which happen to be ignored or contradicted by other sources. A more reliable methodology would be to seek a pattern in Alexander's reported behaviour, which is discernible in otherwise unconnected reports from different primary sources. Such a pattern would provide better confidence that we are perceiving historical reality through the obfuscation introduced by second and third hand reporting.

Alexander's Lovers by Andrew Chugg

In fact Arrian has indicated a possible templet for Alexander's conduct in mourning Hephaistion by pointing out that by shearing his hair he was copying Achilles' behaviour at the funeral of Patroclus. Arrian may have derived this insight from a primary source, since the comment is repeated by Aelian. Among these primary sources, it appears that Cleitarchus' lost history of Alexander particularly emphasised the analogy between the relationship of Alexander & Hephaistion and that of Achilles & Patroclus, so he is one possible common source on this point.

We have also seen that Alexander looked upon Hephaistion as his alter ego, a second self, so we should also expect to see some evidence of Alexander treating Hephaistion's funeral almost as though it were his own. With this in mind we will proceed by reviewing the rest of the ancient testimony, whilst tabulating the various funeral rites against the instances of their occurrence in the sources (see the end of this chapter for the resulting Tables). An extra column has been reserved for comments on the possible allusions to royal or literary precedents in each recorded ritual.

Plutarch's several references to the immensity of Alexander's desolation rank next in importance after Arrian:-

Alexander's grief at [Hephaistion's death] knew no bounds. He immediately ordered that the manes and tails of all horses and mules should be shorn in token of mourning, and took away the battlements of the cities round about; he also crucified the wretched physician, and put a stop to the sound of flutes and every kind of music in the camp for a long time, until an oracular response from Ammon came bidding him honour Hephaistion as a hero and sacrifice to him. Moreover, making war a solace for his grief, he went forth to hunt and track down men, as it were, and overwhelmed the nation of the Cossaeans, slaughtering them all from the youth upwards. This was called an offering to the shade of Hephaistion. Upon a tomb and obsequies for his friend, and upon their embellishments, he purposed to expend ten thousand talents, and wished that the ingenuity and novelty of the construction should surpass the expense. He therefore longed for Stasicrates[191] above all other artists... in consequence of oracular responses regarding Hephaistion which were brought to him, he laid aside his grief...

Plutarch, Alexander 72 & 75.2

Another difference happened between [Eumenes] and Hephaistion concerning a gift, and a great deal of ill language passed between them, yet Eumenes still continued in favour. But Hephaistion dying soon after, the King in his grief, presuming all those that differed with Hephaistion in his lifetime were now rejoicing at his death, showed much harshness and severity in his behaviour with them, especially towards Eumenes, whom he often upbraided with his quarrels and ill language to Hephaistion. But he, being a wise and dexterous courtier, made advantage of what had done him prejudice, and struck in with the King's passion for

---

[191] A.k.a. Deinocrates of Rhodes (preferred form), Dinocrates (Vitruvius & Ammianus Marcellinus & Latin Alexander Romance), Dimocrates of Rhodes (Armenian Alexander Romance) or Cheirocrates (Strabo).

Hephaistion, The Chiliarch

glorifying his friend's memory, suggesting various plans to do him honour, and contributing largely and readily towards erecting his monument.

Plutarch, Life of Eumenes 2.4-5

...Alexander the Great, when Hephaistion died, not only cut off the manes of his horses and mules, but even demolished the battlements of city walls in order to show the cities in mourning and make them present a shorn and dishevelled appearance in place of their former beauty.

Plutarch, Life of Pelopidas 34

There is an interesting and corroborative anecdote concerning Alexander's campaign against the Cossaeans in Polyaenus, though he is mistaken in stating that Hephaistion died in Babylon. His source had probably merely stated that Hephaistion's corpse had arrived in the metropolis:-

Alexander was surveying the territory of the Cossaeans – rough terrain, high, inaccessible mountains and a large number of excellent men in the mountains. There was no hope, therefore, of taking it. Someone arrived with the report, "Hephaistion has died in Babylon." He decreed general mourning and rushed to Hephaistion's burial. When the Cossaean scouts saw them breaking up their camp, they dispersed. By sending horsemen at night Alexander seized the unguarded entrance to the mountains. Turning back from his journey, he joined the horsemen and with them subdued the Cossaeans' territory. This act, they say, was a consolation to Alexander for his grief at Hephaistion's death.

Polyaenus, Stratagems of War 4.3.31

Justin gives a brief mention of the subject, probably epitomised from a much fuller account in Trogus, his source:-

At this time one of [Alexander's] personal friends died – Hephaistion, a favourite of Alexander's because of his good looks and boyish charms as well as his complete compliance with the King's wishes. Disregarding kingly decorum, Alexander spent a long time mourning him, built him a tomb at a cost of 12,000 Talents and ordered that he be worshipped posthumously as a god.[192]

Justin 12.12.11-12

Aelian echoes some details from Arrian and Plutarch, but also adds a few unique points, such as Alexander altering his dress and the consignment of panoplies and precious metals to the inferno of Hephaistion's pyre:-

When Hephaistion died Alexander threw armour on to his pyre, and melted down with the corpse gold, silver, and clothing much prized by the Persians.[193] *He cut off his own hair, a gesture in the Homeric manner, in imitation of the poet's Achilles.*[194] *But Alexander was more violent and hotheaded than Achilles: he destroyed the acropolis of Ecbatana and*

---

[192] *Dum haec aguntur, unus ex amicis eius Hephaestion decedit, dotibus primo formae pueritiaeque, mox obsequiis regi percarus. Quem contra decus regium Alexander diu luxit tumulumque ei duodecim milium talentum fecit eumque post mortem coli ut deum iussit.* Justin 12.12.11-12.
[193] Perizonius suggested that this was the dress worn by the Persian king and subsequently by Alexander: this would therefore be a further instance of Alexander treating Hephaistion as his alter ego and therefore affording him kingly honours.
[194] Homer, Iliad 23.141.

knocked down its walls. As far as his hair is concerned, I think he acted in accordance with Greek custom; but when he pulled down the walls, that was a barbaric expression of grief by Alexander. He changed his dress and allowed himself to be completely controlled by anger, love and tears. Note that Hephaistion died at Ecbatana. A story circulates that these ceremonies, while planned for Hephaistion, were carried out for Alexander on his death, because mourning for the young man was not yet completed when death overtook Alexander.

Aelian, Varia Historia 7.8

Lucian has an extended anecdote from an exceptionally hostile source. Perhaps this comes from the libellous pamphlet "On the Funerals of Alexander and Hephaistion" by Alexander's contemporary, Ephippus of Olynthus. Elsewhere in this propagandist document Ephippus accused Alexander of dressing up as the goddess Artemis, though this seems in fact to have been a sardonic reference to the king's adoption of certain elements of Persian regalia, which resembled the robes of the Huntress to a Greek eye.[195] The attested fragments of Ephippus' pamphlet, as preserved by Athenaeus, have connections with Samos, which is the homeland of Agathocles in this anecdote.[196] Lucian's story is notable for its scornful treatment of Hephaistion's deification and its mockery of Alexander's gullibility, but it would seem that his source embroidered the facts, since we know from Arrian and Plutarch that Hephaistion was only officially accorded the status of a hero.

In the court of Alexander it was once the greatest of all slanderous charges to say that a man did not worship Hephaistion or even make obeisance to him – for after the death of Hephaistion, Alexander for the love he bore him determined to add to his other great feats that of appointing the dead man a god. So the cities at once erected temples; plots of ground were consecrated; altars, sacrifices and feasts were established in honour of this new god, and everybody's strongest oath was 'By Hephaistion.' If anyone smiled at what went on or failed to seem quite reverent, the penalty prescribed was death. The flatterers, taking hold of this childish passion of Alexander's, at once began to feed it and fan it into flame by telling about dreams of Hephaistion, in that way ascribing to him visitations and cures and accrediting him with prophecies; and at last they began to sacrifice to him as "Coadjutor" and "Saviour." Alexander liked to hear all this, and at length believed it, and was very proud of himself for being, as he thought, not only the son of a god but also able to make gods. Well, how many of Alexander's friends, do you suppose, reaped the results of Hephaistion's divinity during that period, through being accused of not honouring the universal god, and consequently being banished and deprived of the King's favour? It was then that Agathocles of Samos, one of Alexander's captains, whom he esteemed highly, came near being shut up in a lion's den because he was charged with having wept as he went by the tomb of Hephaistion. But Perdiccas is said to have come to his rescue, swearing by all the gods and by Hephaistion to boot that while he was hunting the god had appeared to him in the flesh and bidden him to tell Alexander to spare Agathocles, saying that he had not wept from want of faith or because he

---

[195] Alexander the Great, Robin Lane Fox.
[196] Gorgos the hoplophylax was granted honorary citizenship of Samos, see Athenaeus, 12.537e–538b and L. Pearson, The Lost Histories of Alexander the Great (New York 1960), pp. 63-65.

Hephaistion, The Chiliarch

thought Hephaistion dead, but only because he had been put in mind of their old-time friendship.   Lucian, Slander 17

Diodorus' account is notable for its elaborate details of the funeral - especially Hephaistion's huge and elaborate pyre. This description suggests that the pyre was constructed in imitation of the nearby seven-storey ziggurat, which was probably also the inspiration for the Biblical story of the Tower of Babel. A 19th century reconstruction, based on the details given by Diodorus, is shown in Figure 3.12. There is a coin type of the Roman Emperor, Antoninus Pius, which depicts a similar high status pyre (Figure 3.13). The Greek term *pyra* can also refer to a permanent funerary monument. Some have therefore argued that the edifice described by Diodorus was actually a mausoleum, but this is improbable, firstly because Diodorus states that it was supported on palm tree trunks and secondly because Achilles cremated Patroclus on an exceptionally large pyre, so it is likely that Alexander was emulating this precedent.[197] Furthermore, the archaeologist Robert Koldewey has located a possible site for the pyre at a scorched and reddened platform beneath a mound of brick rubble close to the inner wall of Babylon due east of the "Southern Palace" of Nebuchadnezzar (see location in Figure 3.14).[198] Koldewey even described having found the imprints of incinerated palm trunks on the platform, reflecting Diodorus' description fairly precisely. Finally, we have already seen that Aelian actually describes armour and precious metals being melted down on Hephaistion's pyre, which indicates a fairly intense blaze. Nevertheless, Diodorus may well be using *pyra* to refer to a planned mausoleum for Hephaistion in his 18th book (last paragraph in the following group of extracts).

The King was intensely grieved at [Hephaistion's death] and entrusted his body to Perdiccas to conduct to Babylon, where he proposed to celebrate a magnificent funeral for him...

When the embassies had been dismissed [April-May 323BC], Alexander threw himself into preparations for the burial of Hephaistion. He showed such zeal about the funeral that it not only surpassed all those previously celebrated on earth but also left no possibility of anything greater in later ages. He had loved Hephaistion most of the group of Friends who were thought to have stood high in his affections, and after his death showed him superlative honour. In his lifetime he had preferred him to all...

As part of the preparations for the funeral, the King ordered the cities of the region to contribute to its splendour in accordance with their ability, and he proclaimed to all the peoples of Asia that they should sedulously quench what the Persians call the sacred fire, until such time as the funeral should be ended. This was the custom of the Persians when their kings died, and people thought that the order was an ill omen, and that heaven was foretelling the King's own death...

---

[197] Robin Lane Fox, Alexander the Great, Ch. 31, p.456-457; AB Bosworth, Conquest & Empire, XIX, p.164.
[198] Hephaestion's Pyre & the Royal Hunt of Alexander by Olga Palagia in Alexander the Great in Fact & Fiction, edited by A. B. Bosworth and E. J. Baynham, Oxford 2000, p.173; R. Koldewey, The Excavations at Babylon, London 1914, p.310-11; Joan Oates, Babylon, London, 1979, p.159.

Alexander's Lovers by Andrew Chugg

Each of the generals and Friends tried to meet the King's desires and made likenesses of Hephaistion in ivory and gold and other materials which men hold in high regard. Alexander collected artisans and an army of workmen and tore down the city wall to a distance of 10 stades. He collected the baked tiles and levelled off the place, which was to receive the pyre, and then constructed this square in shape, each side being a stade in length. He divided up the area into thirty compartments and laying out the roofs upon the trunks of palm trees wrought the whole structure into a square shape. Then he decorated all the exterior walls. Upon the foundation course were golden prows of quinqueremes in close order, two hundred and forty in all. Upon the catheads each carried two kneeling archers four cubits in height, and (on the deck) armed male figures five cubits high, while the intervening spaces were occupied by red banners fashioned out of felt. Above these, on the second level, stood torches fifteen cubits high with golden wreaths about their handles. At their flaming ends perched eagles with outspread wings looking downwards, while about their bases were serpents looking up at the eagles. On the third level were carved a multitude of wild animals being pursued by hunters. The fourth level carried a centauromachy rendered in gold, while the fifth showed lions and bulls alternating, also in gold. The next higher level was covered with Macedonian and Persian arms, testifying to the prowess of the one people and to the defeats of the other. On top of all stood Sirens, hollowed out and able to conceal within them persons who sang a lament in mourning for the dead. The total height of the pyre was more than one hundred and thirty cubits.

All of the generals and the soldiers and the envoys and even the natives rivalled one another in contributing to the magnificence of the funeral, so, it is said, that the total expense came to over twelve thousand talents. In keeping with this magnificence and the other special marks of honour at the funeral, Alexander ended by decreeing that all should sacrifice to Hephaistion as god coadjutor. As a matter of fact, it happened just at this time that Philip, one of the Friends, came bearing a response from Ammon that Hephaistion should be worshipped as a god. Alexander was delighted that the god had ratified his own opinion and was himself the first to perform the sacrifice, and entertained everybody handsomely. The sacrifice comprised ten thousand victims of all sorts…

Diodorus 17.110.8, 17.114-17.115

When [in June 323BC] Perdiccas found in the memoranda of the King orders for the completion of Hephaistion's pyre [tomb?], which required a great deal of money,… he decided that it was inexpedient to carry the plans out.

Diodorus 18.4

In 2009 I proposed a specific plan for Hephaistion's pyre on the basis of Diodorus' description in a sub-section of my book on *The Death of Alexander the Great: A Reconstruction of Cleitarchus*, which is reproduced in this edition of *Alexander's Lovers* in Figure 3.15. The key to my new proposal was the observation that the construction from thirty chambers mentioned by Diodorus corresponds neatly to a pyramidal structure with 4 x 4 chambers in its base, 3 x 3 chambers in its second stage, 2 x 2 chambers in its third level and a single chamber constituting its top stage. A more detailed explanation of this design together with a thorough analysis of the pyre's decoration has been incorporated in Appendix B of this edition of *Alexander's Lovers*.

Hephaistion, The Chiliarch

It may be remarked at this point that the reported cost of Hephaistion's obsequies at variously 10,000 or 12,000 talents was roughly equivalent to 25 tonnes of gold, which makes this easily the most expensive funeral in history.

To conclude regarding the testimonies, one voice from Athens speaks to us directly from a date within a year or two of Hephaistion's death. It is that of Hypereides, an Athenian who was a renowned orator in his day.[199] His words have come down to us solely from Egyptian papyri preserved from ancient times in the dry sand of the desert.

Figure 3.12. Reconstruction of Hephaistion's funeral pyre according to Diodorus (F Jaffé)

The practices that even now we have to countenance are proof enough: sacrifices being made to men; images, altars and temples carefully perfected in their honour, while those of the gods are neglected, and we ourselves are forced to honour as heroes the servants of these people. If reverence for the gods has been removed by Macedonian insolence, what fate must we conclude would have befallen the rules of conduct towards man?

Hypereides (Athenian orator), Epitaphios col. 8.21-22 in 322BC

---

[199] Hypereides probably made this speech during the Lamian War which broke out in Greece after Alexander's death; more famously he proposed the award of honours to Iollas, Alexander's cupbearer and a son of Antipater, when it was rumoured he had poisoned Alexander (Plutarch, Moralia 849F); his tongue was cut out and he was executed on Antipater's orders when the latter marched on Athens after the battle of Crannon in August 322BC (Plutarch, Life of Demosthenes 28 and Moralia 849B).

Figure 3.13. Funeral pyre on a denarius of Antoninus Pius (sketch by the author)

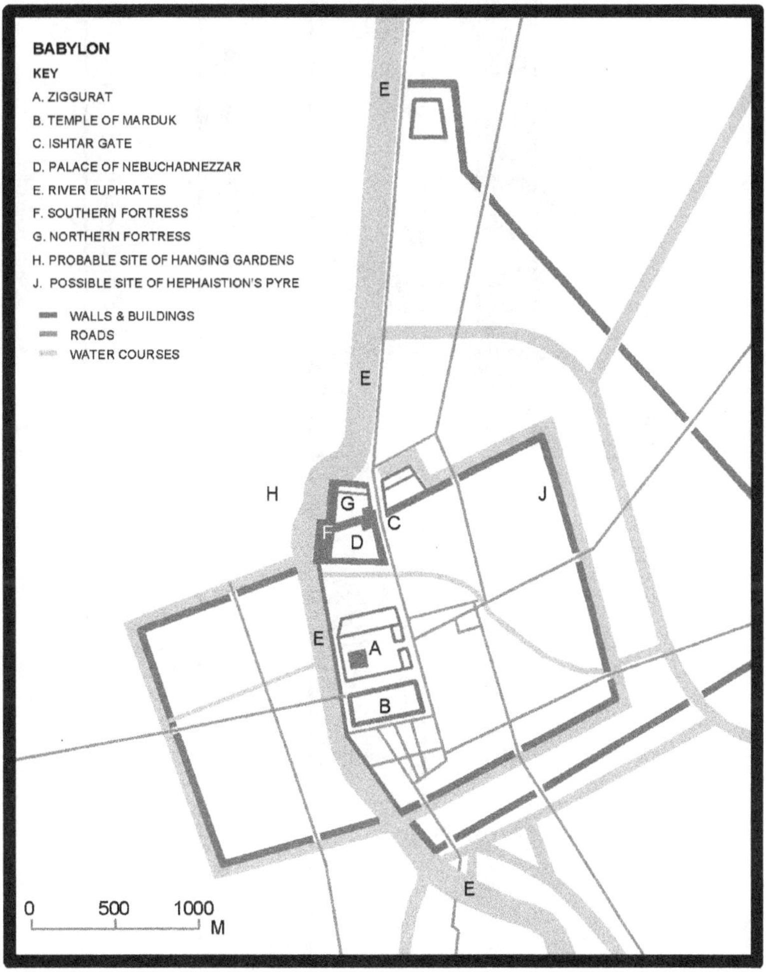

Figure 3.14. Map of Babylon after Koldewey (possible traces of the pyre at J)

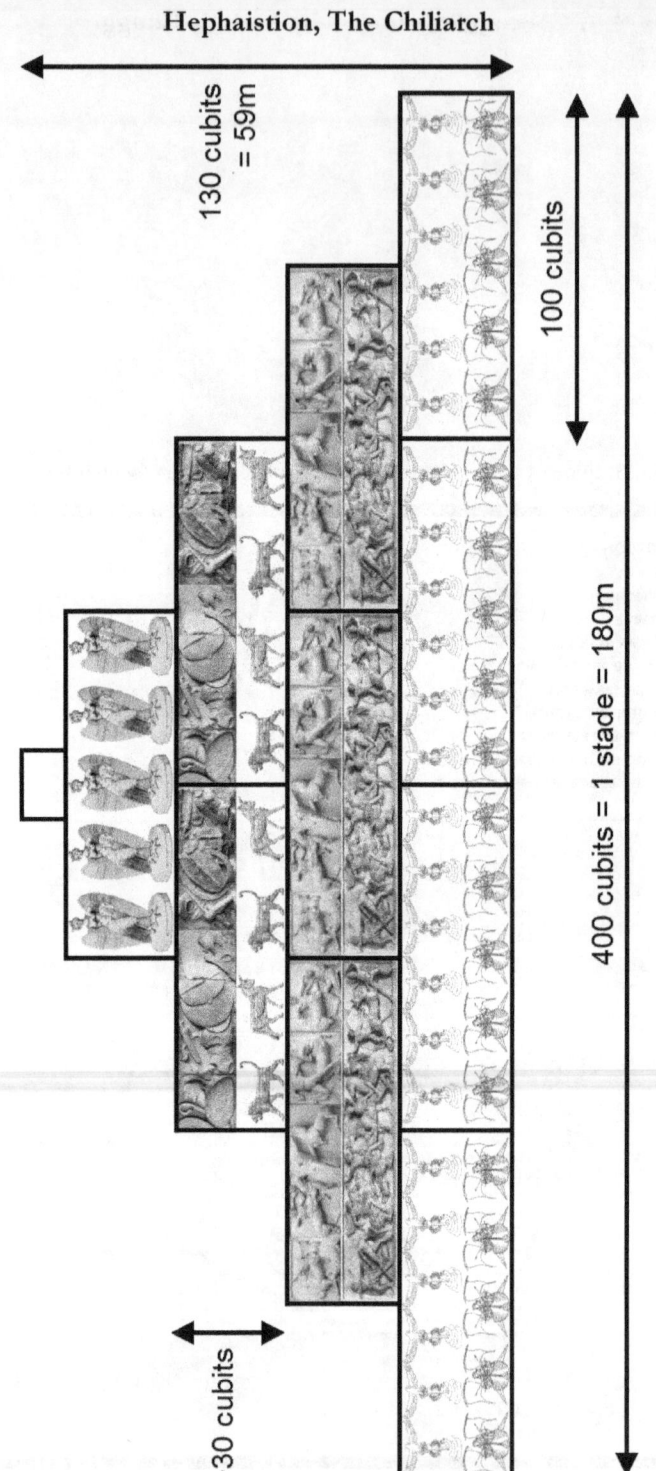

Figure 3.15. A conceptual reconstruction of Hephaistion's pyre by the author.

Alexander's Lovers by Andrew Chugg

Given the dating of Hypereides' speech and its context, it is extremely probable that the "servant" who must be honoured as a hero is a reference to Hephaistion. This tends to corroborate the statements of Arrian and Plutarch, that Alexander only officially endorsed sacrifice to Hephaistion as a hero and even that only after having secured the endorsement of the oracle of Ammon at Siwa. We have also seen that the relief from Thessalonike similarly represents Hephaistion as a hero. Furthermore, Achilles calls the dead Patroclus a hero in the Iliad, which explains why Alexander was content with Ammon's decision. A hero had a status in Greek religion not dissimilar to a saint in Christianity. It seems therefore to have been permissible to sacrifice to a hero just as Christians often pray to a favourite saint.

The title that has been translated as "Coadjutor" (*paredros*) is slightly mysterious. It appears to mean a kind of assistant god or demigod: literally, one who sits beside deities. This comes close to being a synonym for "hero" in its religious sense. Although the accounts of Lucian and Diodorus are clearly hostile to Alexander, the very strangeness of "paredros" in this context suggests that it may be an authentic compromise term adopted by Alexander himself. Perhaps there is a hint of a hope that Hephaistion would sit beside the deified Alexander in their afterlife, as he had been at Alexander's side on Earth.

A number of direct parallels between Alexander's mourning for Hephaistion and Achilles' behaviour following the killing of Patroclus have already been noticed. Specifically, Alexander's participation in the funeral procession of the corpse, the shearing of his hair, the exceptionally large pyre and recognition of his dead friend as a hero are all paralleled in the Iliad. However, the analysis shown in the Tables at the end of this chapter indicates that Alexander's prolonged lamentation over the corpse, his refusal to eat, the sacrifices at Hephaistion's funeral and his funeral games are also all consistent with an objective of emulating or even excelling Achilles' mourning for Patroclus. Furthermore, as has been noticed by modern historians, Alexander's reported declaration that the Cossaean bandits he killed in the winter campaign of early 323BC were offerings to Hephaistion's shade resembles a less barbarous emulation of Achilles' sacrifice of twelve sons of the Trojans before Patroclus' pyre. Most telling of all is Arrian's report that Alexander publicly declared that Hephaistion had been a companion whom he valued as much as his life. This was almost certainly an intentional paraphrasing by the king of Homer's Achilles, who used strikingly similar words to assert that Patroclus had been a companion whom he valued above all others and as much as his life. The fact that neither Arrian nor his source (who may well have been an eyewitness) seems to have noticed this argues strongly for the authenticity of the quotation. So too does the fact that the additional detail specifying the envoys to have come from the cult centre of Asclepius at Epidaurus would have been superfluous and risky in a forgery. This quotation also provides an instance of another pattern in Alexander's actions: the apparent policy of treating Hephaistion as his alter ego. Hence the command that the temple fires be extinguished and the incineration of royal robes (as Perizonius has suggested)[200] on the pyre are also interrelated with the emulation of Achilles.

The removal of the parapets, presumably meaning the crenellations, from the city walls seems merely to be an extrapolation of the practice of shearing the hair in mourning, as is specifically asserted by Plutarch in his life of Pelopidas. In this light, Aelian's assertion that Alexander actually destroyed the Acropolis of Ecbatana looks like another of the exaggerations of Ephippus or some other hostile commentator.

On the matters of banning of music, ordering mourning throughout the realm and shearing the manes of the horses, Alexander is probably following Euripides' description of the mourning commanded by Admetus for Queen Alcestis[201]:-

CHORUS LEADER:

My King, thou needs must gird thee to the worst.
Thou shalt not be the last, nor yet the first,
To lose a noble wife. Be brave, and know
To die is but a debt that all men owe.

ADMETUS:

I know. It came not without doubts and fears,
This thing. The thought hath poisoned all my years.
Howbeit, I now will make the burial due
To this dead Queen. Be assembled, all of you;
And, after, raise your triumph-song to greet
This pitiless Power that yawns beneath our feet.
Meantime let all in Thessaly who dread
My sceptre join in mourning for the dead
With foreheads sorrow-shorn and sable weeds.
Ye chariot-lords, ye spurrers of the steeds,
Shear close your horses' manes! Let there be found
Through all my realm no lute, nor lyre, nor sound
Of piping, till twelve moons are at an end.
For never shall I lose a closer friend,
Nor braver in my need. And worthy is she
Of honour, who alone hath died for me.

It is spine-tingling that Alexander, through the obsequies he performed for Hephaistion, is seemingly pointing us at these words from the pen of his favourite playwright in order to speak to us across the centuries of the depth of his feelings for his dead friend. In a way he is saying that he thinks that his

---

[200] See note to item 7.8 in the Loeb edition of Aelian's Varia Historia.
[201] This translation is by Gilbert Murray (George Allen & Unwin, London 1915); thanks are due to Linda de Santis for having noticed the parallels with the funeral of Alcestis.

relationship with Hephaistion was similarly close as that of Admetus with Alcestis. Perhaps he is telling us that Hephaistion is the one who would have died to save him, just as Alcestis perished to preserve the life of Admetus.

There are far too many instances of the pattern of copying Achilles mourning for Patroclus and Admetus mourning Alcestis for them to be attributable to coincidence. The evidence is sufficiently strong as to suggest a deliberate plan to emulate the funeral rites described by Homer and Euripides. This being established, it is now possible to recognise that Alexander's superficially wild behaviour was actually too systematic for allegations of irrationality by both ancient and modern authors to have any validity. From this perspective, Alexander's actions were a perfectly sane way for him to exploit the cathartic power of a spectacular funeral to mitigate his extreme grief.

Despite the cynical view that Hephaistion was scarcely missed by any save the king, Curtius attested that the Chiliarch's Persian wife, Drypetis, had sincerely mourned her husband.[202] Tragically, Alexander himself died just six or seven months after his friend, before he had completed any of the permanent monuments to Hephaistion's memory. Perdiccas persuaded the Assembly of the Macedonians to abandon the construction of Hephaistion's tomb shortly after the king's death and virtually all other memorials to the Chiliarch suffered similar neglect. The same might be said of his reputation as well: once Alexander had passed away, no one had any motive to glorify his chief lieutenant or to recollect the extent of his influence.

Synthesis

As we have seen, Alexander and Hephaistion had probably always been a partnership in private, at least from their early youth. What is more remarkable is the extent to which by 324BC their private relationship had been translated into a double-act on the public stage. Whereas Alexander undoubtedly remained very much the senior partner, the reality of the double-act is nevertheless clearly evinced in the marriage of Hephaistion to the sister of Alexander's own bride and in his appointment as Chiliarch. In modern terms, this made Hephaistion the chief executive officer responsible for day-to-day management issues in the multi-national corporation that the Empire in some ways resembled. This had the effect of freeing up Alexander to perform the Chairman's role, dealing with issues of longer-term strategy, such as the proposed campaigns in Arabia and North Africa. Even more telling of the perceived duality of their rule are the comments of their contemporaries. Thus, for example, Apollodorus wrote to his brother that he feared Alexander *and* Hephaistion, whilst Ephippus of Olynthus penned a diatribe On the Funerals of Alexander *and* Hephaistion.

---

[202] Curtius 10.5.20.

Hephaistion, The Chiliarch

It would require a degree of disingenuousness to deny a sexual aspect of this relationship in the light of the copious hints, clues and insinuations and the conducive environment of the profoundly homoerotic Macedonian court. It is beyond reasonable doubt that Alexander deliberately and publicly equated his feelings for Hephaistion with those of Achilles for Patroclus. Furthermore, there is overwhelming evidence that Alexander's contemporaries interpreted the Achilles-Patroclus relationship as the archetype of a homoerotic affair. Above all else, it is surely incredible that Alexander's reaction to Hephaistion's death could indicate anything other than the closest relationship imaginable. Also in the context of the funeral, the fact that Alexander is attested to have had the sacred flames extinguished in the temples provides a corroborative instance of the king publicly treating Hephaistion as his alter ego. This makes it particularly difficult to dismiss the first instance, during the audience with the Persian royal ladies after Issus. As we have seen Plutarch illustrates the case where the friend is deemed a second self with a list of well-known homosexual couples. Finally, even the sceptical Tarn would have had difficulty (had he noticed it) in explaining away the fact that Arrian stated that Hephaistion was Alexander's *eromenos*, albeit in the obscure context of the Discourses of Epictetus.

Arrian wrote that Alexander *excelled in physical beauty* and Aelian calls the king *casually handsome*, yet Diodorus asserted that Hephaistion was the taller and more comely of the pair and Justin remarked upon his boyish charms.[203] The extant portraits, some at least of which are probably authentic, tend to support these accounts. In general, they depict a clean-shaven ephebe or comparatively young man, who was boyishly good-looking with short, slightly curly hair.

Regarding Hephaistion's personality, the evidence is relatively slight. A case for quarrelsomeness and irascibility is usually substantiated with reference to his arguments with Craterus and Eumenes and the evident hostility of Olympias, but it may equally be argued that Hephaistion's position would have tended to bring him into conflict with precisely these individuals. Furthermore, to observe that the court and the army were highly factionalised would be considerably to understate the reality. Fighting between the factions actually broke out in Babylon within hours of Alexander's death. Most likely, we hear about Hephaistion's particular quarrels, because of his key role within the integrationist faction and his general importance within the regime. There are also hints that Hephaistion was rather less inclined to forgive those who turned against Alexander, such as Philotas and Callisthenes, than the king himself, which may well have made him an unpopular figure in some quarters.

In general attempts to damn Hephaistion's character should be regarded as unproven. It should be mentioned in the Chiliarch's defence that he was clearly trusted implicitly by the king and that there is no evidence or suggestion that Alexander's faith in his principal lieutenant was ever disappointed or betrayed.

---

[203] Arrian, Anabasis 7.28.1; Aelian, Varia Historia 12.14; Diodorus 17.37.5; Justin 12.12.11.

As far as Hephaistion's diplomatic and political influence is concerned, we can probably only discern a fraction of the floe, since nine tenths of the diplomacy and political negotiations required to operate a Macedonian administration were necessarily shadowed in confidentiality and outright secrecy. Nevertheless, what we do know is impressive:-

a) Hephaistion was specifically responsible for the appointment of a new king for Sidon, which makes it credible that he was frequently consulted regarding the selection of local rulers within the empire.

b) Hephaistion was instrumental in achieving a peace agreement with Demosthenes, which may have saved the Macedonians from defeat during the rebellion of Agis in Greece.

c) On circumstantial evidence, Hephaistion may have had a part in winning over Mazaeus, the governor of Babylon.

d) Hephaistion was central to the process of reconciliation with the Persian aristocracy following the death of Darius.

e) Hephaistion played a key and probably decisive role in the downfall of Philotas and his father Parmenion.

f) Hephaistion organised the proskynesis experiment and was the leading proponent of integration with the Persians among Alexander's courtiers.

g) Hephaistion seems to have negotiated extensively with local rulers in northern India.

No other individual in Alexander's administration, save the king himself, appears to have exerted a comparably strong influence on events. In these scattered instances, we can glimpse the exceptional power wielded by the Chiliarch.

Modern historians have traditionally denigrated Hephaistion's military skills, but there seems to be no tangible evidence to justify this habitual reflex. On the contrary, Arrian states that Hephaistion was wounded in close-quarter fighting in perhaps the most critical engagement of the battle of Gaugamela. Furthermore, Hephaistion is recorded as having led large army groups in independent campaigns in Bactria, Sogdiana and India with unbroken success. On the factual evidence, his military record reveals an impeccable combination of bravery and competence.

Hephaistion's official rank among Alexander's retinue was probably always high. He is likely to have been a member of Alexander's formally appointed circle of "Friends" from the beginning of the reign. He was probably made a member of the king's Bodyguard either at Halicarnassus in 334BC or perhaps even earlier and he retained this exclusive rank for the rest of his life. His absence from lists of senior army officers prior to Gaugamela is explicable in terms of his leadership of the Bodyguard. This was incompatible with a formal army command, since it required Hephaistion to fight beside the king. After the fall of Philotas, Alexander found it expedient to extend Hephaistion's authority through his joint-command of the Companion Cavalry. He continued to command the top regiment of this unit (evidently entailing the overall command of the Companion Cavalry) until his untimely death and in spirit even beyond the grave, since Alexander commanded that his Hipparchy should forever retain his name and standard. Some time during the so-called "orientalising" phase, after the death of Darius, most probably in Hyrcania upon the surrender of Nabarzanes, the previous incumbent, and certainly before the proskynesis experiment, Hephaistion was appointed Chiliarch. This made him Alexander's deputy and chief minister and elevated him clear above his rivals among the king's retinue. Ultimately, in 324BC his marriage to the younger sister of Alexander's bride made him a de facto associate member of the Royal Family, cementing his position with the king through kinship at just the time when Craterus, his nearest rival at court, was sent away to govern Macedon.

It is most likely that Hephaistion's sudden death at Ecbatana near the end of 324BC resulted from the complications of typhoid or a similarly severe gastro-enteric infection. Specifically, his meal of chicken washed down with much wine may have caused a severe rupture of disease-damaged bowel tissue, although this remains conjectural. Poisoning is substantially inconsistent with the reported range of symptoms and details of the course of the illness, but it cannot be definitively excluded, due to the paucity of the evidence.

Both Alexander's extravagant mourning for his friend and the flamboyance of the funeral have been seen as wildly excessive and symptomatic of melancholy madness by both ancient and modern critics. However, a detailed comparison of these events with Achilles' behaviour following Patroclus' death in the Iliad and the mourning commanded by Admetus for Alcestis demonstrates that Alexander was substantially following Homer's and Euripides' models for Hephaistion's exequies. Aelian and Arrian both noted that Alexander shaved his head in emulation of Achilles' mourning for Patroclus. They are probably following a common primary source, so the imitation of the funeral of Homer's Patroclus must have seemed blatant to Alexander's contemporaries. Some modern scholars have noted one or two other parallels with the events of the Iliad, but I have shown that there are many other allusions to the actions of Achilles and the orders of Admetus in Alexander's behaviour following Hephaistion's death, most of which are actually clearer and more striking than those previously recognised. Even Alexander's supposedly wild weeping, irrational forsaking of royal decorum and obstinate refusal of sustenance in the immediate aftermath of his bereavement, whilst perfectly sincere and heartfelt, were clearly inspired by the corresponding events in the Iliad. Far from being symptoms of madness, these responses actually demonstrate a profoundly rational attempt by the king to come to terms with his vast grief.

Alexander's Lovers by Andrew Chugg

Alexander made it manifest to his contemporaries on at least several occasions through various different statements and actions that he considered Hephaistion to be his alter ego. The relationship between the two of them was apparently sexually and psychologically intense. They represented themselves as reincarnations of Achilles and Patroclus, but the reality was a vastly richer and more productive partnership than that portrayed in Homer's heroic parable of the tragic consequences of arrogant pride. In the rare instances where we can still discern Hephaistion's influence at work, it was generally positive and decisive. In all probability, there were many other circumstances where Hephaistion's private councils swayed Alexander's public policy, but they are irrevocably obscured from our gaze. Even so, there are strong hints that Hephaistion was instrumental in negotiating the reconciliation with Demosthenes, that his influence was decisive in the downfall of Philotas and Parmenion, that he was charged with the implementation of the policy of integration with the Persians and that he spearheaded a programme to deliver control of the army into the hands of the Bodyguards, who were by that time all carefully selected Alexander-loyalists. In summary, Hephaistion was no mere minion of the king, nor an ineffectual and lightweight cavalry commander, but rather he should more correctly be recognised as Alexander's fully empowered Prince-Consort.

Hephaistion, The Chiliarch
Alexander's actions following the death of Hephaistion (Part I)

Reaction	References	Allusions
Weeps prostrated over corpse for a day and a night and is eventually dragged away by his Companions	Arrian Anab. 7.14.3-4 (Aelian VH 7.8)	Cf. Achilles weeps over Patroclus and lies in his arms for a day and a night surrounded by his companions. Iliad 18.340, 19.4
Fails to eat for several days	Arrian Anab. 7.14.8	Cf. "But the lords of Achaia were gathered about Achilles beseeching him to eat, but he with a groan denied them." Iliad 19.303-8
Execution of Glaucus, Hephaistion's doctor	Arrian Anab. 7.14.4 Plutarch, Alexander 72.2	
Shaves his hair	Arrian Anab. 7.14.4-5 Aelian VH 7.8	Cf. Achilles for the death of Patroclus. Iliad 18.27 & 23.141
Changes his dress	Aelian VH 7.8 Cf. Euripides, Alcestis	Cf. Admetus tells Thessalians to wear black robes in mourning for Alcestis (and does so himself)
Shaves manes & tails of horses	Plutarch, Alexander 72.2 Plutarch, Pelopidas 33-34 Cf. Euripides, Alcestis	Cf. Admetus orders the shearing of the horses' manes for the death of Queen Alcestis in Euripides' tragedy Also done by the Thessalians to mourn the death of Pelopidas in 364BC
Demolition of battlements of Ecbatana etc.	Plutarch, Alexander 72.2 Plutarch, Pelopidas 34 Aelian VH 7.8	Extension of shearing of hair and horses' manes
Bans music in the camp	Plutarch 72.2 Cf. Euripides, Alcestis	Cf. Admetus orders that music be banned for 12 months in mourning the death of Queen Alcestis in Euripides' tragedy
Orders mourning throughout realm	Arrian Anab. 7.14.8 Cf. Euripides, Alcestis	Cf. Admetus asks all his realm to mourn the death of Queen Alcestis in Euripides' tragedy
Orders cities to contribute to funeral	Diodorus 17.114.4	
Orders fires extinguished in temples	Diodorus 17.114.4-5	Treating Hephaistion as his alter ego by according him royal obsequies

Alexander's actions following the death of Hephaistion (Part II)

Reaction	References	Allusions
Drives funeral car	Arrian Anab. 7.14.5	Cf. Achilles bore Patroclus' head in his funeral procession. Iliad 23.136-7
"The companion whom I valued as much as my life"	Arrian Anab. 7.14.6	Hephaistion as Alexander's alter ego; Cf. "The companion whom I valued above all others and as much as my life." Achilles of Patroclus. Iliad 18.81
Temples, shrines etc.	Arrian Anab. 7.23.7-8 Lucian, Slander 17 (Hypereides, Epitaphios col. 8.21-22)	
Regiment to retain Hephaistion's name	Arrian Anab. 7.14.10	
Kills Cossaeans as offerings to Hephaistion's shade	Plutarch, Alexander 72.3	Cf. Achilles' sacrifice of a dozen "sons of the Trojans" at Patroclus' pyre. Iliad 18.336-7 & 23.175 & 23.181
Enquiry of Ammon: permission for worship as a hero	Arrian 7.14.7 & 7.23.6 Diodorus 17.115.6 Plutarch, Alexander 72.2 (Lucian, Slander 17) (Justin 12.12.12) (Hypereides, Epitaphios col. 8.21-22) (Thessalonike relief)	Cf. Patroclus referred to as a hero by Achilles. Iliad 23.151
Giant funeral pyre and tomb at high cost 10,000 talents (Arrian & Plutarch) 12,000 talents (Diodorus & Justin)	Diodorus 17.114-115,18.4 Arrian Anab. 7.14.8 Plutarch, Alexander 72.3 Plutarch, Eumenes Justin 12.12.12	Cf. Patroclus' pyre "a hundred feet long this way and that" Iliad 23.164
Gold, silver and (royal?) raiment on pyre	Aelian VH 7.8	(Further evidence of Hephaistion being treated as Alexander's alter ego?)
Sacrifices at funeral	Diodorus 17.115.6 Arrian Anab. 7.23.6	Cf. Sacrifices around and upon Patroclus' pyre. Iliad 23.165-177
Gathered 3000 athletes and performers for funeral games	Arrian Anab. 7.14.10	Cf. Achilles provides prizes for Patroclus' funeral games. Iliad 23.259

4. Barsine, Daughter of Artabazus

Barsine was by birth a minor princess of the Achaemenid Empire of the Persians, for her father, Artabazus, was the son of a Great King's daughter.[204] It is known that his father was Pharnabazus, who had married Apame, the daughter of Artaxerxes II, some time between 392 - 387BC.[205] Artabazus was a senior Persian Satrap and courtier and was latterly renowned for his loyalty first to Darius, then to Alexander. Perhaps this was the outcome of a bad experience of the consequences of disloyalty earlier in his long career. In 358BC Artaxerxes III Ochus had upon his accession ordered the western Satraps to disband their mercenary armies, but this edict had eventually edged Artabazus into an unsuccessful revolt. He spent some years in exile at Philip's court during Alexander's childhood, starting in about 352BC and extending until around 349BC,[206] at which time he became reconciled with the Great King. It is likely that his daughter Barsine and the rest of his immediate family accompanied him in his exile, so it is feasible that Barsine knew Alexander when they were both still children. Plutarch relates that she had received a "Greek upbringing", though in point of fact this education could just as well have been delivered in Artabazus' Satrapy of Hellespontine Phrygia, where the population was predominantly ethnically Greek.

As a young girl, Barsine appears to have married Mentor,[207] a Greek mercenary general from Rhodes. Artabazus had previously married the sister of this Rhodian, so Barsine *may* have been Mentor's niece, although it is also possible that Barsine was the daughter of a different wife. The marriage cemented a grand alliance between the two families. They were also allied in a political sense, since it seems that Memnon, the brother of Mentor, commanded Artabazus' mercenary troops during his abortive rebellion and accompanied Artabazus in his exile. Following Mentor's premature death, probably in 338BC, Memnon took over Barsine as his wife, perhaps partly to perpetuate the alliance, but surely also in tribute to Barsine's reputed loveliness. The princess's familiarity with the language and culture of the Greeks probably also contributed to the conviviality of these liaisons with men who had by then become the leading commanders of the Great King's large Greek mercenary contingents.

In the first half of 333BC Memnon was at the forefront of the Persian Empire's doomed resistance to the precocious onslaught of Alexander the Great. The

---

[204] Plutarch, Life of Alexander 21.4.
[205] P A Brunt, Alexander, Barsine and Heracles in Rivista di filologia e di istruzione classica 103 (1975) 22-34; rejecting Curtius 6.5.1-6, which makes the unlikely claim that Artabazus was 94 in 330BC.
[206] Diodorus 16.52.3; Curtius 5.9.1.
[207] Arrian, Anabasis 7.4.6.

Alexander's Lovers by Andrew Chugg

Rhodian condottiere was appointed to the command of a fleet of 300 warships and an army of 60,000 men. He enjoyed some success in reducing the islands and the Ionian coastline. However, soon after he sat down to besiege Mytilene in April or May, he fell seriously ill and perished some time around June. Thus Barsine found herself widowed for a second time, whilst still probably in her early twenties. Diodorus says (17.23.5) that she had already been sent to her father for safety and as a guarantee of Memnon's loyalty. Her father accompanied Darius as he mustered a massive army to meet the Macedonian invasion with what he doubtless hoped might prove an overwhelming force. However, when the Macedonian and Persian forces clashed at Issus in November of 333BC, Darius was utterly vanquished and fled the field in disarray.

Artabazus and most of the Persian aristocracy escaped back to the heartlands of their empire together with their king, but their women and much of the Persian baggage train were overtaken by the Macedonian pursuit. Curtius[208] observes that the "wife and son of the renowned general Memnon were taken" at Damascus together with numerous other Persian ladies, whilst Justin[209] records that it was through admiring the magnificence of the captured baggage train of Darius, that Alexander "first began to indulge in luxurious and splendid banquets, and fell in love with his captive Barsine for her beauty, by whom he had afterwards a son that he called Hercules [i.e. Heracles in its Greek form]."

As we shall see, the name of Heracles is cited for the son of Alexander and Barsine in numerous passages from the ancient sources. Alexander's family traced its descent from the Heracles of the twelve labours and the hero is featured wearing the skin of the Nemean lion on the obverses of Alexander's silver drachm and tetradrachm coins (and some of his bronzes), so the prince's name is a highly credible and apt choice for a son of the king.

The fullest account of Barsine's capture is given by Plutarch:-

But Alexander, as it would seem, considering the mastery of himself a more kingly thing than the conquest of his enemies, never came near the [captured Persian] women, nor did he associate with any other before marriage, with the sole exception of Barsine. This woman, the widow of Memnon, the Greek mercenary commander, was captured at Damascus. She had received a Greek upbringing/education, was of a gentle disposition, and could claim royal descent, since her father was Artabazus, the son of a Great King's daughter. These qualities made Alexander the more willing – at the instigation of Parmenion, so Aristobulus tells us – to form an attachment to a woman of such beauty and noble lineage.

Plutarch, Life of Alexander, 21.4

The most interesting details here are the attribution of the story of Alexander's liaison with Barsine to Aristobulus and the matchmaking role played by

---

[208] Curtius 3.13.14; Arrian, Anabasis 2.11.9-10 confirms that Persian noblewomen were found at Damascus.
[209] Justin 11.10.

Barsine, Daughter of Artabazus

Parmenion. Aristobulus is generally considered to be amongst the more reliable of the first-hand, eyewitness accounts of Alexander's expedition. Consequently, Arrian chose him as one of his two principal sources for his austerely proper history of Alexander's campaigns. His word therefore imputes some authenticity to this affair.

Parmenion's involvement is equally intriguing at this juncture. A theme is developed elsewhere in the ancient sources, wherein Alexander continually ignores or overrides the advice of Parmenion, who occupies the role of an overcautious elder statesman as a kind of foil to Alexander's passion for the pursuit of glory. However, here we have an instance of avuncular encouragement, which seems to have proved congenial to the young king. It is perhaps reassuring to find the history for once reflecting the influence that Parmenion must indeed have wielded at this stage of events, uncontaminated by the shadow of Parmenion's subsequent elimination, which still lay several years into the future.

Nothing specific is heard of Barsine again until the final year of Alexander's reign. However, Hieronymus (cited by Diodorus) makes Heracles about 17 years of age in 310BC,[210] which would date his conception to 328BC or 327BC, around five years after Issus. At Alexander's death, Heracles and Barsine are said to be living in Pergamon by Justin. Diodorus provides partial corroboration of this by stating that the boy was reared in Pergamon. This city lay in Artabazus' old Satrapy, where the family probably still held estates, so this detail is likely to be authentic.

If Barsine was with Alexander until 328BC, but was living in Pergamon in 323BC, the question arises of the date of her departure from court. We cannot say for certain, but two other events, which might well be connected with the termination of Barsine's relationship with Alexander, also occur in Bactria around 327BC. Firstly, this was the time of Alexander's marriage to Roxane (the first time he took the hand of a woman in wedlock) and secondly "Alexander relieved Artabazus of the satrapy of Bactria at his own request on account of old age."[211] Especially if Heracles had just been conceived, there would have been a potentiality for conflict between the influential and competing families of Roxane and Barsine. The "retirement" of Artabazus might thus have afforded an excellent pretext for defusing the situation by having Barsine accompany her father when he returned to his estates at the opposite end of the empire.

In the summer of 324BC Alexander organised spectacular nuptials for himself and his senior officers and courtiers at Susa. In a majestic gesture of reconciliation and integration, their partners were chosen from among the

---

[210] Justin 15.2 makes Heracles "nearly 14" in 310/309BC, but this is about the correct age for Alexander IV, so there may be some confusion on the part of Justin (or Trogus).
[211] Arrian, Anabasis 4.17.3; Curtius 8.1.19.

daughters of former Persian kings and aristocrats. Daughters of Artabazus and Barsine were prominent among these brides according to Plutarch and Arrian:-

...besides his other honours, Eumenes had been deemed worthy by [Alexander] of relationship in marriage. For Barsine the daughter of Artabazus (Alexander's first mistress in Asia, and by whom he had a son, Heracles) had two sisters; of these Alexander gave one, Apame, to Ptolemy, and the other, also called Barsine, to Eumenes. This was at the time when he distributed the other Persian women as consorts among his Companions.

Plutarch, Life of Eumenes, 1.3

[Alexander] also held weddings at Susa for himself and for the Companions... to Ptolemy the Bodyguard and Eumenes the royal secretary, the daughters of Artabazus, Artacama and Artonis respectively; to Nearchus the daughter of Barsine and Mentor.

Arrian, Anabasis 7.4.4&6

Ostensibly, these two accounts seem to be at odds with one another in the matter of the names of the women. Certainly, it is probable on this ground alone that they derive from different sources. Plutarch introduces this passage from the Life of Eumenes by citing Duris as his source. The account of Arrian is likely to have been abstracted from Ptolemy's history (possibly augmented by Aristobulus), so it may be argued that it really ought to be accurate, since Ptolemy was himself one of the bridegrooms. However, Plutarch's version also presents some hints of authenticity. Elsewhere, it is indicated that Artabazus' mother's name was Apame, so it is fitting that one of his daughters should have borne the same appellation, considering the almost universal tendency for names to persist in families. Furthermore, Plutarch's specific points that Eumenes became connected to Alexander through his marriage to a daughter of Artabazus and that Ptolemy married another are repeated in Arrian's account. Although the names of these brides differ between the two accounts, this need not be significant, since Arrian refers to the daughter of Darius, whom Alexander married, as another Barsine, whereas she is called Stateira elsewhere. It appears that aristocratic and royal Persian ladies may have borne more than one name or else (as Tarn suggests[212]) they may have changed their name upon marriage. It is even possible that some of these supposed names are actually Persian titles. There are also cases of duplicate names among royal Greek women in this period, the best-known case being Cleopatra/Eurydice, the wife of Philip II, who seems to have taken the name (or title?) of Philip's mother upon entering wedlock. Some of the kings are also known to have assumed new names on their accession: for example, Ochus became the third Artaxerxes.[213] Indeed, among the Macedonians too, Arrhidaeus became Philip III upon Alexander's demise.

Excepting the equivocal discrepancies in the names, the accounts of the Susa weddings are concordant with one another, but derive from different primary

---

[212] W W Tarn, Heracles Son of Barsine, Journal of Hellenic Studies, 1921, p.21 note 9.
[213] Diodorus 15.93.1.

sources. It follows that they are very likely to be authentic. Arrian's source was Ptolemy or Aristobulus, whereas Plutarch was using Duris of Samos, who was a contemporaneous observer whose lifespan roughly covered the period 340-260BC.[214] It is therefore clear that Barsine, her father Artabazus and their entire clan remained high in Alexander's favour in 324BC, for Ptolemy, Eumenes and Nearchus were among the king's closest lieutenants, deserving of high status brides.

A year later, on the evening of 10th June 323BC Alexander died in the Palace of Nebuchadnezzar at Babylon. Appian summarises the situation:-

[Alexander] died leaving one very young son [i.e. Heracles] and another yet unborn [i.e. Alexander IV], and the Macedonians, who were loyal to the family of Philip, chose Arrhidaeus, the brother of Alexander, as king during the minority of Alexander's sons (for they even guarded the pregnant wife [i.e. Roxane]), although he was considered to be hardly of sound mind, and they changed his name from Arrhidaeus to Philip.

Appian, The Syrian Wars 52[215]

Curtius provides a dramatic account of the debate on the succession, which occurred the day after Alexander was declared dead. In particular, he records a misjudged attempt by Nearchus to advocate the selection of Heracles as the new king:-

Nearchus then said that, while nobody could express surprise that only Alexander's blood-line was truly appropriate for the dignity of the throne, to await a king yet unborn and pass over one already living suited neither the inclinations of the Macedonians nor their critical situation. The King already had a son by Barsine, he said, and he should be given the crown. Nobody liked Nearchus' suggestion. They repeatedly signalled their opposition in traditional fashion by beating their shields with their spears and, as Nearchus pressed his idea with greater insistence, they came close to rioting.

Curtius 10.6.10-12

According to Arrian's account of the Susa marriages, Nearchus had become Heracles' brother-in-law, so it must have been clear to the Assembly that Nearchus had a vested interest in supporting Heracles' succession to the throne. There seems also to have been considerable antipathy among the army to the idea of handing the Empire over to a boy who was both half-Persian and illegitimate. Being so young, Heracles could probably have been controlled by his Persian relatives. The Macedonians would hardly have tolerated any arrangement, which appeared to hand their hard won empire back to their vanquished foes.

---

[214] Robert B Kebric, In the Shadow of Macedon: Duris of Samos, Wiesbaden: Franz Steiner, 1977.

[215] See also Appian, The Syrian Wars 54, where he states that "the two sons of Alexander" were dead before Antigonus and Demetrius proclaimed themselves kings (306BC); Justin 12.15 also mentions Heracles' existence at the point of Alexander's death.

Alexander's Lovers by Andrew Chugg

Illegitimacy among the Macedonians probably lacked the stigma that it later acquired in Christian societies. However, on a purely practical level, illegitimate sons were normally automatically excluded from the succession (and all other inheritance rights). Hence Alexander's indignation when Attalus volubly prayed for a *legitimate* heir at the party celebrating Philip's marriage to Cleopatra, implying that Alexander was a bastard. The preference for legitimate heirs was probably motivated by a desire to maintain the stability of the regime. Rumour made Philip II the father of numerous illegitimate sons, including, for example, Ptolemy. If they had all competed for the throne, mayhem would have resulted. Upon Alexander's death, there was a severe shortage of legitimate heirs, but the troops still remained reluctant to consider a bastard. Old habits die hard and many present would have been the fathers of illegitimate sons, whom they could not afford to countenance as competitors for the rights and property of the offspring from their official marriages.

Nearchus' remarks imply that it was common knowledge, at least among the officers, that Alexander was survived by a son by Barsine at the point of his death. If Heracles was an imposter, as Tarn has sought to argue, then Nearchus' interjection has to have been a fiction. In the first place, we can exclude the possibility that it was Curtius' fiction by observing that Justin (and therefore his source Trogus) also recorded that Heracles' case was pressed at this Assembly:-

Meleager argued that their proceedings should not be suspended for the result of an uncertain birth; nor ought they to wait till kings were born when they might choose from such as were already born; for if they wished for a boy, there was at Pergamon a son of Alexander by Barsine, named Hercules; or, if they would rather have a man, there was then in the camp Arrhidaeus, a brother of Alexander...

Justin 13.2

If it were possible to show that the sources used by Curtius and Trogus were independent of one another, then it would be virtually certain that Heracles really was Alexander's son. Their versions are indeed dissimilar in that Nearchus mentions Heracles in Curtius and Meleager names him in Justin. However, the possibility cannot be excluded that Curtius and Trogus used a common source or at least that their versions originated in a common source (probably Cleitarchus). Nevertheless, general considerations make it difficult to see how or why such an original source could have succeeded in promulgating such a blatant lie about this very public event. The ultimate murder of Heracles in 310/309BC would have removed the motive to lie about him later on, whereas before that date there would have been many soldiers and officers still living who had attended the Assembly after Alexander's death and could easily have denounced any attempt to rewrite the historic statements made there. In fact no surviving ancient source disputes the fact that Alexander was Heracles' father, despite the fact that Cassander and others would have had strong motives to do so had it been feasible. It should be clear therefore, that it would be a tortuous trail to pursue the argument that Heracles was not genuinely presented as a candidate for the throne immediately after Alexander's death, and that it is therefore equally difficult to argue that he was an impostor.

Having been rejected decisively by the Assembly at Babylon, Heracles presumably remained in obscurity at Pergamon with his mother for the time being. However, Strabo speaks of the *"children of Alexander"* accompanying Perdiccas in his fateful invasion of Egypt in 321BC and Nepos has Olympias refer to *"Alexander's children"*.[216] This can only mean both Alexander IV, the son of Roxane, *and* Heracles, the son of Barsine, for no other child is recorded (except for a child by Roxane that had died in India). If this is true, then Perdiccas had presumably summoned Heracles from Pergamon during his Anatolian campaigns in 322BC. This would indicate that the Regent felt that the boy was potentially a significant pawn in the manoeuvring that was to prove the prelude to outright civil war. His purpose must particularly have been to ensure that Heracles did not fall into the hands of his enemies.

Subsequently, perhaps after the second distribution of the satrapies at Triparadeisos late in 321BC, Heracles must have returned to Pergamon, for that is where he was still living a decade later, when dramatic events conspired to bring him once more to center-stage in the drama of the succession.

Most probably in the summer of 310BC Cassander commanded that the young king, Alexander IV, and his mother Roxane should be poisoned. Judging by their reactions, news of this atrocity would seem to have reached Cassander's enemies, Antigonus in Asia Minor and Polyperchon in the Peloponnese, within months. As Alexander's sole surviving son, it was now viable that Heracles might be prevailed upon to make a bid for the throne. Presumably with Antigonus' backing, for Pergamon lay within his sphere of influence, Polyperchon acted swiftly to play Heracles as his new political pawn. The most complete account comes from Diodorus, who in turn had probably sourced his material from the contemporaneous history of Hieronymus of Cardia, a protégé of Eumenes[217]:-

Meanwhile Polyperchon, who was biding his time in the Peloponnesus, and who was nursing grievances against Cassander and had long craved the leadership of the Macedonians, summoned from Pergamon Barsine's son Heracles, who was the son of Alexander but was being reared in Pergamon, being about seventeen years of age. Moreover, Polyperchon, sending to his own friends in many places and to those who were at odds with Cassander, kept urging them to restore the youth to his ancestral throne. He also wrote to the governing body of the Aetolians, begging them to grant a safe conduct and to join forces with him and promising to repay the favour many times over if they would aid in placing the youth on his ancestral throne. Since the affair proceeded as he wished, the Aetolians being in hearty agreement and many others hurrying to aid in the restoration of the king, in all there were assembled more than

---

[216] Strabo, Geography 17.1.8; Nepos, Eumenes 6, Olympias mentions Alexander's *children*.
[217] Arrian, Indica 18.7 makes Eumenes the son of an Hieronymus, so the historian might well have been a son or nephew of the Secretary.

Alexander's Lovers by Andrew Chugg

20,000 infantry and at least one thousand horsemen. Meanwhile Polyperchon, intent on the preparations for the war, was gathering money; and sending to those of the Macedonians who were friendly, he kept urging them to join in the undertaking.

Diodorus 20.20

Aetolia lies adjacent to the Peloponnese on the northern side of the Corinthian Gulf, so it controlled Polyperchon's land route to Epirus, yet a little further to the north. The Aetolians were allies of Antigonus in this period and had been friendly to Polyperchon in the past. Olympias, Alexander's mother, had been a princess of Epirus and in 318BC Polyperchon had awarded her the guardianship of Roxane and Alexander IV. She had marched on Macedonia and killed Philip-Arrhidaeus and his young queen Adea-Eurydice, who had declared for Cassander. In Epirus, therefore, Polyperchon, acting as the sponsor of Heracles, could be relatively confident of finding enthusiastic support and a strong base from which to launch a renewed assault upon Macedonia, which lay immediately to its northeast. Diodorus' account shows that the plan to place Heracles upon his father's throne was proving highly popular in Greece, such that Heracles' bandwagon had begun to roll in a seemingly inexorable fashion. Cassander must have been seriously alarmed, especially recalling the setback, which had been inflicted on him by Olympias in similar circumstances eight years beforehand. Diodorus takes up the story again a few pages later:-

Meanwhile Polyperchon, who had collected a strong army, brought back to his father's kingdom Heracles, the son of Alexander and Barsine; but when he was encamped at the place called Stymphaea, Cassander arrived with his army. As the camps were not far distant from each other and the Macedonians regarded the restoration of the king without disfavour, Cassander, since he feared lest the Macedonians, being by nature prone to change sides easily, should sometime desert to Heracles, sent an embassy to Polyperchon. As for the king, Cassander tried to show Polyperchon that if the restoration should take place he would do what was ordered by others; but, he said, if Polyperchon joined with him and slew the stripling, he would at once recover what had formerly been granted him throughout Macedonia, and then, after receiving an army, he would be appointed general in the Peloponnese *and would be partner in everything in Cassander's realm, being honoured above all. Finally he won Polyperchon over by many great promises, made a secret compact with him, and induced him to murder the king. When Polyperchon had slain the youth and was openly co-operating with Cassander, he recovered the grants in Macedonia and also, according to the agreement, received four thousand Macedonian foot-soldiers and five hundred Thessalian horse.*

Diodorus 20.28.1-3

It may seem that Cassander turned Polyperchon against Heracles with curious ease. However, it should be remembered that Heracles was an unacknowledged bastard son, so his claim to the throne was relatively weak in Macedonian law. Polyperchon and his faction must have been concerned at the legal weakness of his candidacy, so it is not so surprising that they betrayed Heracles as soon as Cassander tabled a reasonably attractive alternative offer. Yet the cynicism and brutality that imbued their dealings is nonetheless shocking and repugnant.

Figure 4.1. Locations of Tymphaea, Aethicia and Trampya

Stymphaea is a region on the border between Epirus and Macedonia, which is also known as Tymphaea. Polyperchon had commanded the battalion from Stymphaea at the battle of Gaugamela,[218] so this must have been especially friendly territory for him. Indeed it was probably his ancestral homeland. Specifically, the poet Lycophron mentions in his Alexandra that the betrayal and murder of Heracles took place at the Tymphaean town of Trampya (see Figure 4.1):-

> *When dead, as seer the Eurytanian folk*
> *Shall honour him, and those who have as home*
> *High Trampya, where the Tymphaean snake,*
> *The Aethic leader, shall while feasting slay*
> *One Heracles, the seed of Aeacus*
> *And Perseus, close kin to Temenus.*
>
> Lycophron, Alexandra 799-804

In this passage Cassandra is foretelling the fate of Odysseus, but as an aside Lycophron makes her prophesy the murder of Heracles. Lycophron probably wrote the Alexandra in Alexandria under Philadelphus, not too long after

---

[218] Diodorus 17.57.2.

283BC, but the feasible range of dates stretches over a half-century range commencing at the close of the 4th century BC.[219] The "snake" is Polyperchon, whilst Aethicia is a small region just south of Tymphaea, which may have been Polyperchon's own birthplace. Aeacus was the grandfather of Achilles, from whom Alexander the Great claimed descent on his mother's side. On his father's side, Alexander was a Temenid; that is a descendant of Temenus, a great-grandson of the Heracles of the twelve labours, who was in turn a great-grandson of Perseus. Lycophron's allusion to an event of his own lifetime is therefore quite unambiguous. In the matter of the feasting he corroborates Plutarch's moving account of Heracles' last supper, at which Polyperchon deceived and betrayed his youthful lord with Judas-like wickedness:-

Polyperchon agreed with Cassander for a hundred talents to do away with Heracles, Alexander's son by Barsine, and proceeded to invite him to dinner. When the youth, suspecting and dreading the invitation, alleged an indisposition, Polyperchon called on him and said: "Young man, the first quality of your father you should imitate is his readiness to oblige and attachment to his friends, unless indeed you fear me as a plotter." The youth was shamed into attending; and they gave him his dinner and strangled him.

Plutarch, Moralia, On Compliancy 530D

Justin augments our information with the detail that Barsine was killed at the same time as her son. In a typical gloss on the truth, he attributes the murders to secret orders of Cassander, which also specified a clandestine funeral:-

Afterwards, lest Heracles, the son of Alexander, who had nearly completed his fourteenth year, should be recalled to the throne of Macedonia through the influence of his father's name, he sent secret orders that he should be put to death, together with his mother Barsine, and that their bodies should be privately buried in the earth lest the murder should be betrayed by a regular funeral [with a pyre].

Justin 15.2

Polyperchon very probably murdered Heracles in 309BC. Apart from the fact that this is broadly consistent with the chronology of Diodorus, we have the completely independent testimony of the Parian Marble on this point:-

From the time when Alexander [Alexander IV, the son of Alexander the Great] died and also another son Heracles from the daughter of Artabazus, and Agathocles crossed over to Carthage..., 46 years [before the inscription of the chronology in 264/3BC, i.e. 310/9BC] and Hieromnemon was archon at Athens.

Parian Marble FGrH 239B

These words were sculpted within living memory of the events and other entries on the Parian Marble are known to be accurate. It follows that Justin is probably in error concerning Heracles' age, for it would make him virtually exactly coeval with Alexander IV, dating his birth to 323BC, yet Nearchus already knew that Heracles was living in Pergamon on the 11th June 323BC. Furthermore, Justin

---

[219] See George W Mooney, The Alexandra of Lycophron, London, 1921, pp. xi-xii.

contradicts Diodorus, who was probably citing the highly authoritative history of Hieronymus on this point. The most reasonable conclusion is that this is another of Justin's numerous inaccuracies, perhaps arising from confusion of Alexander IV with Heracles, since both were murdered at Cassander's instigation within a year or so of one another. This is probably why Justin mentions their murders in the wrong order. In fact, Justin seems to have perpetrated an identical confusion previously at 14.6.2, where he states that Olympias retreated into Pydna with Roxane *and her grandson Heracles*.

Plutarch reveals in his Life of Alexander that he obtained much of his information about Barsine and Heracles from Aristobulus, but he cites Duris as his source, when he mentions them in his Life of Eumenes. Diodorus is believed mainly to have relied upon the account of Hieronymus of Cardia in his 19th and 20th books, whereas Aristobulus probably did not cover this period after Alexander's death. Lycophron was probably relying on contemporaneous news reports of Heracles' fate, whereas Trogus (Justin) "kept clear of the Macedonian writers such as Ptolemy, Aristobulus and Marsyas" and mainly relied upon Cleitarchus for Alexander's reign according to N. G. L. Hammond.[220] The Parian Marble is likely to have been based on official records. It would therefore seem that the ancient accounts of Barsine and Heracles derive from at least five or six primary sources, at least several of which were independent of all of the others. None of these sources seems to have expressed any doubt as to the validity of Heracles' claim to be Alexander's son. As Brunt has amply demonstrated, Tarn's objections to Heracles' authenticity range from the flimsy to the vacuous. It would be correct rather to assert that the evidence overwhelmingly favours the view that Alexander was indeed Heracles' father.

Regarding Tarn's theory[221] that the Heracles of 309BC was an impostor, his only significant observation is to point out a number of references in Diodorus, which appear to ignore Heracles' existence. In particular, Diodorus states that Alexander was "childless" at his death,[222] that "he left no sons as successors to the kingdom"[223] and that Cassander believed there would be no successor to the kingdom if he killed Alexander IV.[224] However, it is also Diodorus who tells the story of Heracles' bid for the throne in the ensuing book of his history. Evidently, this author did not recognise his earlier statements as denials of Heracles' existence. It is obvious why not: it is implicit in his previous terminology that there had been no *legitimate* child or successor, which was quite true. Diodorus (or his source - Hieronymus?) probably let the matter of legitimacy remain implicit, so as dramatically to unveil the unpleasant surprise

---

[220] NGL Hammond, Three Historians of Alexander the Great, CUP 1983, p. 114.
[221] W W Tarn, Heracles Son of Barsine, Journal of Hellenic Studies, 1921.
[222] Diodorus 18.2.1.
[223] Diodorus 18.9.1.
[224] Diodorus 19.52.4 & 19.105.3.

for Cassander, when a bastard son of Alexander suddenly claimed his father's kingdom following Cassander's murder of his legitimate younger half-brother.

Tarn also seems to have overlooked the allusion to Heracles' existence in Strabo in the context of 321BC, where he says that more than one child of Alexander accompanied the Grand Army in Egypt and the same plurality of Alexander's offspring mention by Cornelius Nepos. Even diehard Tarn enthusiasts may find this a little difficult to accommodate within the hypothesis that Heracles was invented a decade later. Dio Chrysostom (Discourse 64.23) also mentions that "Heracles was Alexander's son, yet did not become a king".

Pausanias has provided an epilogue on the murders of Alexander's relatives, which shows that Cassander, the orchestrator of these horrors, was himself doomed to suffer an agonising end:-

My own view is that in rebuilding Thebes Cassander was mainly influenced by hatred of Alexander. He destroyed the whole house of Alexander to the bitter end. Olympias he threw to the exasperated Macedonians to be stoned to death; and the sons of Alexander, Heracles by Barsine, and Alexander by Roxane, whom he killed by poison. But he himself was not to come to a good end. He was filled with dropsy, and from the dropsy came worms while he yet lived.

Pausanias 9.7.2

Poetic justice perhaps, but a little delayed, since Cassander survived until 297BC.

A team from the Aristotle University of Thessaloniki led by Chrysoula Saatsoglou-Paliadeli inscribed an archaeological footnote to the tragic history of Alexander's bastard son in the course of excavations at Aegae in August of 2008. A large copper vessel was unearthed on the site of the ancient marketplace near the theater where Philip II was assassinated, but at some distance from the cemetery area. It was found to contain a cylindrical gold jar with a lid, inside of which were human bones together with a spectacular golden wreath of style and quality comparable to those found in the royal tombs of the Great Tumulus of Aegae. Archaeologists suggested that the remains had been extracted from another grave in ancient times and reburied. Subsequently, there was much speculation that these were the remains of a late 4th century BC individual of virtually royal status. Within a year it had been established that the bones belonged to a teenage youth and the name of Heracles was put forward as a candidate for his identity, although there is as yet no proof.

*　　*　　*　　*　　*　　*　　*　　*　　*

The tragic history of Barsine and her son Heracles poses some intriguing questions, which merit some further deliberation.

Why did Alexander fail to marry Barsine, when he subsequently insisted upon marrying Roxane? In the first place, Barsine had already been married twice to Alexander's enemies and had children from those previous marriages. An heir would have been the younger half-brother of those children, which would have been a potentially uncomfortable situation, especially vis-à-vis the succession. Secondly, and perhaps more significantly, what indications we have (excepting the unreliable Justin) suggest that the relationship with Barsine was more a matter of convenience for Alexander than an affair of the heart. The king will have been under some political pressure to beget an heir, especially in view of a reportedly conspicuous lack of any sexual liaisons with women prior to the battle of Issus. This was not at all a question of morality, but a matter of political stability and state security. If a king should die without an heir, there was a very real threat of a chaotic and bloody power struggle over the succession, which would have been in the interests of few. Furthermore, a king with no apparent heir was arguably more exposed to assassination attempts, since the rebels might believe that their objectives were more easily achievable with a lesser risk of retribution. In fact, we have the direct testimony of Aristobulus, a reputable primary source, that Alexander took Barsine as his first mistress at Parmenion's instigation, which confirms both the existence of the pressure and the dispassionate nature of the decision. This is underlined by indications that Alexander packed Barsine off to Pergamon without compunction, when he found a princess whom he actually desired to make his bride. In fact, the particular choice of Barsine was probably due to her knowledge of Greek and of Greek culture and sensibilities, her reputed beauty and possibly also because Alexander had known her in childhood. Amorous feelings were subordinate to pragmatic considerations.

Why did Alexander's affair with Barsine seemingly result in only one child, when it extended over a period of at least 6 years? We cannot be certain that there were no other miscarried pregnancies or that another child did not become a victim of the high rate of infant mortality. We are told that Philip II fathered many sons, but most of them seem to have been killed in infancy by disease or in warfare whilst they were still youths.[225] However, there is no mention of another child in any source, so the more straightforward explanation would be that Alexander did not sleep with his mistress very frequently. This observation tends to reinforce the view that the relationship was more a business partnership than a love-match.

Why did Polyperchon betray Heracles when the enterprise of his bid for the throne seemed to be going so well?[226] The true answer to this question remains something of an enigma. Ostensibly, Polyperchon gave up a chance to dominate all Greece in order to become merely Cassander's henchman in the Peloponnese. But he was old, probably over 70, and he may have had little appetite for a risky fight. He undoubtedly had nearly as much reason to be suspicious of Antigonus, the probable ultimate backer of the enterprise, as of Cassander, for he had been the friend and the enemy of both in the recent

---

[225] Justin 9.8.
[226] See also NGL Hammond, History of Macedonia, III, 100 & 165.

past.[227] He may also have been nervous of Heracles' family, since they were mainly Persians. However, these factors do not in themselves provide a convincing justification for an act of perfidy that would forever damn his name. There was probably something going on, of which we know nothing. Did Cassander have some hold over Polyperchon? Perhaps he held hostage some of the latter's family or friends or threatened the destruction of Polyperchon's home region. Alternatively, it could be that Cassander presented some intelligence of a plot by Antigonus and/or Heracles to betray Polyperchon once the struggle against Cassander was won. Whether true or invented, this would have played naggingly on the fears of a suspicious old man, especially if Heracles was proving a less pliable puppet than had been hoped.

Whatever the ulterior reason, Heracles certainly perished for it, and any realistic hope for a restitution of the Temenid dynasty as kings of the entire empire died with him.

---

[227] See Waldemar Heckel, The Marshals of Alexander's Empire, London 1992, pp.188-204.

5. Bagoas the Eunuch

Although he makes only eight or nine named appearances in the ancient sources, Bagoas the eunuch has always been one of the most controversial figures in Alexander's career. Some authorities, notably Tarn and possibly even Arrian, have attempted to write him out of history, because his existence poses problems for their versions of Alexander's character. Others have sought to invent a second Bagoas, who is supposed to have been a Persian prince, in order to deny the evidence that Alexander's eunuch lover ranked among the most prominent and influential of his courtiers. Instead they relegate him to the status of a mere slave and body-servant of the King. However, the eight ancient references to Bagoas can be shown to derive from no fewer than four independent primary sources written within living memory of Alexander's reign. Furthermore, there are strong circumstantial reasons to believe that all these instances refer to the same individual and there is even a probable ninth reference, which has erstwhile been overlooked. On most other points this weight of evidence would hardly be questioned, but both modern Christian and ancient Roman writers have harboured deep prejudices and superstitious misapprehensions concerning eunuchs. Consequently, Alexander's apologists have been prepared to take great pains to purge his reputation of the supposed stain of Bagoas' existence. Ironically, it is implausible that Alexander himself would have thanked them for their tendentious and propagandist efforts.

It is appropriate to begin by posing the question of what Alexander's attitude to eunuchs might have been prior to his relationship with Bagoas. Two particular points are worth making. Firstly, a eunuch named Hermias had been a fellow student of Aristotle.[228] He became the Persian governor of Atarneus in Ionia, but rebelled against the Great King and ruled independently for a while. Aristotle was invited to his court and married his niece and ward. Alexander's father, Philip, possibly with the assistance of Aristotle, forged an alliance with Hermias, but the eunuch was captured and executed by the Great King through treachery. Clearly, Alexander's father and his tutor were on friendly terms with at least one powerful eunuch.

Secondly, there is considerable circumstantial evidence that Alexander was strongly influenced by the writings of Xenophon and especially by his Cyropaidia. For instance, Strabo writes that Alexander was "a lover of Cyrus" and it is difficult to see how this fondness can have arisen other than through reading the Cyropaidia.[229] This book contains a notably pragmatic comment on the nature and efficacy of Persian Royal Eunuchs:-

---

[228] Diogenes Laertius, Aristotle 5; Lucian, The Eunuch.
[229] Strabo, Geography 11.11.4.

Alexander's Lovers by Andrew Chugg

[Cyrus] knew that men with children or wives or favourites in whom they delight must needs love them most: while eunuchs, who are deprived of all such dear ones, would surely make most account of him who could enrich them or help them if they were injured or crown them with honour. And in conferring such benefits he was disposed to think he could outbid the world. Moreover the eunuch, being degraded in the eyes of other men, is driven to seek the assistance of some lord and master. Without such protection there is not a man in the world who would not think he had the right to over-reach a eunuch: while there was every reason to suppose that the eunuch would be the most faithful of all servants. As for the customary notion that a eunuch must be weak and cowardly, Cyrus was not disposed to accept it.... No men have shown more faithfulness than eunuchs when ruin has fallen on their lords. In bodily strength, perhaps, the eunuch seems to be lacking, but steel is a great leveller and makes the weak man equal to the strong in war. Holding this in mind, Cyrus resolved that his personal attendants, from his doorkeeper onwards, should be eunuchs one and all.

These formative influences may have predisposed Alexander to perpetuate the Persian tradition of appointing eunuchs to senior positions at court, so evidence that he actually did so in the case of Bagoas should not be considered inherently questionable or surprising.

Moreover it is a matter of historical fact that Persian eunuchs commonly bore arms and regularly governed cities and kingdoms on behalf of the Great King. Alexander himself was put to some trouble by a eunuch commander called Batis, who led the surprisingly stiff resistance of Gaza in 332BC. According to a fragment of Hegesias, Batis sent an assassin, who pretended to surrender to Alexander as a ruse to gain an opportunity to stab him.[230] Alexander dodged the blow and suffered only a slight wound. After capturing Batis, he made an example of the eunuch by dragging him behind his chariot in imitation of Achilles' treatment of Hector. The magnitude of the power that could be wielded by Persian Royal Eunuchs is exemplified by the career of an earlier Bagoas, who rose to prominence as the favourite of the Great King, Artaxerxes Ochus. This Bagoas was one of Ochus' generals in the Persian recovery of Egypt in 343BC. Diodorus lauds him as "exceptionally daring and impatient of propriety" and he was instrumental in the success of the invasion.[231] Later he became Chiliarch, the Persian equivalent of a Grand Vizier, and he is said to have dispatched Ochus by poisoning him in 338BC. He ruled the empire in all but name for several more years, virtually exterminating the royal family to preserve his authority. Eventually in 336BC he chose to place Darius Codomannus on the throne as his puppet, but the new Great King, hearing or fearing that Bagoas was seeking to poison him, compelled the Chiliarch to drink poison from his own cup.[232]

---

[230] FrGrH 142F5 = Dion. Hal., De comp. Verb. 18 p.123-126 R; cf. Curtius 4.6.15-16.
[231] Diodorus Siculus, Book XVI, where he is following a favourable source who refers to the Great King by his regnal name of Artaxerxes.
[232] Diodorus Siculus, Book XVII, where he uses a hostile source who calls the Great King "Ochus".

Bagoas the Eunuch

Returning to the story of Alexander's Bagoas, Curtius has recorded his introduction to the king's retinue in Hyrcania in late July or August 330BC. He probably took his information from the lost history of Alexander by Cleitarchus, composed within a generation of the King's death.[233] Bagoas had been a personal attendant of Darius, who had just been deposed and murdered by a conspiracy among his senior courtiers led by Bessus the Satrap of Bactria and supported by Nabarzanes the Chiliarch. But Nabarzanes fell out with Bessus and sought a pardon from Alexander:-

> *At this time he came to that Hyrcanian city that housed the palace of Darius, where, having accepted the king's pledge of safe-conduct, Nabarzanes came before him proffering prodigious presents. Amongst these was Bagoas, a eunuch of uniquely lovely looks and just then in the very flower of his youth, whom Darius had been wont to penetrate and with whom Alexander used later to mate. Mainly through this youth's pleas he was driven to agree that Nabarzanes be forgiven.*
>
> Curtius, 6.5.22-23

Arrian also mentions Nabarzanes' surrender at about this time.[234] Furthermore, as we shall see, at least two other ancient sources confirm that Bagoas subsequently became Alexander's lover. The basic facts of Curtius' account are therefore difficult to dispute. However, the slant or spin that Curtius imposes on the meeting, that Alexander was beguiled by the eunuch's charms, need not be the correct interpretation of the facts. Plutarch states that Alexander severely rebuked a commander and one of his Friends on separate occasions for offering to procure handsome slave boys for him.[235] It is not completely satisfactory that Nabarzanes should have managed successfully to ingratiate himself with Alexander using a tactic that dismally backfired on two other occasions.

In fact, less pandering motives existed for Nabarzanes to have brought Bagoas before Alexander on this occasion. If Nabarzanes wished to persuade Alexander that the part he had played in the downfall of Darius had been honourable and driven by necessity, then Bagoas, as Darius' personal attendant, was perhaps the most credible witness he could bring forward in his defence. Bagoas probably also spoke Greek, furnishing him with the ability to translate Nabarzanes reliably, which is the obvious implication of Curtius' assertion that Bagoas addressed pleas directly to Alexander on Nabarzanes' behalf. Linguistic skills would necessarily have been taught to young eunuchs to equip them for the far-flung governmental posts in a multi-ethnic empire that we know they occupied. This also helps to explain how Bagoas was so readily absorbed into Alexander's

---

[233] Hammond, Three Historians of Alexander the Great, p.135, 137.
[234] Arrian, Anabasis Alexandrou, 3.23.4; Badian has argued reasonably that Arrian's announcement of Nabarzanes' surrender is slightly premature (it probably dates the opening of negotiations) and that Curtius' version is more credible, see The Eunuch Bagoas: A Study in Method, Classical Quarterly 8 (1958).
[235] Plutarch, Life of Alexander, 22.

entourage. That he also possessed persuasive personal charms may simply have been an incidental bonus from Nabarzanes' perspective.

Even if his linguistic and diplomatic capabilities were sometimes more pertinent to his duties, it is axiomatic among ancient writers that Alexander's Bagoas was indeed a paragon of loveliness. He is referenced as such in a passage from Quintillian:

When the masters of sculpture and hand desired to carve or paint forms of ideal beauty, they never fell into the error of taking some Bagoas or Megabyzus as models, but rightly selected the well-known Doryphorus (spear-bearer), equally adapted either for the fields of war or for the wrestling school, and other warlike and athletic youths as types of physical beauty. Shall we then, who are endeavouring to mould the ideal orator, equip eloquence not with weapons but with tambourines? Quintillian, *Inst. Orat.* V 12

His point is that the Persian eunuchs Bagoas and Megabyzus constituted flamboyant but impotent exemplars of male beauty. And this must have been a famous cliché, in order for his comparison to have been intelligible to his readership.

The term consistently used by Curtius to describe Bagoas' particular state of emasculation is *spado*. This seems to have the specific meaning in classical Latin of a eunuch created by having his testes torn off, a method said to derive from the Persian town of Spada. Other types included the *castrati*, who were originally those eunuchs who had had both their penis and their testes severed.[236]

In the late summer of 329BC in the aftermath of Alexander's pursuit of the Scythians across the Jaxartes, the King received an embassy from the Sacae, who were Scythian tribesmen from east of the Jaxartes, who wished to promise their submission to him. Curtius records that Alexander engaged a member of his retinue, who is named in most modern texts as "Euxenippus", to escort the deputation:-

Therefore [Alexander] welcomed the emissaries from the Sacae and gave them Euxenippus as their escort. He was as yet a mere youth and beloved by the king for his cuteness of those years, but, although he was equally as handsome as Hephaistion, he could not match his masculine charm, being barely manly at all it appears.

The manuscript Latin being:

Benigne igitur exceptis sacarum legatis comitem excipinon dedit, adhuc admodum iuvenem, aetatis flore conciliatum sibi, qui cum specie corporis aequaret hephaestionem, ei lepore haud sane virili par non erat.[237]

There are good reasons to believe that "Euxenippus" is in fact a garbling of a reference to Bagoas the Eunuch. Bagoas was certainly in Alexander's service at this time and Curtius stated that he had a sexual relationship with the King. This

---

[236] Charles Humana, The Keeper of the Bed (London, 1973) pp. 14-15.
[237] Curtius 7.9.19; see also H. Berve, Das Alexanderreich…, 318 *Euxenippos* on *excipinon*.

passage implies that the relationship of "Euxenippus" with Alexander was also homoerotic in character. The wording "flower of his youth" (*aetatis flore*) recalls "flower of boyhood" (*flore pueritiae*) with which Curtius had earlier introduced Bagoas.[238] The name "Euxenippus" given in current editions is in fact a modern (19th century) textual revision by Hedicke and it is the only appearance of this name in the antique sources on Alexander. The manuscripts of Curtius actually read *excipinon* or *escipinon*. It is possible that this is some kind of attempt by Curtius to transliterate a Greek title meaning "Welcomer" or "Greeter" in the sense of a Court Usher by adapting the Latin verb *excipio*. This would fit well with the task of escorting the delegation and is consistent with the kind of duties that might fall upon a eunuch in Bagoas' position: the Sacae probably knew Persian, but not Greek, so they required a translator. Diodorus (17.77.4) states that Alexander "installed Asiatic ushers in his court" at just the time that Bagoas joined his retinue. *Excipio* also means to take out or extract. It is similar to the verb *excido*, to extract by cutting, one of the attested meanings of which is to castrate. It is feasible that Curtius was indulging in some awkward punning on the theme of a eunuch usher or else that an originally subtle pun has been corrupted perhaps due to the incomprehension of transcribers. Another possibility could be that *excipinon* is a corrupted adjective and that the sense was originally that "Alexander assigned his castrated companion to the Sacae".

Furthermore, the emphatic stress in the Latin of the statement that *excipinon* was *"not at all manly"* demands some kind of explanation. It is jarringly inappropriate terminology for one of Alexander's teenage pages, for they were virile sons of the Macedonian nobility. Especially in the light of the manuscript ambiguities, we should not allow Hedicke arbitrarily to invent a second unmanly male in the flower of his youth and conversant with both Greek and Persian with whom Alexander had a sexual relationship, when we already know of an individual who fits the circumstances perfectly.

With "Euxenippus" revealed to be a phantasm, Bagoas may in fact have been the only younger male lover of Alexander and indeed the only other male lover besides Hephaistion. There is one other candidate known to me, a certain Charmides, but he appears only at Alexander's deathbed (Section 3.33) in the late (not earlier than the 8th century AD) and highly historically unreliable gamma recension of the Alexander Romance:

When Alexander had finished greeting everybody, Charmides the son of Polycrates came in. He was a strong lad, well-reputed even among his enemies, and Alexander was in love with him. He embraced Alexander and did not want to leave him. He wailed terribly and poured forth a long lament. Even the earth seemed to mourn with him. At last the boy turned to the horse Bucephalus, and addressed him tearfully, 'You too, I imagine, are just as unhappy; you are a Pegasus who has lost his Belerophon; but you were stronger than Pegasus among horses, just as Alexander is mightier than Belerophon. Alas, who will ride you now? Who could look

---

[238] Curtius 6.5.23.

Alexander's Lovers by Andrew Chugg

Bucephalus in the eye with another rider on his back?' So said Charmides, weeping as he spoke; and the crowd beat their breasts. Alexander did not want to let the lad go, but flung his arms about his neck. Alexander made a speech... All the while he clung to Charmides.

Very touching and almost certainly fictitious, though the question of its inspiration remains an unsolved matter of interest.

Bagoas next appears in the sources in a surprisingly eminent context. In his Indica, Arrian cites a list of thirty-three "trierarchs" (triereme commanders) for the fleet, which Alexander assembled to sail down the Indus. These posts were essentially honorary in the sense that the actual sailing command of ancient vessels was the responsibility of a separate pilot or helmsman. Furthermore, it is doubtful whether these ships were literally triremes, with three banks of oars that the term itself references. In effect, therefore, this list of trierarchs, which almost certainly comes from Nearchus, Alexander's admiral, is possibly the most complete list of Alexander's senior courtiers, which has come down to us. In addition to the senior military commanders, for all of the King's Bodyguards were made trierarchs, Alexander's secretary Eumenes, his doctor Critobulus and his friend Medius of Larissa all figure among those so honoured. At the end of the list Arrian tells us that Alexander "even appointed a Persian" as a trierarch, namely *Bagoas ho Pharnoucheos* (Βαγώας ὁ Φαρνούχεος) which is usually translated as "Bagoas son of Pharnuches".

It is certainly not impossible that the father of Bagoas the eunuch was named Pharnuches. However, there is a more tempting and cogent explanation in that the degree of correspondence between the phrase in Arrian's manuscript and *Bagoas ho Eunouchos* (Βαγώας ὁ εὐνοῦχος, i.e. Bagoas the Eunuch) is rather striking in the original Greek, particularly if the accentuation is taken into account.[239]

No Persian called Pharnuches is mentioned anywhere else in the sources for Alexander, although a Lycian translator of that name appears in Arrian's Anabasis.[240] A Persian captain named Pharnuches is also a character in Xenophon's Cyropaidia. Someone familiar with these sources could have been responsible for the probable transcription error. Notably, this would include Arrian himself, who entitled his history of Alexander the *Anabasis* in homage to Xenophon's *Anabasis*.[241] It is absolutely telling of such an error that in the original Greek *Pharnuches* appears to be the name that most closely resembles *eunuchos* in the whole of Arrian's surviving works on Alexander. To underline

---

[239] It is believed that Arrian's Anabasis and Indica have been transmitted to us via a single manuscript (the Vienna Codex A of about 1200AD – see Brunt, Intro. xiv), so it is not surprising that there seem to be numerous corruptions among the less well known names in the list of trierarchs. Some of these have been corrected by the editors, but others seem to have gone unnoticed: for example, the trierarch Andron of Teos is very probably Alexander's friend Hagnon of Teos, who is mentioned several times by Plutarch and by Athenaeus 12.539c & Aelian VH 9.3.
[240] Arrian, Anabasis 4.3.7, but not elsewhere.
[241] Arrian's full name was Flavius Arrianus Xenophon (see Intro to the Penguin Arrian).

the point: anyone who wishes to resist this conclusion needs in some other way to account for the amazing coincidence that a person in Alexander's retinue with the name of his eunuch lover also had a father with a name that is more similar to *eunuchos* than any other among the thousand or so names found in Arrian. But actually, it looks suspiciously as though Arrian found it difficult to accept that Alexander had appointed a eunuch as a trierarch and therefore decided to emend his reading of Nearchus' manuscript to the most similar name to *eunuchos* that appeared elsewhere in his accounts of Alexander.

Especially in the light of these considerations, the contention of some modern authorities that the trierarch is not the eunuch, but some other princely Persian, who just happened to share a name elsewhere only known to have been applied to eunuchs,[242] seems a little preposterous. It also explicitly contradicts Pliny, Natural History 13.41, who writes ...*uno in horto Bagou; ita vocant spadones, qui apud eos etiam regnavere*, which translates "...only in the garden of Bagoas [in Babylon]; that is what they call eunuchs, who also exercise royal power amongst them [i.e. the Persians]."[243] In other words Bagoas was a Persian name or title for important eunuchs who acted on behalf of the king and therefore could not have been the name of an intact Persian noble. Hence we should instead conclude that Bagoas the eunuch had risen to become the most senior Persian in Alexander's retinue during the four years between their first encounter in Hyrcania and the embarkation of the fleet for the Indus River voyage.

This conclusion is consistent with a mention by Plutarch, who lists Bagoas among five of Alexander's worst flatterers in an essay on *How to Tell a Flatterer* in Moralia 65D. He is joined in this list by two other Indus trierarchs: Medius of Larissa and Hagnon of Teos, both of whom are well-attested members of Alexander's immediate entourage.

A further named historical appearance of Bagoas comes during musical contests and games following the crossing of the Gedrosian Desert. They took place in the capital of Carmania[244] in around January of 324BC. The incident is reported both by Plutarch and independently by Athenaeus in the following terms:-

> *Once when Alexander was viewing some contests, after wine had warmed the mood, it is recorded that Alexander's lover* [eromenos], *Bagoas the Eunuch, won the prize for singing and dancing, whilst the king presided. Decked in his festal adornments, the champion quit the stage and went across the theatre to sit down right next to Alexander. On seeing this, the*

---

[242] The only other characters called Bagoas that I am aware of are: Ochus' eunuch Chiliarch; the fictional eunuch in Lucian's parable entitled The Eunuch; the bedchamber attendant Bagous in Ovid, Amores 2.2; a Bagoas mentioned in Appian, Mithridatic Wars 10, who drove out King Ariobarzanes of Cappadocia and replaced him with Ariarathes (evidently he did not himself become the king, because he was a eunuch and did not qualify).

[243] The garden was also mentioned by Theophrastus, Enquiry into Plants 2.6.7.

[244] I follow Badian [The Eunuch Bagoas: A Study in Method, Classical Quarterly 8 (1958)] in determining that the event occurred at the contests in the Carmanian capital, which are also mentioned in Arrian and Diodorus.

Alexander's Lovers by Andrew Chugg

Macedonians clapped their hands and shouted for the king to kiss the victor, until their persistence was rewarded by the spectacle of Alexander embracing the eunuch and kissing him passionately.
Plutarch, Life of Alexander, 67

King Alexander also was a passionate boy-lover. Dicaearchus, at any rate, in his book On the Sacrifice at Troy *says that he was so overcome with love for the eunuch Bagoas that, in full view of the entire theatre, he, bending over, caressed Bagoas fondly, and when the audience clapped and shouted in applause, he, nothing loathe, again bent over and kissed him.*
Athenaeus, Deipnosophistae, 13.603a-b

Dicaearchus is a reasonably reputable contemporaneous source. He was a pupil of Aristotle, like Alexander himself. Badian has proposed a credible argument that Plutarch used a different, unspecified source for the incident (perhaps Cleitarchus), but the case is not proven.[245] The title of Dicaearchus' treatise appears to refer to Alexander's sacrifice at Troy. Given that Alexander and Hephaistion are said to have crowned the tombs of Achilles and Patroclus respectively at Troy, the essay may have discussed the parallels between the relationship of Alexander with Hephaistion and that of Achilles with Patroclus in the Iliad. In other words it probably discussed Alexander's amorous liaisons with males, since that would be the relevance of Bagoas. It is anyway fairly clear that at least two primary sources (Cleitarchus in Curtius and Dicaearchus in Athenaeus) firmly believed that Alexander enjoyed a sexual relationship with Bagoas: such a weight of early evidence is difficult to refute.

Shortly after the Carmanian celebrations Alexander progressed westwards into Persia. Numerous accounts of the abuse of power by his governors in his absence now reached his ears. It seems that they had not reckoned on his safe return from the remote reaches of India. Harpalus, the Satrap of Babylon, fled to Athens with 6000 mercenaries, 5000 talents and a very guilty conscience in anticipation of the King's wrath. Worst of all, upon visiting the former Persian capital at Parsagada, Alexander discovered that the tomb of his hero Cyrus had been ransacked. According to Curtius, Orsines, the self-appointed Satrap of Persia (Alexander's appointee having died whilst the king was away), brought valuable presents to win the favour of Alexander and his Friends. However, he gave no gift to Bagoas the eunuch, who Curtius implies ranked among the Friends of the King,[246] but who had "won the regard of Alexander through prostitution."[247] Orsines excuse for the omission was incendiary from Bagoas' point of view. Here is the full account in Curtius' own words:

Afterwards the king arrived at Parsagada, where the people are Persians. Their satrap was Orsines, pre-eminent among all the inhabitants due to a combination of noble ancestry and wealth. His family were descended from that Cyrus who had once reigned over the Persians. He had inherited the family fortune, which he had considerably augmented in the course of a

---

[245] E Badian, The Eunuch Bagoas: A Study in Method, Classical Quarterly 8 (1958), n.3 on p.151.
[246] This further corroborates the identification of the trierarch as Bagoas the eunuch.
[247] Curtius, 10.1.25.

lengthy tenure of the Satrapy. He showered gifts upon Alexander and purposefully directed his largesse upon the king's Friends as well. Herds of ready-broken horses trotted in his train, together with gilded chariots, magnificent furniture, flawless gems, massive golden vases, rich purple robes and three thousand talents of silver coin. Yet this immense profligacy of the barbarian was to lead to his death. For having bestowed presents exceeding all expectations upon the rest of Alexander's Friends, he conspicuously neglected similarly to honour Bagoas, the eunuch who had won Alexander's affection by making himself sexually available to the king. Orsines was actually cautioned by certain individuals that Bagoas was very dear to Alexander, but he quipped: "I wished to show my respect for the king's noblemen, rather than for his whores, for it is not the Persian custom to treat as men those who adopt the female sexual role."   Curtius 10.1.22-26

But Curtius is virtually contradicting himself here, since he had previously stated that Bagoas had been the lover of Darius, the Persian king. Furthermore, a public remark of this degree of offensiveness to Alexander would have been extraordinarily rash. In all probability Curtius is embroidering the facts somewhat. He continues on the theme of the wrath of Bagoas:

On hearing of [Orsines' disparaging remark], the eunuch directed all his power and energy towards the downfall of the satrap. By making surreptitious enquiries he discovered Persians who were willing to bear witness to the misdeeds of Orsines, but he counselled them to refrain from making their accusations public until he should order it. Meanwhile in private he began to undermine Orsines' reputation with the king, so that although the satrap had not yet been charged, he was already less highly regarded. Bagoas even began to take advantage of the opportunities afforded by his sexual liaisons with Alexander, so that whenever he had aroused the king's passion for him he made accusations of acquisitiveness or even of sedition against the satrap.   Curtius 10.1.27-29

He next makes the vengeful Bagoas charge Orsines with responsibility for raiding Cyrus' tomb and asserts that the eunuch contrived that unnamed Persians, whom he had suborned, brought various charges against the Satrap.

Then it happened that Alexander ordered that the tomb of Cyrus should be opened, since he wished to reverence the corpse of the former monarch, which had been laid to rest within. He had supposed it to be a treasury crammed with gold and silver, for such was its widespread repute among the Persians. Yet in fact Alexander found nothing, save the king's decaying shield, two Scythian bows and a sabre. He set a golden crown upon the sarcophagus containing the body and draped it with his own cloak, musing that it was surprising that a monarch of such power and fame had been entombed with no more splendour than many an ordinary man. The eunuch, who was close beside him, gazed intently at Alexander: "What's so surprising about the tombs of kings being bare, when the mansions of satraps cannot hold all the gold gleaned from there? As for myself, I have never seen inside this vault before, but I heard from Darius that three thousand talents were buried with Cyrus. So the generous donations that Orsines has made to you were designed to purchase your favour using funds that he knew that he could not anyway retain with impunity." Thus Alexander already harboured some antipathy towards Orsines, when the witnesses to the satrap's criminality procured by Bagoas came before him. On the one hand Bagoas and on the other the testimonies of Orsines' own subjects filled the king's ears with capital charges. Before he even suspected that allegations had been made against him, the satrap found himself arraigned in fetters. Bagoas himself manhandled Orsines to his execution. Curtius 10.1.30-37

However, there is further identifiable embroidery here in that Bagoas is cited as the source of information on the treasure stolen from the tomb. In fact it is beyond reasonable doubt that Alexander had already visited the tomb whilst it was intact six years beforehand and knew very well what it had contained. This was explicitly stated by Aristobulus, who is quoted almost verbatim on the matter by Strabo.[248] Furthermore, It is fairly certain that Alexander took the road which passed through Parsagada on his way north after the burning of Persepolis. Given his fondness for Xenophon's book about the Upbringing of Cyrus (*Cyropaidia*), it is hardly credible that he had failed to visit the tomb when this opportunity had arisen. The manuscript of Arrian states that Alexander intended to visit Cyrus' tomb "whenever he might conquer the Persians" when Arrian introduces the King's second visit to Parsagada, but this is nonsensical, especially since Alexander had already conquered them at the time of his first visit. Brunt has adopted a simple and logical emendation of the manuscript text, which instead makes it read that Alexander made a point of paying his respects at the tomb *whenever* he visited the Persian capital.

Ultimately, Bagoas dragged the "blameless" Orsines to his execution and Curtius made the Satrap complain, "I had heard that women were once rulers in Asia, but this really is something new – a eunuch as king!" As we have seen, another eunuch called Bagoas had in fact virtually ruled the Persian empire just twelve years before these events, so Orsines' words are hopelessly anachronistic and a transparent invention. It is Curtius' habit of occasionally misrepresenting events through just such embellishments that has deprived him of the respect among historians that his account of Alexander would otherwise merit.[249]

Nevertheless, further analysis often reveals that Curtius' basic historical framework for the events is substantially genuine and the instance of the execution of Orsines is no exception. In particular, Arrian corroborates the bare facts of Orsines' downfall:-

And now many allegations were made by the Persians against Orxines too, who governed them after the death of Phrasaortes. It was proved that he had rifled temples and royal tombs, and that he used to put many Persians to death unjustly. He was hanged by persons Alexander appointed. Arrian, Anabasis, 6.30

Hammond argues that Curtius is taking his version from Cleitarchus, whilst Arrian is mainly reliant on Aristobulus.[250] Here we see that the hint by Curtius

---

[248] Strabo, Geography, 15.3.7.
[249] The habit exposes Curtius to scholarly attempts to disprove everything he says by ridiculing the embroidery: cf. Lloyd Gunderson, Quintus Curtius Rufus: Historical Methods in Philip II, Alexander the Great and the Macedonian Heritage, eds. Adams and Borza, 1982.
[250] N. G. L. Hammond, Three Historians of Alexander the Great, 1983, p.157.

that a whole range of charges were brought against the Satrap was precisely true and that the informants against him were indeed themselves Persians. Arrian also confirms that the charges included robbing royal tombs. The extract from Aristobulus given by Strabo includes an expression of doubt as to whether the raid on Cyrus' tomb was sufficiently organised to have been the work of Orsines:-

> ...*on a later visit the place had been robbed and everything had been carried off except the couch and the coffin, which had only been broken to pieces, and that the robbers had removed the corpse to another place, a fact which plainly proved that it was an act of plunderers, not of the satrap, since they left behind only what could not easily be carried off...* Strabo, 15.3.7

This is of doubtful worth as evidence of Orsines' innocence, but it does confirm as fact that he was accused of orchestrating the crime.

It is also suspicious that Arrian is deliberately vague concerning the identity of the executioners. Arrian's basic motivation was a desire to rehabilitate Alexander in the eyes of the Roman patrician audience in the Antonine age. This was an audience that had within living memory been outraged by the eunuch lovers of Nero and Domitian. In general, there are good grounds to suppose that Arrian was often economical with the truth, when it suited this purpose. We know from Plutarch, Curtius and others that Bagoas was a significant personage at Alexander's court, yet Arrian seems (as here) to go out of his way to avoid mentioning him, even when he recounts events in which the eunuch was a key player.

There are also circumstantial reasons to believe that Bagoas would almost inevitably have become involved in Orsines' downfall. If, as seems likely, Persian complainants and accusers did come before Alexander, then Bagoas would have had a special interest in the case, being the highest-ranking Persian among the courtiers. Alexander would probably have asked him to act as interpreter and might well have sought his opinion regarding the truth of the charges and the reliability of the plaintiffs. In other cases it was Alexander's policy to put offenders into the custody of their victims for punishment and a Persian team of executioners was not without precedent: for example, in the case of Bessus.[251] In all probability, convincing evidence was presented to Alexander, if not on the charge of robbing Cyrus' tomb,[252] then in respect of the killings. That Alexander did not lightly execute his subjects is demonstrated by his eventual freeing of the Magi, who had been the guardians of Cyrus' tomb, when they maintained their innocence, even under torture.[253]

---

[251] For example, Bessus was sent to be executed in the Assembly of the Medes and the Persians, against whom he was considered to have offended by executing Darius; Arrian, Anabasis, 4.7.3.
[252] Plutarch, Life of Alexander, 69, states that a Macedonian named Polymachus was executed for despoiling Cyrus' tomb; perhaps Orsines was actually acquitted of this particular offence.
[253] Arrian, Anabasis, 6.29.11.

Alexander's Lovers by Andrew Chugg

The last appearance of Bagoas is recorded by Aelian,[254] who cited Alexander's Secretary, Eumenes of Cardia, as his source. This is now generally recognised as an edited excerpt from the "Ephemerides" or Royal Journal for the Macedonian month of Dios in 324BC.[255] This was the first month of the Macedonian calendar and it began at the first New Moon following the autumnal equinox (~22nd September in the Gregorian Calendar, but ~27th September in the Julian Calendar that we customarily adopt for ancient dates to maintain congruency with Roman writers). At the beginning of the month Alexander was still en route to Ecbatana, but by the time of the mention of Bagoas he must have arrived in that city. The relevant sentence is:-

He [Alexander] had dinner on the twenty-seventh [of Dios] with Bagoas – the distance from the palace to Bagoas' house was ten stades [~1800 metres] – and on the twenty-eighth he slept.   Aelian, Varia Historia, 3.23

We learn from this that Bagoas remained high in Alexander's favour at this time, seven months before the King's death and immediately prior to the death of Hephaistion. Furthermore, he was sufficiently well-funded and independent of the King as to be able to maintain his own household, which is, of course, completely consistent with the influential picture we have construed for the eunuch from the other evidence.

It can now be recognised that Bagoas apparently figured in at least four primary sources: namely Alexander's Royal Journal, Nearchus' account of India and his sea voyage, Dicaearchus' treatise "On the Sacrifice at Troy" and Cleitarchus' history "Concerning Alexander". It is also likely that Plutarch got his information from yet another source, either for his account of the episode in the Carmanian theatre, which is not entirely congruent with that from Dicaearchus, or for his list of Alexander's flatterers. Given this weight of first-hand evidence the proposition of Tarn and others that Bagoas is an invented character is not at all tenable.

We may also firmly conclude that Alexander's contemporaries believed that Bagoas was the King's lover (technically, his *eromenos*) and this belief is very likely to have been correct. But we have also seen that a modern assumption that a beautiful teenage eunuch lover must have been a lowly body slave is mere prejudice and entirely anachronistic. It ignores general evidence on the status of Persian Royal Eunuchs and necessitates the absurd invention of a second (intact) Bagoas in Alexander's immediate entourage. It is also thoroughly inconsistent with Alexander's reportedly indignant refusal of several offers of slave boys for sexual purposes. In actuality it seems that the historical Bagoas was entrusted with numerous important diplomatic and governmental duties, such as escorting the Sacae and executing delinquent governors.

---

[254] Aelian, Varia Historia, 3.23; Athenaeus, Deipnosophistae, 10.434b states that this was Alexander's *Ephemerides* (diaries/journals) and that Eumenes' co-author was Diodotus of Erythrae.
[255] A. B. Bosworth, From Arrian to Alexander (Oxford 1988) 170-172.

Bagoas the Eunuch

By the time Alexander sailed down the Indus in 326BC, Bagoas ranked among the Friends of the King[256] as was demonstrated by his appointment as an honorary captain of one of the ships of Alexander's fleet along with most of the other senior members of the royal retinue. He seems to have been a talented, capable and influential individual. He won a singing and dancing contest in Carmania and he seems genuinely to have been instrumental in the downfall and execution of Orsines, self-appointed Satrap of Persia. On balance it is likely that Orsines was deserving of his fate, since Alexander must have been convinced of his culpability and there is widely attested evidence for abuse of power by Alexander's lieutenants during his absence in the east.

Alexander's generosity to Bagoas was sufficient that he was able to set up his own household at Ecbatana in 324BC and entertain the king to dinner, which reputedly cost about 40kg of silver per banquet.[257] Plutarch accounted him one of Alexander's "flatterers", but it would be remarkable, in the light of their intimacy and Bagoas' background at Darius' court, if the eunuch had been overtly critical of his lord.

The picture of the eunuch, which has emerged from this analysis, enables us to recognise a probable contemporaneous representation of Bagoas in the lost painting by Aetion of the marriage of Alexander and Roxane, which was exhibited at the Olympic games in about 324BC. We know this painting mainly from an eyewitness description by Lucian from the 2nd century AD when the painting was in Italy (Lucian, Herodotus sive Aetion 4-7). Despite Lucian's view that the "handsome youth" was Hymenaios, the god of marriage, Bagoas fits the context far better and all the other main characters in the painting were real people. Though ostensibly a marriage scene, the painting seems in fact to have been a study of Alexander's various loves at a critical point in his career. (See the cover for a Renaissance recreation of this painting by Sodoma, which he based on Lucian's eyewitness description; Hephaistion, who holds the torch, rests his left hand on Bagoas' shoulder.)

Finally, some (e.g. Mary Renault in The Nature of Alexander p.136-7) have detected the authentic voice of an eyewitness in some of the testimony related by Curtius concerning events at Darius' court during Alexander's invasion. If so, then Bagoas is perhaps the most ceredible ultimate source for this insider information. Even Patron, Darius' commander of Greek mercenaries, lacked sufficiently intimate access to the Great King to have provided eyewitness testimony concerning some details in Curtius.

---

[256] This was a formally appointed group of senior courtiers: for example, Philip the Acarnanian was admitted to the Friends as a reward for curing Alexander of a fever in Cilicia (Diodorus, 17.31.6); Curtius, 10.1.26, literally states that Bagoas ranked among the "amicos regis".
[257] Plutarch, Life of Alexander, 23.6.

6. Thalestris, Queen of the Amazons & Cleophis, Queen of Massaga

Thalestris, Queen of the Amazons

The Greeks are especially renowned for the Freudian themes that pervade much of their mythology. Oedipus' marriage to his mother, Orestes' matricide and Thyestes' rape of his daughter and cannibalisation of his sons are salient instances. It is therefore quite characteristic of the genre that it should have spawned some dubious tales concerning a tribe of belligerent dominatrices known as the Amazons. It is more surprising, however, that these legendary warrior women should have cantered out of their mythological realms and into the pages of the history books in the context of Alexander's expedition as it trudged through Hyrcania and Parthia. Curtius tells the standard version of the story:-

There was, as was said before, neighbouring on Hyrcania, a race of Amazons, inhabiting the plains of Themiscyra, about the river Thermodon. They had a queen, Thalestris, who ruled all who dwelt between the Caucasus mountains and the river Phasis. She, fired with a desire to visit the King, came forth from the boundaries of her kingdom, and when she was not far away sent messengers to give notice that a queen had come who was eager to meet him and to become acquainted with him. She was at once given permission to come. Having ordered the rest of her escort to halt, she came forward attended by 300 women, and as soon as the King was in sight, she herself leapt down from her horse, carrying two lances in her right hand. The clothing of the Amazons does not wholly cover the body; for the left side is nude as far as the breast, then the other parts of the body are veiled. However, the fold of the robe, which they gather in a knot, does not reach below the knee. One nipple is left untouched and with it they nourish their female children; the right is seared, in order that they may more easily stretch their bows and hurl their spears. With fearless expression Thalestris gazed at the King, carefully surveying his person, which did not by any means correspond to the fame of his exploits; for all the barbarians feel veneration for a majestic presence, and believe that only those are capable of great deeds whom nature has deigned to adorn with extraordinary physical attractiveness. However, on being asked whether she wished to make any request, she did not hesitate to confess that she had come to share children with the King, being worthy that he should beget from her heirs to his kingdom; that she would retain any female offspring but would return a male to his father. Alexander asked her whether she wished to serve in war with him; but she, giving as an excuse that she had left her realm without a guard, persisted in asking that he should not suffer her to go away disappointed in her hope. The passion of the woman, being, as she was, more keen for love than the King, compelled him to remain there for a few days. Thirteen days were spent in satisfying her desire. Then she went to her kingdom, and the King to Parthia.

Curtius 6.5.24-32

Thalestris & Cleophis

A more cursory account by Diodorus has so many details in common with Curtius as to suggest a common source. Where these two historians draw on the same source for any story, that source is almost invariably Cleitarchus:-

When Alexander returned to Hyrcania, there came to him the queen of the Amazons named Thallestris, who ruled all the country between the rivers Phasis and Thermodon. She was remarkable for beauty and for bodily strength, and was admired by her countrywomen for bravery. She had left the bulk of her army on the frontier of Hyrcania, and had arrived with an escort of 300 Amazons in full armour. The King marvelled at the unexpected arrival and the dignity of the women. When he asked Thallestris why she had come, she replied that it was for the purpose of getting a child. He had shown himself the greatest of all men in his achievements, and she was the superior of all women in strength and courage, so that presumably the offspring of such outstanding parents would surpass all other mortals in excellence. At this the King was delighted and granted her request and consorted with her for thirteen days, after which he honoured her with fine gifts and sent her home.

Diodorus 17.77.1-3

Figure 6.1. Thalestris, Queen of the Amazons visits Alexander (1696)

Justin mentions the visit of Thalestris (Figure 6.1) at several points in his epitome of Trogus' Philippic History. He repeats the details from Cleitarchus (13 day visit, escort of 300 Amazons, etc.), but adds an alternative name for the queen, the duration of her journey and the information that she died soon after returning home, whilst noting that the story was to be found in many sources. It therefore appears likely that he is supplementing Cleitarchus with at least one other early version of the tale:-

After Orithya, Penthesilea occupied the throne, of whose valour there were seen great proofs among the bravest heroes in the Trojan War, when she led an auxiliary force thither against the Greeks. But Penthesilea being at last killed, and her army destroyed, a few only of the Amazons, who had remained at home in their own country, established a power that continued (defending itself with difficulty against its neighbours), to the time of Alexander the Great. Their queen Minithya, or Thalestris, after obtaining from Alexander the enjoyment of his society for thirteen days, in order to have issue by him, returned into her kingdom, and soon after died, together with the whole name of the Amazons.

Justin 2.4

[In Hyrcania] Thalestris, or Minithya, queen of the Amazons, came to meet [Alexander], having travelled for twenty-five days, with three hundred women in her train, and through extremely populous nations, in order to have issue by him. Her appearance and arrival was a cause of great astonishment to all, both from her dress, which was weird for a woman, and from the object of her visit. To gratify her, thirteen days' rest was allowed by the king; and when she thought herself pregnant, she took her leave.

Justin 12.3.5-7

On the Albanians border the Amazons, whose queen Thalestris, as many authors relate, sought the couch of Alexander.

Justin 42.3

Geographically, the area said to be the Amazons' homeland on the banks of the river Thermodon lies at the southeast corner of the Black Sea, in the vicinity of the modern border of Turkey with Georgia. Strabo tells us that Cleitarchus in particular cited this location for Thalestris' realm, thus tending to confirm the inference that he is the most influential primary source for the story:-

Only a few writers make assertions as to where [the Amazons] are at the present time, but their assertions are without proof and beyond belief, as in the case of Thalestria, queen of the Amazons, with whom, they say, Alexander associated in Hyrcania and had intercourse for the sake of offspring; for this assertion is not generally accepted. Indeed, of the numerous historians, those who care most for the truth do not make the assertion, nor do those who are most trustworthy mention any such thing, nor do those who tell the story agree in their statements. Cleitarchus says that Thalestria set out from the Caspian Gates and Thermodon and visited Alexander; but the distance from the Caspian country to Thermodon is more than six thousand stadia.

Strabo 11.5.4

Strabo scorns the story firstly because it did not occur in the sources he regarded as most trustworthy, secondly because the accounts were contradictory and finally on grounds of supposed geographical impracticality. However, the last objection should be disallowed, since it is not at all clear that that the journey from the south-eastern Black Sea region to Hyrcania on the southern shores of the Caspian would have presented any insuperable difficulties. The distance is a little less than indicated by Strabo, perhaps 600 miles, which might well have been possible in the 25 days of travel specified by Justin, considering that Curtius implies that the Amazon party was mounted.

The Alexander Romance has a curious exchange of letters between Alexander and the Amazons, by means of which the King negotiated access to the territory of the warrior women together with appropriate tribute and the mercenary services of a brigade of Amazon cavalry. The Romance agrees that the Amazons inhabited a region near the river Thermodon, but it makes no mention of Thalestris or of any amorous liaisons between any Amazon and Alexander.[258] Since Herodotus[259] also placed the realm of the Amazons in the vicinity of the river Thermodon more than a century before Alexander's time, the region was well established as the traditional home of the tribe in Greek folklore.

The authenticity of the Amazon episode within the history of Alexander's expedition is the subject of close attention by Plutarch (Life of Alexander 46.1-2). He cites Cleitarchus and four other early authors as sources for the visit of the Queen of the Amazons, but notes that most of the more credible of the early sources denounced it as a fiction. Plutarch also presents an anecdote, which strongly suggests that Onesicritus' account of the Amazon queen was at least a heavily embroidered version of the truth:-

Here [on the border between Parthia and Scythia] the queen of the Amazons came to see him, as most writers say, among whom are Cleitarchus, Polycleitus, Onesicritus, Antigenes and Ister; but Aristobulus, Chares the royal usher, Ptolemy, Anticleides, Philo the Theban, and Philip of Theangela, besides Hecataeus of Eretria, Philip the Chalcidian, and Duris of Samos, say that this is a fiction. And it would seem that Alexander's testimony is in favour of their statement. For in a letter to Antipater, which gives all the details minutely, he says that the Scythian king offered him his daughter in marriage, but he makes no mention of the Amazon. And the story is told that many years afterwards Onesicritus was reading aloud to Lysimachus, who was now king, the fourth book of his history, in which was the tale of the Amazon, at which Lysimachus smiled gently and said: "And where was I at the time?" However, our belief or disbelief of this story will neither increase nor diminish our admiration for Alexander.

Plutarch, Life of Alexander 46.1-2

Plutarch's hypothesis for an origin of the story in the genuine offer of the hand of the Scythian king's daughter in marriage is highly apposite. The more so because recent archaeological finds of frozen mummies in the Siberian mountains have indicated that some young Scythian women in Alexander's era really did bear arms.[260]

---

[258] Greek Alexander Romance, Book III, 25-27; Armenian Alexander Romance 251-254, 257.
[259] Herodotus 4.110.
[260] At least one Siberian burial of a Scythian woman included weapons (Ice Maiden TV documentary, BBC, 1997).

Arrian also makes occasional mention of the Amazons, but seems deliberately to have expurgated any reference to the Thalestris affair. He was inclined to suppress some of the more colourful stories, he purports out of an idealistic regard for the truth, but perhaps more honestly because they conflicted too jarringly with his rather prudish conception of his hero. Arrian appears generally to have been circumspect in his references to Alexander's love life, by virtue of a moral stance that it was improper for historians to delve into such matters.

Nevertheless, Arrian confirms Plutarch's account of the marriage offer from the king of the European Scythians in the winter of 329-328BC. He presumably found this in either Ptolemy or Aristobulus. Interestingly, he further corroborates Plutarch's theory for the origin of the Thalestris legend by linking the Scythian offer with historical rumours of an Amazon kingdom:-

The purpose of the embassy was to express the willingness of the Scythians to do whatever Alexander commanded; they brought the gifts for Alexander from the king of Scythia that are most highly regarded in Scythia, and said that the king was willing to give Alexander his daughter in marriage to confirm his friendship and alliance. If, however, Alexander should not think fit to marry the Scythian princess, he was still willing to give the daughters of the satraps of the Scythian territory and of the chief personages in Scythia to Alexander's most trusted followers; he would also come to visit Alexander, if summoned, and hear Alexander's commands from Alexander himself. At the same time Pharasmanes, king of the Chorasmians, came to Alexander with fifteen hundred horsemen; he said he lived on the border of the Colchians and the Amazons, and if Alexander desired to attack Colchis and the Amazons and subdue all the races that extended in these regions to the Euxine Sea, he promised to act as guide and to provide supplies for the army. Alexander then replied to the Scythian envoys graciously and as his interest at the time demanded, that he had no need of a Scythian marriage.

Arrian 4.15.2-5

The Scythian offer is also mentioned by Curtius, but transposed to the summer of 328BC (Curtius' chronology differs from that of Arrian for the Bactrian and Sogdian campaigns):-

Alexander...returned to Maracanda. Here he was met by Derdas, the emissary he had sent to the Scythians beyond the Bosphorus, with a deputation of that people.... The Scythians requested that Alexander marry a daughter of their king or, if he thought this marriage alliance beneath him, that he permit the leading Macedonians to intermarry with the nobility of their race. They also assured him their king would visit him in person.

Curtius 8.1.7 & 9

The final mention of Amazons in Arrian is placed among the events of 324BC during a visit to the plain where the Nesaean horses were bred:-

They say that there Atropates, the satrap of Media, gave Alexander a hundred women, saying that they belonged to the Amazons; they were equipped like cavalry troopers, except that they carried hatchets instead of spears, and small targets instead of shields. Some say their right breast was smaller, and was uncovered in battle. According to the story Alexander sent

Thalestris & Cleophis

them away from the army, in case they suffered any outrage from the Macedonian or barbarian troops, but he told them to inform their queen that he would come to see her to get children by her. This, however, neither Aristobulus nor Ptolemy nor any other reliable author on such matters has attested.

Arrian 7.13.2-3

It is likely that this event was another ingredient in the genesis of the Thalestris legend, since Alexander's bravado in inviting the Amazons' queen to have his children might easily have been extrapolated into an actual physical liaison in the florid prose of his more extravagant biographers. Atropates delivered his gift of cavalrywomen after Alexander returned from India, much later than the purported tryst with Thalestris, but the location was not far south from Hyrcania.

Figure 6.2. Alexander with Thalestris in a fresco from Pompeii (sketch by the author)

There are no generally acknowledged ancient representations of Thalestris. However, there is a fresco found in a villa at Pompeii, which depicts a nude Alexander before an unknown woman (Figure 6.2). She is a queen because she bears a sceptre. It is usually supposed that she is Roxane. But this looks like an introductory meeting with Alexander and Roxane was not a queen, when she first met the King. It has also been assumed that the helmet at her feet belongs to Alexander, but it might be her own, if she is Thalestris.[261]

It is likely that the ancient sceptics were right to conclude that the story of Alexander's liaison with Thalestris is essentially mythical in the form in which we know it. This version derives principally from the account given in the lost history of Alexander by Cleitarchus, which in turn probably reworked the version by Onesicritus. Nevertheless, it is also likely that this tale is far from being a complete invention by those authors. Rather they would seem to have conflated and embroidered several of Alexander's actual experiences and encounters with warrior women to produce a fictional romance of a nature that they knew would beguile their readerships. In common with many of the most tantalising and enduring fables, the story of the Thalestris affair sprouted from a rich manure of the truth.

Cleophis, Queen of Massaga

The story of Alexander is replete with Oedipal mother figures. Apart from Olympias herself, Alexander was adopted by Ada, Queen of the Carians,[262] and doted upon by Sisygambis, Queen Mother of Persia. The King even encountered the semi-mythical figure of Queen Candace of Meroe in Ethiopia according to the far-flung and further-fetched legends of the Alexander Romance (though, in fact, this may be a transposition of historical events from the early decades of the Roman provincial government of Egypt.)[263] Yet among all these maternally inspired dowagers, there is only one with whom Alexander is anywhere said specifically to have had sexual relations (I discount the very late writings of John of Nikiu, George the Monk and the anonymous author of the Ethiopic Alexander Romance: they assert that Alexander made Candace his wife, but this is complete myth.)

This lady, perhaps the most unlikely of all Alexander's putative lovers, was an Indian grandmother, who had fought him vigorously in defence of her city. Though we know little about her and despite the fact that her claim to have had sexual relations with Alexander is tenuous at best, she was nevertheless very much a real person, who is mentioned in most of the surviving ancient sources.

---

[261] A. Stewart, Faces of Power: Alexander's Image & Hellenistic Politics (California, 1993), p. 186.
[262] Arrian, Anabasis 1.23.8.
[263] A. K. Bowman, Egypt after the Pharaohs (London, 1986), p. 40.

Thalestris & Cleophis

At the Indian border town of Massaga, Arrian notes briefly that Alexander captured the mother and daughter of Assacenus, its deceased king.[264] He must surely have been aware of rumours of an affair between Alexander and this queen mother, but he disdains to mention them. In Diodorus' account, the submission of this queen is noted in the first surviving sentence after a long lacuna[265]: *a truce was concluded on these terms, and the queen, impressed by Alexander's generosity, sent him valuable gifts and promised to follow his orders in everything.* In Curtius she is named as Cleophis:-

Next [Alexander] crossed the Choaspes and, leaving Coenus to besiege a large city, which its inhabitants called Beira, pressed on himself to Mazagae [a.k.a. Massaga]. This had been the Kingdom of the recently deceased Assacanus and was now, both the province and its capital, under the rule of his mother, Cleophis.

Curtius 8.10.22

Only Justin (perhaps following Cleitarchus[266]) alleges that Alexander had sexual relations with Cleophis and fathered an eponymous son by her:-

He next proceeded to the Daedalian mountains, and the dominions of queen Cleophis; who, after surrendering to Alexander, recovered her throne from him by admitting him to her bed; saving by her charms what she had been unable to secure by her valour. A son she had by him she named Alexander; and he afterwards sat upon the throne of the Indians. Queen Cleophis, for allowing her chastity to be violated, was thenceforward called by the Indians the royal harlot.

Justin 12.7.9-11

Curtius describes in some detail Alexander's survey of Massaga's defences, during which he was reputedly wounded in the leg by an arrow. The King then spent nine days recuperating and preparing an assault with siege engines. When at last his assault began, the inhabitants retreated to their citadel. Curtius continues:-

Since the besieged townspeople now had no option but to surrender, a deputation came down to the King to seek a pardon, which was granted to them. Then the queen came with a group of ladies of noble birth, who made libations from golden bowls. The queen herself placed her little son at Alexander's knees, and from him gained not only a pardon, but also the restitution of her former status, for she retained the title of queen. Some have held the belief that it was the queen's beauty rather than Alexander's compassionate nature that won her this, and it is a fact that she subsequently bore a son who was named Alexander, whoever his father was.

Curtius 8.10.33-36

Curtius metamorphoses Cleophis' granddaughter (in Arrian) into an infant son. He has read the story asserted by Justin of a romance between Alexander and the queen, yet evidently considers it dubious. Despite this, he believes it to be

---

[264] Arrian, Anabasis 4.27.4.
[265] Diodorus 17.84.
[266] NGL Hammond, Three Historians of Alexander the Great, (Cambridge, 1983), p.104.

an historical fact that Cleophis named a son after Alexander. This is significant, because Curtius' source, Cleitarchus, enjoyed relatively wide-ranging access to the lost eyewitness sources on Alexander's campaigns and wrote within living memory of the events, so he is unlikely to be wrong when he is so emphatic.

The Metz Epitome (section 45) also records that Cleophis came before Alexander accompanied by her leading citizens and her little grandson. The party was decked with sacred fronds and proffered produce to signal their supplication. Though it states that Alexander considered her a beautiful woman, it makes no mention of a sexual liaison:

The Macedonians returned to the town [Massaga] and were met by Cleophis, who came with her most prominent citizens and her little grandson. All of them bore before them veiled produce and fronds of foliage to signal their supplication. Alexander was struck by the fair features of Cleophis. From her status and authority, it was quite apparent that she was of noble breeding and worthy of regal power. Afterwards Alexander entered the citadel with a few of his retinue and tarried there for several days.

Metz Epitome 45

It looks suspiciously as though Alexander's affair with Cleophis was discussed as a topic of scandalous gossip by Cleitarchus, inspired by the King's generosity to the queen and her reciprocal gesture of naming a son or grandson after him. Conceivably, Cleitarchus merely distilled the essence of fanciful rumours, which were already in circulation among his fellow citizens in Alexandria, when he composed his sensationalist masterpiece.

There remains to be mentioned one final twist. Today in the Chitral region of Pakistan in the vicinity of ancient Massaga there live the Kalash people, who continue vociferously to claim descent from Alexander's army. The historian Michael Wood visited the clan for his TV series and book: In the Footsteps of Alexander the Great (London 1997, pp. 7-9). Furthermore, it is reputed that the leader of the Kalash asserts that Alexander himself is his direct ancestor. The legend of the mountain queen and Alexander's lost son would seem to have achieved a kind of perpetuity.

7. Roxane, The Starlet

O, she doth teach the torches to burn bright!
It seems she hangs upon the cheek of night
Like a rich jewel in an Ethiope's ear;
Beauty too rich for use, for earth too dear!
So shows a snowy dove trooping with crows,
As yonder lady o'er her fellows shows.

William Shakespeare, Romeo & Juliet, Act I, Scene V

Much of the toughest resistance Alexander ever experienced in his campaigns was encountered in the wild, mountain-riven kingdoms of Bactria and Sogdiana in 328-327BC. Here his elite troops were embroiled during two long years in the suppression of a multitude of evanescent insurrections. No sooner was overwhelming Macedonian force brought to bear, than their antagonists vanished amongst the cloud-draped peaks, where impregnable mountain eyries had long served as the surety of local independence. Nothing daunted, in the Spring of 327BC according to Arrian[267] the King determined to capture perhaps the most forbidding of these lofty lairs, the so-called Sogdian Rock.[268] Being nobody's fool, however, he eschewed the doomed tactic of a frontal assault in favour of a flamboyant ruse. Through a combination of exhortation and bribery, Alexander persuaded such of his men as possessed some basic rock climbing skills to scale a supposedly impassable face of the rock by night, so as to appear the next morning joyfully waving flags from a crag overlooking the lofty plateau occupied by the startled defenders. This degree of intimidation was sufficient to secure a prompt offer of surrender on terms, which Alexander accepted with grace and alacrity in view of the fact that his climbing team had had to leave behind most of their arms. It would have rested as just another impossible victory, but for the fact that, among his captives from the Rock, the King discovered the only woman he was ever truly to love.

Her name was Roxane, which translates as Little Star[269] and might have been pronounced something like "hrox-AHN-ay" or "hroc-SHAHN-ay" in the light of the nuanced range of transliterations presented by the ancient sources. She was the daughter of a Bactrian Prince called Oxyartes, who had sequestered his wife and daughters on the pinnacle when he had revolted against Alexander a

---

[267] Arrian, Anabasis 4.18.4-19.4.
[268] However, Curtius 7.11.1-29 and the Metz Epitome 15-18 say that Alexander captured the Rock of Ariamazes with his team of mountaineers, but that Roxane was taken later at the Rock of Cohortandus or Corianus - they may well be correct, since Arrian seems a little confused in his account of the Sogdian campaigns; Strabo 11.11.4 says Roxane was at the Rock of Sisimithres.
[269] John Maxwell O'Brien, Alexander the Great: The Invisible Enemy, (London, 1992) p.140; HG Rawlinson, Bactria, (London 1912) p.46 n.2; Jona Lendering has more recently argued that her Persian name, Roshanak, might mean "bright-faced girl".

year or so earlier.[270] She is likely to have been in her early teens at the time, given her eligible yet still maiden status. Her beauty is famous in legend, though some contemporaneous witnesses seem to have ranked her second after Darius' wife.[271] Unfortunately, no persuasively authentic ancient representations of Roxane have survived.

Desperate to appease their conqueror, the Lord of the Rock, probably a Sogdian called Chorienes, organised a sumptuous banquet at which Alexander was the guest of honour. Roxane first made her appearance among the other captive maidens, as they furnished the entertainment by performing an exotic dance act, but the king had eyes for none but her. There is persuasive unanimity among the ancient sources that Alexander genuinely fell in love with her and Plutarch further insisted that she was in fact the only woman that the king ever loved and that he married her to suit his personal feelings, rather than for any political motive.[272] Neither does there seem to be any good reason to doubt the truth of these assertions, but rather they help to explain Alexander's spontaneous decision to make Roxane his bride (Figure 7.1), when there was little to inhibit him from simply seizing her as his concubine.

In his Life of Alexander (47.4) Plutarch elaborates on comments that he had initiated in his essays on Alexander in the Moralia by suggesting that, although Alexander's motives had been personal, his marriage with Roxane was nonetheless instrumental in finally pacifying the local warlords:-

His marriage to Roxane, whom he saw in her youthful beauty taking part in a dance at a banquet, was a love affair, and yet it was thought to harmonise well with the matters, which he had in hand. For the Barbarians were encouraged by the partnership into which the marriage brought them, and they were beyond measure fond of Alexander, because, most temperate of all men that he was in these matters, he would not consent to approach even the only women who ever mastered his affections, without the sanction of law.

Arrian (Anabasis 4.19.5) introduces Roxane as the *second* lovliest woman in Asia:-

[On the Sogdian Rock] were captured the wives and daughters of Oxyartes. Now Oxyartes had a maiden daughter of age to marry called Roxane, and those who served with Alexander said that she was the loveliest woman they had seen in Asia next to Darius' wife, and that when Alexander saw her he fell in love with her; despite his passion he was not prepared to violate her as a war captive, but did not think it beneath him to take her in marriage.

He continues (4.20.4) by noting that Alexander's marriage plans promptly secured the submission of her father, Oxyartes, who had (in his version) been elsewhere when the Rock was surrendered:-

---

[270] Arrian, Anabasis 4.18.4.
[271] Arrian, Anabasis 4.19.5.
[272] Plutarch, Moralia 332E & 338D.

Roxane, The Starlet

When Oxyartes heard that his daughters were captives, but also that Alexander was showing solicitude for his daughter Roxane, he ventured to come to Alexander and was honourably treated by him, as was appropriate on so happy an event.

Figure 7.1. The Marriage of Alexander and Roxane (A. Castaigne 1899)

Later in the same year Oxyartes was rewarded for his reconciliation with the king by his appointment as Satrap of the Paropamisus,[273] a post he managed to retain for at least the next decade. Diodorus records the official confirmation of Oxyartes as overlord of this region on three separate occasions after Alexander's death: in the first division of the satrapies in the Summer of 323BC,[274] in the reallocation undertaken by Antipater in 321BC[275] and finally in the third division imposed by Antigonus in 316BC, because Oxyartes (though

---

[273] Arrian, Anabasis 6.15.3; the Paropamisus was the mountainous region between Bactria and India.
[274] Diodorus 18.3.3; Justin 13.4, "Extarches"; Photius on Dexippus, 82.62B.
[275] Diodorus 18.39.6-7; Photius, Arrian's Events after Alexander, F1.34-38; see Walter J. Goralski, Arrian's Events After Alexander in Ancient World 19 (1989), pp.81-108.

he had supported Eumenes, the enemy of Antigonus) *could not be removed without a long campaign and a strong army.*[276]

Curtius (8.4.21-30) has the most elaborate account of the marriage with Roxane, but he also incorporates some species of error concerning the circumstances of the initial meeting of the king with his destined bride. Curtius' interpretation of the marriage as a sign that Alexander was losing control of his passions is especially preposterous in view of the fact that other writers correctly recognised it as an example of the king's restraint and moderation in sexual matters that he did not simply seize Roxane as his concubine. Even in this case, where the evidence is opposed to Curtius' thesis of an Alexander who was progressively corrupted by absolute power, he still ploughs on resolutely with his theme. Nevertheless, it is possible that Curtius is simply reflecting the attitude of his source, Cleitarchus, who was associated with the Cynics, a school of philosophers that especially preached the benefits of imperviousness to sexual passion. Furthermore, despite Curtius' judgemental attitude, much of his factual detail is likely to have been abstracted fairly directly from authentic first-hand sources and merits our close attention. In particular, Alexander's reported reference to Achilles is highly characteristic and deserving of credulity:-

Thence Alexander entered the territory that was in the sway of the celebrated satrap Cohortandus, who submitted himself to the mastery and magnanimity of the monarch. Alexander restored him to his rule, requiring nothing more than that two of his three sons serve as soldiers in the king's campaigns. In fact the satrap also surrendered the son he had kept into the custody of the king and he convened a banquet equipped with outlandish luxury, to which he welcomed Alexander. Whilst this was being conducted with considerable conviviality, the satrap instructed that thirty thoroughbred virgins should be introduced. These included the satrap's own maiden daughter, Roxane by name, who was most remarkably radiant and also distinguished in her deportment to a degree that is rare among the barbarians. Though she strode among a select band, yet she garnered the gape of all and most especially engaged the gaze of Alexander, who was no longer so much the master of his lust, having been fawned upon by Fortune, whom mortal men too little distrust. Hence he who had beheld with hardly more passion than that of a parent Darius' queen and her pair of virgin daughters, to whom none except Roxane could compare in comeliness, was then so infatuated with feelings for this little virgin of vulgar roots relative to royalty that he said it was conducive to the durability of his domains that Persians and Macedonians be matched in matrimony, for only so might the humiliation of the vanquished and the vanity of the victors both be banished. And among his own ancestors, he said, Achilles, of course, coupled with a captive wench [Briseis]. *To forestall all ill-feeling he wished by lawful wedding to take to wife Roxane. The father was happy beyond his hopes for this to happen and Alexander, in the heat of his ardent desire, ordered that a loaf of bread be brought in accordance with his country's customs. This was sliced with a sword and tasted by the two of them, which is the most sacrosanct surety of marriage among the Macedonians.* Curtius 8.4.21-27

---

[276] Diodorus 19.48.2.

Roxane, The Starlet

Arrian is clear that Oxyartes was not present when Alexander met Roxane, but the reader will find it stated in most modern texts of Curtius 8.4.21 that it was Oxyartes who introduced them. However, this is a horrible mistake, dating back to Renaissance attempts to disambiguate Curtius' text in a section where there are indeed some significant manuscript problems. In fact the name rendered as "Oxyartes" in modern versions of Curtius read "Cohortandus" in the manuscripts. Aldus spuriously altered it to Oxyartes. This was done to reconcile Curtius' ensuing statement that Roxane was the daughter of this Cohortandus. But in fact it was this latter statement that was the true error. The reason this was not clear to Renaissance editors like Aldus is that they were unaware of the parallel text (also derived from Cleitarchus) in Sections 28-29 of the *Metz Epitome*, which states that Roxane danced among Corianus' daughters, but was herself the daughter of one of his friends:

Corianus convened a banquet and introduced his own maiden daughters as well as those of his friends as dancers at the dinner. The most remarkably radiant among them was Roxane, the daughter of Oxiatris.

This Cohortandus/Corianus appears to be the chieftain called Chorienes by Arrian. It seems probable on balance that Arrian himself is in error in placing the meeting with Roxane at the Sogdian Rock rather than at the Rock of Chorienes, as must have been asserted by Cleitarchus. It is clear from the version of Cleitarchus in the *Metz Epitome* that Curtius might easily have assumed that Roxane was one of Chorienes' daughters, if he had not read his source carefully.

Confusingly, Strabo 11.11.4 suggests yet a third location for Alexander's meeting with Roxane at the Rock of Sisimithres, although he is also explicit that it did not happen at the Sogdian Rock, which he notes was also known as the Rock of Ariamazes[277] (as is also its name in Curtius and the Metz Epitome):

Through a betrayal Alexander took also two strongly fortified rocks, one in Bactriana, that of Sisimithres, where Oxyartes kept his daughter Rhoxana, and the other in Sogdiana, that of Oxus, though some call it the rock of Ariamazes. Now writers report that that of Sisimithres is fifteen stadia in height and eighty in circuit, and that on top it is level and has a fertile soil which can support five hundred men, and that here Alexander met with sumptuous hospitality and married Rhoxana, the daughter of Oxyartes; but the rock in Sogdiana, they say, is twice as high as that in Bactriana.

It is clear that Diodorus dealt with Alexander's marriage to Roxane in some depth in the 17th book of his history, for in his list of contents he states that he will narrate:-

---

[277] A possible resolution might be that the individual called Sisimithres in some eyewitness sources was called Chorienes in others (there are signs that names and titles of Asian dignitaries were sometimes used interchangeably by the Greeks: e.g. Mophis versus Taxiles in India.)

Alexander's Lovers by Andrew Chugg

How Alexander, enamoured of Roxane, daughter of Oxyartes, married her and persuaded numbers of his friends to marry the daughters of the prominent Barbarians.

His actual account is lost in a major lacuna of our manuscript, but the reference to the marriages of his friends has been thought to indicate that Diodorus also discussed the Susa weddings at this point, albeit several years ahead of their chronological occurrence (he later spared just two sentences in mentioning these weddings in their proper context). However, the *Metz Epitome* 29-31 seems to follow the same line as Diodorus (presumably echoing Cleitarchus), so Alexander's policy of intermarriage, made famous by the Susa weddings, may already have been in place at his marriage to Roxane in Bactria 3 years earlier:

Enraptured at the sight of [Roxane] and filled with desire, Alexander asked who she was and who her father was. On discovering that she was the daughter of Oxiatris [Oxyartes], also a diner at the dinner, the king took up his cup and tipped a libation to the gods, then began to declaim: "Much that befalls many men and women commonly occurs against expectations. Thus countless kings have sired sons on women won in war or dispatched daughters to distant domains to seal an alliance with wedlock." Then the king focused upon the foreigners: "In my view the Macedonians are not a better breed than you and nor, even if you would come into alliance with us as losers, do I believe you to be unworthy of intermarriage with us. I am going to make such [a union] myself and I shall have a care that the other Macedonians do the same also." He himself having exhorted his Friends with these words, each of them led away a virgin that he wedded at the banquet. Oxyartes and the rest of the foreigners were happy beyond their hopes for this to happen.

The marriage was also celebrated in a famous contemporaneous painting by the Greek artist Aetion, which is sadly long since lost. Fortunately, however, a description of this masterpiece is given by Lucian, who saw it in Italy in the 2nd century AD:-

The scene is a very beautiful chamber, and in it there is a bridal couch with Roxane, a maiden of extraordinary beauty, sitting upon it; her eyes are cast down in modesty for Alexander is standing there. There are also some smiling cupids: one, standing behind Roxane, removes the veil from her head showing her to the bridegroom; another takes the sandal off her foot like a true slave, already preparing her for bed; and a third has grabbed Alexander's cloak and is pulling him with all his might towards Roxane. The King himself holds out a crown to the girl...[278]

Various renaissance artists have created the painting afresh from Lucian's description. Perhaps the best of these is Sodoma's version in the Villa Farnesina in Rome (reproduced on the cover).

Finally on the subject of the marriage, the Alexander Romance displays its characteristic confusion by making Roxane the daughter of the Persian Great

---

[278] Lucian, Herodotus sive Aetion 4-7.

King, Darius,[279] who magnanimously grants her hand to Alexander in his dying peroration. Diodorus also has a similar, though more subtle error, when he states that a Persian lady called Amestris, who had married Craterus, was the daughter of Oxyartes and niece of King Darius.[280] This would ostensibly suggest that Oxyartes had married a sister of Darius, in which case Roxane might have been another offspring of this pairing and also therefore a niece of Darius. Sadly, this intriguing interrelationship is exploded by the fact that the brother of Darius, by name Oxyathres (or Oxathres), is said by Arrian to have had a daughter called Amastrine, who married Craterus at Susa in 324BC.[281] Evidently the name of Oxyartes in Diodorus' text is an uncorrected error for Oxyathres.[282]

Between the marriage in 327BC and Alexander's death in 323BC there are few references to Roxane in the ancient sources. At the time of the weddings at Susa in 324BC, Arrian refers back to the marriage with Roxane,[283] whilst Curtius makes Alexander himself raise the subject of his marriage to Roxane in the context of a speech on the occasion of the mutiny of the troops at Opis in the Summer of 324BC.[284]

For the only significant mention of Roxane in this period, we rely upon nearly the most obscure of all the ancient histories of Alexander: the so-called Metz Epitome, an anonymous Latin manuscript dating from around the 4th century AD. In the context of the commencement of the voyage down the Indus, which took place in the Autumn of 326BC, this text has:-

Interim filius Alexandri ex Rhoxane moritur.[285]

Which translates, "Meanwhile the son/child of Alexander by Roxane died."

The authority of the Metz Epitome is not the best, but most of the events it describes are historical and there is considerable evidence to suggest that it is basically a rather selective epitome of Cleitarchus in its first 86 sections (up to Alexander's arrival in the Indus River Delta). Furthermore, it is difficult to see why its author should invent such a detail as Roxane's first child, merely to inject it into his text as an offhand remark. Conversely, it is easy to imagine our other sources ignoring an infant mortality of this kind, since they do not even

---

[279] Alexander Romance: Greek (trans. Stoneman), Book II, 22 & Armenian (trans. Wolohojian), 197 & 204.
[280] Diodorus 20.109.7; I am using the Loeb edition of 1954.
[281] Arrian, Anabasis 7.4.5.
[282] It is interesting that Oxyathres/Oxathres' presence does not seem to be recorded by the ancient sources after 328BC, whereas Oxyartes' existence is not noted before 328BC; however, the idea that they might be the same individual comes up against the objection that Arrian, Curtius and Diodorus all treat them as different persons, so it would be necessary to posit an enormous level of confusion in the lost primary sources on this issue to sustain the theory.
[283] Arrian, Anabasis 7.4.4.
[284] Curtius 10.3.11.
[285] Epitoma Rerum Gestarum Alexandri Magni (Metz Epitome - Teubner edition) 70.

mention the birth of a surviving son by Barsine in its chronological context. The timing is also relatively credible, since sexual relations between Alexander and Roxane would probably have been at their most enthusiastic in the immediate aftermath of their wedding. Consequently, a birth in 326BC, swiftly followed by a peri-natal mortality, fits in well with the established circumstances. Interestingly, the Suda has the following entry:-

DRAKON, grandson of Hippokrates the famous doctor; son of Thessalus; father of Hippokrates, who again had a son Drakon, the latter being the doctor who healed Roxane while she was living with Alexander.

One possible context for Roxane's malady would be her pregnancy in India, since complications in giving birth were a very common cause of illness in young women before the advent of modern medicine.

In early June 323BC Alexander lay dying of a fever in the palace of Nebuchadnezzar at Babylon. Most probably he had contracted falciparum malaria on a boating trip through the nearby marshes a few weeks earlier. In this context, we have a story, ironically preserved in both the most respected and the worst of our sources, telling of how Roxane prevented Alexander from crawling to the river Euphrates with the purpose of suicide. Arrian[286] cites this tale as an example of the silliness of the stories surrounding the king's death, which he found in his sources:-

One writer has had the impudence to record that Alexander, feeling that he would not survive, went to throw himself into the Euphrates, so that he might disappear from the world and make more credible to posterity the belief that his birth was by a god and that it was to the gods that he had departed, but that Roxane, his wife, noticed that he was going and stopped him, whereupon he groaned and said that she was really grudging him the everlasting fame accorded to one who had been born a god.

In the Alexander Romance[287] essentially the same story is transformed into a key element of the plot:-

And at nightfall Alexander ordered everyone to leave the house. Among those he dismissed were Kombaphe and Roxane, his wife. And from his house there was an exit toward the river called Euphrates, which runs through Babylon. He ordered it opened and that no one be at the places they customarily stood guard. And when it was the middle of the night, he got up from his bed, put out the light, and crawled on all fours toward the river. And he saw his wife, Roxane, advancing toward him. He had been planning to act in a manner worthy of his great courage. She followed his final journey in the dark. And Alexander, scarcely making a sound, would groan, and Roxane was directed to the cry. And he stopped and was still. And his wife embraced him and said, "Are you abandoning and leaving me, Alexander, by committing suicide?" And he said: "Roxane, it is a small deprivation for you that my glory be taken

---

[286] Arrian, Anabasis 7.27.3.
[287] Wolohojian (trans.), Armenian Alexander Romance 268; the story also occurs in the Metz Epitome 101-102.

away from you. But let no one hear about this." And he turned away from Roxane and went back home in concealment.

Arrian is probably right to regard as ridiculous the interpretation that Alexander calmly plotted to commit suicide by drowning in order to promote the legend of his divinity. However, the basic framework of the story is much less unreasonable. Alexander is known from reliable sources to have become delirious with a burning fever in the stifling heat of the Babylonian summer. In the early stages of his illness, it is recorded that he bathed frequently. Archaeology has confirmed that the Euphrates did indeed flow past the palace, within a stone's throw of Alexander's rooms. In these circumstances the king might very well have tried, whilst in an agitated state, to crawl to the river with the intention of cooling his fever. If so, then it is also possible that none present save Roxane dared to prevent him and that he made some garbled complaint about her intervention. The story is probably an original element of the propaganda pamphlet known as the *Liber de Morte* (comprising the last 37 sections of the Metz Epitome), which Heckel believes to have been composed by Holkias in about 317BC.[288] However, these early distortions were necessarily embroideries on the truth rather than outright inventions, since the latter would have been untenable, within living memory of the events. If so, then the story retains some evidential value in suggesting that Roxane was at Babylon when Alexander died.

The ancient sources all chose the immediate aftermath of Alexander's death to reveal that Roxane was with child by the king,[289] even though she was evidently already at least six months pregnant at the time.[290] The timing of Roxane's pregnancy might indicate that Alexander had sought solace in sex with Roxane after Hephaistion's death at the end of November. Alternatively, on a more pragmatic level, his friend's premature demise had perhaps impressed upon the king the urgency of his fathering an heir, for Hephaistion appears to have expired without issue (or at least we hear of none).

Both the Alexander Romance and the *Liber de Morte* section of the Metz Epitome recite a putative "Will of Alexander".[291] This document has undoubtedly suffered from a number of additions and distortions by a propagandist of Rhodian affiliation (and probably by others too). However, its core reads like an attempt to legitimise the settlement of the succession and the division of the satrapies, which was implemented by Perdiccas at Babylon in the

---

[288] The *Liber de Morte* forms the last part of both the Alexander Romance and the Metz Epitome; Waldemar Heckel, The Last Days & Testament of Alexander the Great: A Prosopographic Study, Stuttgart 1988; for another theory see Ptolemy and the Will of Alexander by A.B. Bosworth in Alexander the Great in Fact & Fiction, ed. A.B. Bosworth & E.J. Baynham, Oxford 2000.
[289] E.g. Justin 12.15.
[290] Curtius 10.6.9; Justin 13.2.5 has 8 months, but his reliability on such points is poor.
[291] Armenian Alexander Romance 273-274; Greek Alexander Romance, A recension, Book III, 32, Alexander's Will.

weeks after Alexander's death. For this purpose it raises the issue of the sex of Roxane's child and asserts that this infant should ultimately inherit the empire, provided it were male. In this, and in its treatment of Arrhidaeus as a temporary monarch of convenience, it adheres closely to the known political stance of Perdiccas in the summer of 323BC. It also gives a partially correct version of Perdiccas' initial division of the satrapies among Alexander's lieutenants including the assignment of "Paropanisadae" to "Oxydrakes of Bactria, the father of Alexander's wife Roxane." Its ultimate inspiration might therefore be the authentic edict issued by Perdiccas in the name of Alexander shortly after the King's death.

Curtius describes a long and animated debate on the succession at an Assembly of the Macedonians the day after Alexander's death, which ultimately erupted into a violent clash between the cavalry and the infantry. Naturally enough, the status that should be accorded to Roxane's unborn child was at the very heart of the dispute. Perdiccas, the most senior officer present and the recipient of Alexander's ring, introduced the issue:-

This is the sixth month of Roxane's pregnancy. We pray that she produces a male, who, with the gods' approval, will assume the throne when he comes of age.

Curtius[292]

But Ptolemy retorted with an expression of the frustration of the Macedonians at the prospect of a king, who would be raised by a mother from among the conquered peoples.[293] Meleager, a relatively obscure commander of an infantry regiment, then attacked Perdiccas directly by asserting that the commander of the cavalry favoured the candidacy of an unborn child only because this would leave all the real power in his own hands.[294] However, most of the senior officers backed Perdiccas, so the meeting appointed him and his fellow Bodyguard, Leonnatus, to be the guardians of Roxane's prospective son.[295] Meanwhile though, Meleager had slipped away to foment a rebellion of the infantry, which forcibly elected Alexander's imbecile half-brother, Arrhidaeus, as the new monarch, under the regnal name of Philip III. There ensued a week or so of bitter skirmishes and political and military manoeuvring, by the end of which Perdiccas had effectively reasserted his authority. He managed to use his loyal cavalry units to cut the food supplies to the infantry in Babylon, whilst proposing as a compromise to implement a joint-kingship of Arrhidaeus and Roxane's son.[296] This was an offer that Meleager was in no position to refuse,

---

[292] Curtius 10.6.9.
[293] Curtius 10.6.13-14.
[294] Curtius 10.6.21.
[295] Curtius 10.7.8-9; Justin 13.2 gives a briefer version of argument over the succession and states that Leonnatus, Perdiccas, Craterus & Antipater were appointed guardians of the unborn child, destined to become king.
[296] The official status of this joint kingship is well-documented: e.g. OGIS 4 lines 5-7; Hesperia 37 (1968) 222; MDAI(A) 72 (1957) 158; c.f. Photius 82 (Dexippus) & 92 (Arrian's Events after Alexander).

but in agreeing to it he signed his own death warrant, for Perdiccas was now able to wrest control of Arrhidaeus from the rebel leaders. Deprived of their puppet and with their military support neutralised, Meleager and his cronies were perfectly exposed to Perdiccas' implacable revenge. He executed most of the ringleaders by having them trampled by elephants at a "reconciliation parade". Meleager himself was assassinated whilst seeking sanctuary in a temple shortly afterwards. Despite his triumph, Perdiccas' unmitigated brutality won him few friends among his fellow officers, but rather sowed the seeds of fear and distrust that would eventually blossom into a generalised civil war.

In a further example of the pervasive mood of ruthlessness, probably in July 323BC Roxane arranged the murders of her erstwhile rival wife Stateira together with her sister Drypetis, who had been wedded to Hephaistion. According to Plutarch the deed was accomplished with the approval and cooperation of the pitiless Perdiccas:-

Now, Roxane was with child, and on this account was held in honour among the Macedonians; but she was jealous of Stateira, and therefore deceived her by a forged letter into coming where she was, and when she had got there, slew her, together with her sister, threw their bodies into the well, and filled the well with earth, Perdiccas being privy to the deed and a partner in it.[297]

The collusion between Roxane and Perdiccas in this matter further vindicates Roxane's presence at Babylon when Alexander died, as reported by the Alexander Romance and the Metz Epitome. A few months later in the early Autumn the queen duly gave birth to a healthy boy, whom the troops acclaimed as king Alexander IV virtually as soon as he saw the light of day, as is recorded in Photius' epitome of Arrian's lost work on the Events After Alexander.[298] Alexander IV is also sometimes called Alexander Aegus or Aegos or Aegeos in modern works. This appears to be an error deriving from a modern misreading of *aigou* for *allou* in the manuscript of the Astronomical Canon of Claudius Ptolemy. Thus "another Alexander" was transcribed as "Alexander Aegus".

In the two years following Alexander's traumatic demise, Roxane and the infant king accompanied Perdiccas, whilst he sought to consolidate his authority as de facto ruler of the empire. In 322BC he campaigned successfully in Cappadocia before retiring to winter the Grand Army in Pisidia in the southwest of Asia Minor. Justin[299] mentions that Alexander IV attended a council called by the regent to determine whether next to attack Antipater and Craterus in Macedonia or to move against Ptolemy who had taken over Egypt. This was late in 322BC and Ptolemy had just hijacked Alexander's catafalque in Syria and stolen his corpse. This stinging provocation would seem to have swung the planned

---

[297] Plutarch, Life of Alexander 77.4.
[298] Photius 92, Epitome of Arrians's Events After Alexander 1.1 & 1.9A; c.f. Photius 82 (Dexippus' Events after Alexander).
[299] Justin 13.6.

offensive towards the south, for the Grand Army duly arrived on the eastern banks of the Nile in the late spring of 321BC. Here Perdiccas' luck finally deserted him along with the loyalty of his officers, who ran the regent through with their spears, after he had twice failed to force the crossing of the river, whilst sustaining catastrophic casualties among his own troops. Strabo[300] comments that Alexander's children were with Roxane in the camp at this time, so the queen may well have witnessed the downfall of her ally and protector.

The officers of the Grand Army hastily made their peace with Ptolemy, who gracefully declined their offer of the poison chalice of the regency. However, he agreed to supply them for the march as they retraced their journey through Palestine and Syria. Somewhere beyond Damascus at an unidentified location called Triparadeisos (Three-Parks), they met up with an army from Macedon led in person by Antipater, Alexander's erstwhile regent in Greece. Adea-Eurydice, a granddaughter of Philip and a niece of Alexander, who had been betrothed to Philip-Arrhidaeus, had recently been inciting disaffection and unrest among the troops. When Antipater addressed the soldiers at an assembly, they rioted and would have slain him, but for the prompt intervention of several loyal officers, notably including Antigonus and Seleucus. Antipater nonetheless managed eventually to reassert his authority and became the new regent for the joint-kings, for there was no other surviving figure of comparable status to whom the army could turn, Craterus having been killed in a battle with Eumenes months earlier. The aged regent appears initially to have intended to leave the kings in the charge of Antigonus, whom he appointed to the command of the army in Asia. However, he also assigned his son, Cassander, to be Antigonus' chiliarch or deputy. This was probably a monitoring brief, but Cassander speedily fell out with his nominal superior and persuaded his father personally to retain the guardianship of the kings. As soon as it could be arranged, Antipater returned to Macedonia with his royal charges in train. Alexander had intended that Babylon should be the capital of his empire, but from Antipater's more traditionalist point of view, the ancestral seat probably seemed a more proper base for a Temenid king.[301]

We can readily imagine Roxane's reaction to these events. As a "barbarian" in Greek eyes, she could not realistically hope personally to sway the loyalties of the soldiers in emulation of Adea-Eurydice. Her only tactic was to curry the protection of whichever Macedonian generalissimo had acquired control of her son. Already, many of the senior officers she had known in Alexander's lifetime, including Hephaistion, Leonnatus, Craterus and Perdiccas, were dead. Antipater and his sons and supporters were relative strangers to her. She found herself increasingly the victim of circumstances and the personal safety of both herself and her son must have seemed more and more open to question.

---

[300] Strabo 17.1.8.
[301] Mostly from Photius' summary of Arrian's Events after Alexander, which is more detailed than Diodorus 18.39.

Roxane, The Starlet

Nonetheless, Roxane was now drawing nearer to an unstinting ally of great authority and enormous symbolic influence. Olympias, Alexander's imperious firebrand of a mother, was resident just across the mountains in Epirus, the land of her birth, whither she had returned having made her position in Macedon untenable by virtue of her fractious and mutually suspicious relations with Antipater and Cassander. But the regent was frail and ailing. He survived for barely more than a year following his return from Asia. In 319BC he finally expired. Among his last acts was the appointment of the Tymphaean infantry officer, Polyperchon, to be his successor, in preference to his own son, Cassander, who received the consolation prize of appointment as Polyperchon's Chiliarch, which meant his deputy. This surprising decision appears particularly to lend the lie to the wild rumours that Antipater had masterminded a plot to poison Alexander in order to perpetuate the power of his own family. In the light of later events, it appears that the old man may actually have been acting upon some foreboding of Cassander's murderous intentions towards the surviving members of Alexander's family.

As his father's strength had waned, so Cassander's faction had begun to flourish at court and throughout Greece, yet Polyperchon retained sufficient support to maintain his supremacy for the time being. Antipater's ambitious heir therefore pretended his acquiescence to the new arrangements, whilst covertly plotting against the new regent. Eventually, under cover of a hunting expedition, he slipped away to Asia to beg the support of Antigonus, who was only too delighted to be handed an opportunity to foment trouble in Macedon.

Among Polyperchon's preparations for the inevitable conflict was a letter dispatched to Olympias in Epirus requesting that she return to Macedon to take charge of the upbringing of her grandson, Alexander IV.[302] However, Eumenes suggested that she remain where she was when she sought his advice on this point, so she seems for the time being to have eschewed Polyperchon's lure.[303]

At this time the city-states of southern Greece nominally enjoyed a limited degree of self-rule, though subject to the over-arching Macedonian hegemony. Most cities were politically divided between an oligarchic faction, which believed in rule by an aristocratic minority, and a democratic party, which advocated a broadening of the franchise to include the poorer citizens. Antipater had favoured the oligarchs in the aftermath of the rebellions that followed upon Alexander's death, but many of these rulers (and the Macedonian garrisons which sustained their power) favoured Cassander for the succession to the regency. Consequently, Polyperchon, acting on the advice of his council, rapidly implemented a bold new policy. Late in 319BC he issued a proclamation switching the support of the joint-kings to the democratic factions and declaring Macedon to be the champion of freedom for the Greeks.[304] This policy proved

---

[302] Diodorus 18.57.2 & 18.65.1.
[303] Diodorus 18.58.4.
[304] Diodorus 18.55-6.

successful in many instances, but some cities nevertheless held out for Cassander.

War was truly joined in 318BC, when the whole of Greece and much of Asia Minor became engulfed in bitter conflict. Polyperchon marched south towards Athens and the Peloponnesus to enforce the "democratisation" of his vassals, whilst Cassander with the connivance of Antigonus led a fleet to the relief of his supporters at Piraeus, the port of Athens. Initially, Polyperchon achieved some slight success in cowing his opponents among the Greeks and his fleet won a victory against that of Antigonus and Cassander near Byzantium. But the new Regent became bogged down in a protracted siege of Megalopolis, a rebel city in the Peloponnesus. The defenders set a trap at a weak point in their perimeter by concealing numerous frames studded with sharp nails in shallow trenches. Polyperchon duly charged his elephants into the perceived gap, where they were quickly brought to a painful and perplexed halt and bombarded with missiles by the Megalopolitans. Many died and others, thrashing about in agony, trampled large numbers of their own support troops.

Worse was to follow. Through over-confidence in the wake of their recent victory at sea, Polyperchon's fleet was annihilated in a sneak attack, whilst it lay at anchor near Byzantium. At a stroke, Antigonus and Cassander now controlled the sea passage from Asia into Europe and dominated the trade route for the supply of corn from the Black Sea territories that was required to feed the Greek city-states. With his reputation in tatters, a pathway laid open for the invasion of Europe and his allies now dependent upon his enemies' goodwill, Polyperchon's position was decisively weakened. In Macedon, Queen Adea-Eurydice, the wife of Philip-Arrhidaeus, had been concerned by the prospect of the return of Olympias, who could naturally be expected to prefer the kingship of Alexander IV over that of her husband.[305] Now she felt confident enough to declare for Cassander and to strip Polyperchon of the Regency, acting in the name of her mentally deficient spouse.

The whereabouts of Roxane and Alexander IV at this time is not entirely clear in the sources. Diodorus states that the joint-kings were with Polyperchon at Phocis shortly after the Regent had moved into Southern Greece.[306] Adea-Eurydice seems to have had her husband with her in Macedon, when she moved to oust Polyperchon, which makes it possible that Alexander IV and Roxane had also returned to the north. If so, they must have fled to Olympias in Epirus, when Adea-Eurydice seized power, since it was probably to Epirus that Polyperchon took his army to support Alexander IV's restoration to the throne.[307] However, an alternative view has been argued by Grace Macurdy, who points out that the only clear statement that Roxane and her son were ever

---

[305] Justin 14.5.
[306] Diodorus 18.68.2.
[307] Diodorus 19.11.1.

in Epirus is given by Polyaenus, who may be unreliable on this point.[308] Macurdy suggests that the evidence is more consistent with the boy king and his mother having remained with Polyperchon and that the generalissimo may or may not have returned to Macedon via Epirus.

In 317BC, most probably as soon as the mountain passes opened up in the spring, Olympias and Polyperchon launched an invasion of Macedon and confronted Adea-Eurydice's forces at the frontier town of Euia. The latter's troops lacked the stomach for a fight against so august a personage as the mother of Alexander the Great, so they capitulated without a contest and both Adea-Eurydice and Philip-Arrhidaeus were captured and soon after eliminated. Polyaenus describes the exultation at this turn of events even in faraway Persia at the camp of Eumenes' army:

In Persia Eumenes observed the soldiers being won over by Peucestas' wine and gifts. Fearing that Peucestas would draw off all the officers, Eumenes produced, as if it came from Orontes the satrap of Armenia, a letter written in Syrian characters, saying that Olympias had come back from Epirus with Alexander's son and legitimately ruled the kingdom of Macedonia after Cassander had been removed. When the Macedonians heard this news, they forgot Peucestas and spoke of Alexander's mother and son with great pleasure and delight.

Polyaenus, Stratagems of War 4.8.3

However Olympias was far from sated by her success, but now indulged a horrible bloodlust in hunting down and murdering a hundred of the more prominent Macedonians, who were known sympathisers of Cassander.[309] Such immoderate vengeance quickly disillusioned the populace of their rapturous regard for their exalted queen.

In the second half of 317BC, Cassander himself attacked Macedon, whilst Polyperchon was isolated from Olympias and his army was subverted by bribery[310]:-

But Olympias, on learning that Cassander had a large army near Macedonia, designated Aristonous general, ordering him to fight Cassander, and she herself went to Pydna accompanied by the following: Alexander's son, his mother Roxane, and Thessalonike, daughter of Philip son of Amyntas: also Deidameia, daughter of Aeacides king of the Epirotes and sister of that Pyrrhus who later fought against the Romans, the daughters of Attalus, and finally the kinsfolk of Olympias' other more important friends.[311]

Diodorus 19.35.4-5

The presence of Deidameia is significant, because Plutarch indicates that she had been betrothed to Alexander IV, presumably at the behest of Olympias.[312]

---

[308] Grace H. Macurdy, Roxane and Alexander IV in Epirus, Journal of Hellenic Studies 52 (1932), pp.256-261; Polyaenus 4.8.3.
[309] Diodorus 19.11.5-9; Justin 14.6.
[310] Diodorus 19.36.6.
[311] Cf. Justin 14.6.
[312] Plutarch, Life of Pyrrhus 4.

Thessalonike was also important, because she was a legitimising source of connection with the Royal Family for any generalissimo with regal ambitions. Olympias had gathered all the key pawns in the succession around her at Pydna. All the eggs lay in that sequestered basket.

Cassander duly invested Pydna by land and sea. The siege lasted most of the winter and ranks among the most terrible recorded in antiquity. The elephants perished on a diet of sawdust and starvation soon stalked among the human garrison as well. The corpses of the dead were cast over the walls, but nevertheless rotted, further beleaguering the defenders amidst their stinking fumes. Attempts by friends and allies to rescue the besieged queen from her dire plight all came to naught. There is an especially vivid anecdote in Polyaenus describing the failure of an attempt by Polyperchon to rescue the Royal Family:-

Cassander shut Olympias in Pydna, a Macedonian city, and besieged her. At night Polyperchon sent a quinquereme to anchor nearby and urged Olympias in a letter to board it. The letter-carrier, caught and taken before Cassander, confessed the purpose for which he was sent. Cassander ordered him to deliver the letter, sealed with Polyperchon's seal, but not to indicate that Cassander knew about it. So he delivered it, while Cassander captured and removed the quinquereme. Olympias trusted Polyperchon's sealed letter and came out of the city at night. When she did not find the quinquereme, she assumed Polyperchon was tricking her. In despair she surrendered the city of Pydna and herself to Cassander.[313]

Polyaenus, Stratagems of War 4.11.3

As Polyaenus indicates, once all hope had been extinguished, Olympias confronted the inevitability of surrender and managed to negotiate just the guarantee of her personal safety with Cassander. In the spring of 316BC, Pydna capitulated and the Royal Family, including Roxane and her young son, fell into the hands of their bitterest enemy.

Cassander paid scant heed to the terms agreed with Olympias, but rather set about organising her murder by proxy. He brought her case before the Assembly of the Macedonians, where the families of those she had killed testified so vividly to her cruelty and rapaciousness as readily to secure her conviction and a sentence of death. Having failed to persuade a body of regular troops to perpetrate the regicide, Cassander appears instead to have permitted the relatives of the queen's recent victims to wreak their vengeance upon her person. Apparently, she was stoned to death.[314] As she expired, she settled her hair and covered her feet with her robe, in order that she should present a seemly corpse. Thus, at the hands of a mob of the bereaved, Macedon's most illustrious and perilous queen met her end with characteristic stoicism.[315]

It is uncertain how much of the horror and bloodshed the 6-year-old Alexander IV witnessed, but the overall impact of the siege and its aftermath can scarcely

---

[313] Cf. Diodorus 19.50.4-5.
[314] Pausanias 9.7.2.
[315] Diodorus 19.51.4-6; Justin 14.6.

have been less than traumatic for the boy. Ominously, Cassander soon signalled his ambitions by marrying Thessalonike, thus linking himself with the royal line as the son-in-law of Philip II.³¹⁶ It seems likely that he would have had Roxane and the king executed at this point, had he believed that the Assembly would allow it. However, it must have been clear to all that their role in events had been entirely passive, so the army, which had baulked even at the killing of Olympias, would never have countenanced the murder of Alexander the Great's only legitimate son. Nevertheless, Cassander now took the opportunity to place Roxane and Alexander IV under the sinister guard of a certain Glaucias in the citadel of Amphipolis, where they remained incarcerated for six long years.

Cassander had determined to do away with Alexander's son and the son's mother, Roxane, so that there might be no successor to the kingdom; but for the present, since he wished to observe what the common people would say about the slaying of Olympias and since he had no news of Antigonus' success,³¹⁷ he placed Roxane and the child in custody, transferring them to the citadel of Amphipolis, in command of which he placed Glaucias, one of his most trusted henchmen. Also he took away the Pages who, according to custom, were being brought up as companions of the boy, and he ordered that he should no longer have royal treatment, but only such as was proper for any ordinary person of private station.

Diodorus 19.52.4

There is some additional evidence for the royal trappings that Alexander IV had enjoyed prior to his imprisonment. A partially preserved Attic inscription speaks of honours for Philip, Iolaos and a third person whose name is obliterated. It states that these three men were Bodyguards (*Somatophylakes*) of Alexander the king.³¹⁸ It is believed that the king in question must be Alexander IV and that these three Bodyguards complemented the four Bodyguards, which Antipater assigned to Philip-Arrhidaeus.³¹⁹ The total number of Bodyguards under the joint-kingship was therefore seven, which had been the traditional number under previous monarchs.³²⁰

In the course of their protracted imprisonment, Roxane and her son were occasionally the subjects of rather half-hearted and ultimately ineffectual campaigns to secure their liberation. As early as 315BC Antigonus fell out with Cassander and made an alliance with Polyperchon's son, another Alexander. As a tactic to undermine Cassander's position, Antigonus called an assembly of his troops and denounced the treason perpetrated against Olympias, Roxane and Alexander IV by Antipater's scheming son:-

---

[316] Diodorus 19.51.1; Justin 14.6.13, who errs in making Thessalonice the daughter of Arrhidaeus; Pausanias 9.7.3.
[317] Antigonus overcame and executed Eumenes and Pithon in 316BC, thus becoming almost undisputed in his leadership of the Asian satrapies.
[318] Stanley M. Burstein, IG II² 561 and the Court of Alexander IV, Zeitschrift für Papyrologie und Epigraphik 24 (1977) 223-225.
[319] Arrian, Events After Alexander (Epitome of Photius) 1.38.
[320] Waldemar Heckel, IG II² 561 and the Status of Alexander IV, Zeitschrift für Papyrologie und Epigraphik 40 (1980) 249-250.

Alexander's Lovers by Andrew Chugg

Antigonus, after Polyperchon's son had come to him, made a pact of friendship with him, and then, calling a general assembly of the soldiers and of the aliens who were dwelling there, laid charges against Cassander, bringing forward the murder of Olympias and the treatment of Roxane and the king [Alexander IV]... When the crowd showed that it shared his wrath, he introduced a decree, according to the terms of which it was voted that Cassander was to be an enemy unless he... released the king and his mother Roxane from imprisonment and restored them to the Macedonians...[321]

Figure 7.2. Alexander IV in a colossal statue from Karnak (sketch by the author)

Despite Cassander's insistence that Alexander IV had been deposed and now ranked as a mere private citizen, elsewhere in the Empire the captive boy continued to be recognised as the reigning monarch. For example, from Egypt we have an inscription known as the Satrap Stele, which dates from 311BC, since it introduces itself by stating that it was made in the seventh year of the reign of Alexander IV. This means in the seventh year after the end of the joint-kingship, which terminated when Philip-Arrhidaeus was killed early in 317BC. There also survives a colossal Egyptian statue of a boy-Pharaoh from Karnak,

---

[321] Diodorus 19.61.1-3.

which is believed to represent Alexander IV (Figure 7.2). Ptolemy continued to mint coins with the legend ALEXANDROU (of Alexander) until 305BC. Late in 305BC or early in 304BC Ptolemy decided to declare himself pharaoh and commenced asserting that his reign had in fact begun upon Alexander the Great's death, interim announcements to the contrary notwithstanding. This was, of course, an implicit admission of the essentially fictitious nature of the control exerted over Egypt by Philip-Arrhidaeus and Alexander IV.

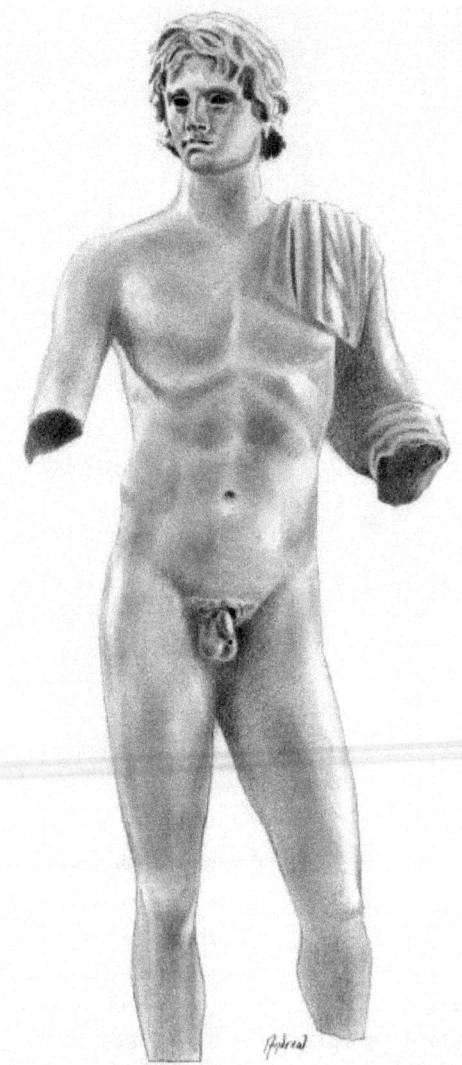

Figure 7.3. The Ephebe d'Agde perhaps representing Alexander IV (sketch by the author)

Professor Paolo Moreno of the University of Rome III has proposed that the bronze statue of a Greek youth (an ephebe) found in the river Hérault in Agde on 13th September 1964 and now displayed in the Musée de l'Ephèbe in Le Cap d'Agde (Figure 7.3) is a representation of Alexander IV.[322] The work is in the style of Lysippus, court sculptor to Alexander, and the mantle is draped over the left shoulder and around the left arm in the Macedonian fashion. The style of the hair, especially the anastole (upward sweep from the forehead), and the facial features are reminiscent of Alexander the Great. However, the statue represents a youth of perhaps 13 to 16 years of age, yet he wears the diadem, a symbol of Macedonian kingship. Alexander the Great was once at the age of sixteen appointed to act as regent in Macedon in his father's absence, but it is dubious whether this would have entitled him to wear the diadem. He did not ascend the throne until aged twenty.

In 311BC, following a further episode of civil war between Antigonus and the other leading commanders, it was agreed as a condition of the truce that Cassander should retain control of Europe "until Alexander the son of Roxane should come of age".[323] The imposition of these terms may well have served to remind Cassander of the increasing magnitude of the threat posed to his position by the young king as he approached adolescence. At any rate, the consensus of the evidence is that Cassander arranged the clandestine murder of Roxane and her son in the year 310BC, when Alexander IV was 12 or 13 years old and Roxane was probably still in her early 30's. In particular, the Parian Marble asserts that Alexander IV died in the year 310/309BC and it is improbable that this contemporaneous source is in error by more than a year. Diodorus provides the most specific account of the atrocity (dating it to 311/310BC):-

Now Cassander perceived that Alexander, the son of Roxane, was growing up and that word was being spread throughout Macedonia by certain men that it was fitting to release the boy from custody and give him his father's kingdom; and fearing for himself, he instructed Glaucias, who was in command of the guard over the child, to murder Roxane and the king and conceal their bodies, but to disclose to no one else what had been done. When Glaucias had carried out the instructions, Cassander, Lysimachus, and Ptolemy, and Antigonus as well, were relieved of their anticipated danger from the king...

Diodorus 19.105.1-4[324]

It must have been Cassander's intention that this should have been the end of the story, so it is likely that the bodies were indeed buried secretly as Diodorus suggests. However, in 1976 Manolis Andronikos began a momentous series of excavations at the Great Tumulus at modern Vergina, which is confidently believed to be the site of the original Macedonian capital of Aegae and the burial place of the Temenid kings. Having in 1977 already found two tombs, one probably belonging to Philip II, Andronikos uncovered a third royal burial

---

[322] Paolo Moreno, Il principe infelice, Archaeo XIII, 7 (July 1997) p. 108-110.
[323] Diodorus 19.105.1.
[324] See also Pausanias 9.7.2 and Justin 15.2.5, though the latter appears to confuse Alexander IV with Heracles; the Heidelberg Epitome 2.3 also mentions the murders.

in 1978.[325] The cremated bones of a youth not yet 16 and most probably 13 were discovered in a silver hydria crowned with a gold oak wreath (Figure 7.4) in Tomb III at Vergina. N. G. L. Hammond has identified them quite credibly as the remains of Alexander IV.[326]

It is possible that some other members of Roxane's household were murdered at the same time, because the Suda has the following entry:

HIPPOKRATES *the fourth, son of Drakon, doctor, also from Kos, of the same family; he treated Roxane, and died at the hands of Cassander the son of Antipater. He also wrote medical works.*

Recalling that the Suda mentioned elsewhere that Hippokrates had cured Roxane of some illness during Alexander's lifetime, it may be inferred that he became her personal physician, then died with her at Cassander's command.

Figure 7.4. Silver hydria of cremated bones, probably Alexander IV (sketch by the author)

Cassander himself died of a lingering illness in 297BC. Soon afterwards Demetrius Poliorketes, the heir of Antigonus, managed to seize the Macedonian kingdom. Plutarch mentions that the Macedonian people welcomed Demetrius

---

[325] Manolis Andronicos, *Vergina* (Athens, 1984); Manolis Andronikos, The Royal Tombs at Vergina *in* The Search for Alexander: An Exhibition, NYGS (Boston, 1980), pp. 26-38.
[326] E.g. NGL Hammond, The Evidence for the Identity of the Royal Tombs at Vergina in Philip II, Alexander the Great and the Macedonian Heritage, ed. Adams & Borza, Boston & London 1982; NGL Hammond, The Miracle That Was Macedonia, Sidgwick & Jackson, 1991.

particularly because they had detested the crimes of Cassander against the family of Alexander the Great.[327] This then is perhaps the most opportune occasion for the hidden corpses to have been tracked down and exhumed, so that the ill-fated boy-king might be granted a worthy entombment in the midst of the sepulchres of his illustrious ancestors.

---

[327] Plutarch, Life of Demetrius 37.

8. Stateira and Parysatis, the Persian Princesses

In 333BC Darius, the Persian Great King, determined to repel Alexander's invasion by the simple tactic of deploying an overwhelming force against him in the field. Accordingly, having assembled a suitably impressive army, comprising perhaps as many as several hundred thousand men (including 30,000 Greek mercenaries), he set off for Asia Minor with virtually the entire Persian court in his train. In particular, the wife, children and mother of the king were brought along to enjoy the prospective spectacle of a famous victory and Curtius has described their stations in the procession of Darius' army:-

Next, at a distance of one stade, came Sisigambis, the mother of Darius, drawn in a carriage, and in another came his wife. A troop of women attended the queens on horseback. Then came the so-called Armamaxae [enclosed wagons] in which rode the king's children, their nurses and a herd of eunuchs (who are not at all held in contempt by these peoples).

Curtius 3.3.22-23

Perhaps Darius' family did indeed witness the spectacular and renowned battle on the shores of the Gulf of Issus in northern Syria, but it was Darius' antagonist who emerged victorious and Alexander pressed home his success with the capture of the Great King's camp, where the Persian queens, an infant prince and two princesses together with their handmaidens and eunuch attendants were all apprehended. The sources imply that Darius' stalwart mother was the de facto leader of the royal ladies.

Darius' camp was stormed at once, and captured with his mother, wife, who was also his sister, and his infant son; two daughters were taken too, with a few noble Persian ladies in their suite.

Arrian, Anabasis 2.11.9

In the lap of their aged grandmother lay Darius' two grown-up but unmarried daughters, grieving for their grandmother as well as themselves.

Curtius 3.11.25

If the princesses were both "grown-up" and yet unmarried and young enough to find solace in their grandmother's lap, it would seem reasonable to infer that they were both in their early teens at this time.

The news that Darius' family had been captured reached Alexander at dusk, soon after he had abandoned the hot pursuit of the Great King himself and was contentedly settling down to an evening meal. Plutarch sets the scene:-

As [Alexander] was betaking himself to supper, someone told him that among the prisoners were the mother, wife and two unmarried daughters of Darius, and that at the sight of his chariot and bow they beat their breasts and lamented, believing that he was dead. Accordingly, after a considerable pause, more affected by their affliction than by his own success, he sent Leonnatus with orders to tell them that Darius was not dead, and that they need have no fear of Alexander...but they should have everything which they used to think their due... But the most honourable and most princely favour which these noble and chaste women received from him in their captivity was that they neither heard, nor suspected, nor awaited anything that would disgrace them, but lived as though guarded in sacred and inviolable virgins' chambers...And yet it is said that the wife of Darius was far the most comely of all royal women...

Plutarch, Life of Alexander 21

Curtius has further vivid details of Leonnatus' embassy to the queens, most probably sourced almost verbatim from the contemporaneous historian Cleitarchus. He conveys a keen sense of the discomfiture of Alexander's lieutenant in this unfamiliar role:-

When Alexander learned of the women's misunderstanding, they say he wept for Darius' reversal of fortune and their devotion to him. At first he ordered Mithrenes, the man who had surrendered Sardis, to go and console them, since he knew the Persian language, but then he became concerned that a traitor might only rekindle the captives' anger and sorrow. So he sent Leonnatus, one of his courtiers, instead, instructing him to tell them that their lamentation was unwarranted since Darius still lived. Leonnatus came with a few guards to the tent that housed the captured women and ordered it to be announced that he had been sent by Alexander. The people at the entrance, however, caught sight of their weapons and, thinking their mistresses were finished, ran into the tent shouting that their final hour had come, that men had been sent to kill the prisoners. The women could not keep the soldiers out, nor did they dare admit them and so, making no reply, they silently awaited their victor's will. Leonnatus waited for a long time for someone to let him in, but, when no one dared to escort him inside, he left his attendants in the entrance and entered the tent. That in itself produced consternation among the women: he had apparently burst in without an invitation. So the mother and sister of Darius fell at his feet and began to beg him to give Darius' body a traditional burial before they were executed, adding that after paying their last respects to the king they would readily face death. Leonnatus' answer was that Darius was still alive and that they would not only come to no harm but would also retain their royal status with all the dignity of their former positions. Only at that point did Darius' mother allow herself to be raised from the ground.

Curtius 3.12.6-12

Arrian agrees with Plutarch in detail on the matter of Leonnatus' visit to reassure the queens, which is not surprising, since we know that both historians made extensive use of Aristobulus, their likely common source for this incident. However, Arrian also tells the further "story" of Alexander visiting the queens in person the following day, which was evidently absent from the accounts of Ptolemy and Aristobulus. Since an identical story is also found in Curtius and in Diodorus (17.37.5-6), it is highly likely that it comes from the lost history of Cleitarchus, who was their common source:-

Nor did he neglect Darius' mother, wife or children. Now some of the accounts of Alexander relate that the very night after his return from the pursuit of Darius he entered Darius' tent, which had been set aside for his own use, and heard a lament and other confused sounds of women's voices near the tent; he enquired what women they were and why they were accommodated so near him; and was told, "Sire, it is Darius' mother, wife and children; as they have heard that you are in possession of his bow and royal mantle and that his shield has been brought back, they are mourning his death." On hearing this, Alexander sent Leonnatus, one of the Companions, to them with instructions to tell them that Darius was alive and had left his arms and mantle in the chariot while escaping, and that these were all Alexander had. Leonnatus entered the tent and gave Alexander's message about Darius, adding that Alexander granted them the right of royal state and all other marks of royalty, with the title of queens, since he had not made war with Darius from personal enmity but had fought for the sovereignty of Asia lawfully. This is the account of Ptolemy and Aristobulus; there is however a story that next day Alexander himself [though wounded in the thigh] visited the tent with Hephaistion and no other Companion; and Darius' mother, not knowing which of the two was king, as both were dressed alike, approached Hephaistion and did him obeisance, since he appeared the taller. Hephaistion drew back, and one of her attendants pointed to Alexander and said he was king; she drew back in confusion at her mistake, but Alexander remarked that she had made no mistake, for Hephaistion was also an Alexander.

Arrian, Anabasis 2.12.3-7

Curtius' version is slightly more elaborate and probably closer to Cleitarchus, its early source:-

The following day... Alexander allowed Darius' mother to bury whomsoever she wished in traditional Persian fashion. She ordered a few close relatives to be buried, and those in a manner befitting their present circumstances, thinking that the elaborate funerals with which Persians paid their last respects to the dead would cause ill-will in view of the simple cremation accorded the victors. When the funeral services had been duly discharged, Alexander sent messengers to the female prisoners to announce his coming and then, leaving the crowd of his attendants outside, he went into their tent with Hephaistion... While he was the king's age, in stature he was his superior, and so the queens took him to be the king and did obeisance before him after their manner. Whereupon some of the captive eunuchs pointed out the real Alexander, and Sisigambis flung herself at his feet, apologising for not recognising him on the ground she had never before seen him. Raising her with his hand, Alexander said, 'Mother, you made no mistake. This man is Alexander too.'

Curtius 3.12.15-17

Although Justin conflates the visit of Leonnatus with that of Alexander with his characteristically careless abbreviation, his details seem otherwise to echo the elaborate account in Curtius 3.12, so Cleitarchus is probably his ultimate source too (via the intermediary of Trogus, whom he was epitomizing):-

In the Persian camp large quantities of gold and other treasures were found, and among the prisoners taken in the camp were the mother of Darius, his wife (who was also his sister) and two daughters. Alexander came to pay them a visit and give them some encouragement, but at the sight of his armed escort the women embraced each other, believing their death imminent, and let out sorrowful cries. Then, throwing themselves before Alexander's feet, they begged not for their lives but only for a stay of execution until they could bury Darius' body. Moved by such loyalty on the women's part, Alexander informed them that Darius was still alive,

Alexander's Lovers by Andrew Chugg

dispelled their fear of execution and gave orders that they should be treated as queens. He also told the daughters to expect marriages not unbefitting their father's rank.

Justin 11.9.11-16

There is a famous old-master painting on the subject of *The Family of Darius Before Alexander* by Paolo Veronese on display in the National Gallery, London. Another famous impression of this scene was created by Charles le Brun, court painter to Louis XIV (Figure 8.1). Versions of this theme have also been created by Giambattista Tiepolo, Sebastiano Ricci, André Castaigne, and Christophe Veyrier amongst others. This artistic plethora reflects the fact that the episode has long been celebrated as one of the great chivalric dramas of Alexander's career.

Figure 8.1. Alexander and the Family of Darius (after Charles le Brun, 1662)

The ancient references suggest that the historicity of Alexander's audience with the Persian queens rests upon the authority of the lost account by Cleitarchus, who has not always been considered the most reliable of the primary sources. Nevertheless, he evidently coupled Alexander's visit with that of Leonnatus the previous evening, which is certainly historical, since it was mentioned in several primary sources. The use of the term 'Mother' in addressing Sisygambis (repeated in Diodorus 17.37.6, hence clearly deriving from Cleitarchus) also reeks of authenticity. This is because we know (e.g. Arrian, Anabasis 1.23.8) that Alexander had previously adopted Ada, Queen of Caria, as a surrogate mother, so it fits a consistent profile of behaviour that Alexander should have accorded the same honour to the Persian Queen-Mother. Furthermore, there is no obvious motive for distortion or invention in the context of this incident and it would be surprising if Alexander had not interviewed the Persian ladies in person shortly after their capture. Finally, there are other instances where Alexander treats Hephaistion as a second self, such as allowing him to read private correspondence and extinguishing the temple fires for his funeral. It would therefore seem highly probable that this audience genuinely occurred and that the quotation of Alexander is virtually verbatim, so we should be grateful to Cleitarchus for having preserved this glimpse of Alexander exuding a degree of grace and charm.

In the aftermath of Issus, Darius was quick to press his suit for the restitution of his family. His messengers reached Alexander in northern Lebanon:-

While Alexander was still at Marathus, envoys reached him from Darius, bringing a letter from him; they were themselves to plead by word for the release to Darius of his mother, wife and children... The letter argued as follows... as a king [Darius] begged a king to restore his captive mother, wife and children.

Arrian, Anabasis 2.14

Curtius 4.1.7 asserts that Alexander was irritated by the haughty and imperious tone of these representations and felt moved to respond in kind by challenging the Great King to come to beg for the release of his family as a suppliant. Diplomacy had got off to a shakey start, but the upshot was that Darius was pressured into adopting a more conciliatory tone. Some six months later as the siege of Tyre drew to its inexorable conclusion a far more pragmatic and relatively diplomatic offer reached Alexander. The heart of the deal was to be the hand of Darius' daughter, Stateira, in marriage.

It was about this time that a letter arrived from Darius finally addressing Alexander as "Your Majesty". Darius requested that Alexander should take his daughter, named Stateira, as his wife, saying that all the land between the Hellespont and the river Halys would be her dowry...

Curtius 4.5.1

Arrian, Anabasis 2.25.1 gives a similar account of the second letter, but he identifies the Euphrates as the prospective new frontier, which would make more sense, since the Halys was in Asia Minor and would have required that Alexander perform an embarrassing retreat from territory he already controlled. The offer itself did prove rather embarrassing to Alexander, since it was generous enough to split opinion among his staff. In particular, Parmenion, his veteran deputy, counselled acceptance, eliciting the famous quip from the King, that he too would have accepted, had he been Parmenion.

The wife (who was evidently also the sister) of Darius, also named Stateira according to Plutarch, died in childbirth (as Plutarch says) or of exhaustion from the rigours of travel (according to Curtius) some time not long before the battle of Gaugamela (Figure 8.2).[328] Possibly, this was actually within nine

---

[328] Plutarch 30; Curtius 4.10.18-34; cf. Arrian 4.20.1-3.

months of the capture of the Persian royal family at Issus, since all sources are clear that Alexander did not allow the Persian women to be molested. However, Curtius places her expiry immediately prior to Gaugamela, in which case the queen may secretly have conducted some kind of illicit liaison with an unknown adulterer. A eunuch named Tyriotes (Curtius) or Teirios (Plutarch) escaped from Alexander's camp and conveyed the news of her death to Darius, who initially supposed his wife to have been impregnated by Alexander. However, the eunuch was adamant that she had instead received exemplary treatment from the king. Darius was eventually convinced and declared to his retinue that, should fate prove committed to bringing about his downfall, then he prayed that none but the noble Alexander should occupy the throne of Persia.

Mary Renault (Nature of Alexander, p.98-9) has noticed that Alexander's treatment of Stateira echoes the treatment of Pantheia, the "Lady of Susa" and wife of Abradatas, by Cyrus in Xenophon's Cyropaidia 5.1.2-18. Xenophon's Great King refuses to sleep with her or even to look upon her for fear of being seduced into ignoble behaviour by her beauty. Still more tellingly, Cyrus subsequently colludes with Pantheia in coaxing the submission of her husband to his rule in exchange for reuniting Abradatas with his wife (Cyropaidia 6.1.45-49). Thereafter, Abradatas becomes a valuable lieutenant of Cyrus. Similarly, Alexander appears to have fostered the intention of preserving the wife of Darius from abuse and employing her and the other captured members of the Great King's family to coax Darius into submission to his rule. In fact, according to Arrian, this plan was explicitly stated by Alexander in his first letter replying to Darius's request for the release of his family after their capture at Issus:

"You must then regard me as Lord of Asia and come to me. If you fear that by coming you may receive some harm at my hands, send some of your friends to receive pledges. Ask for your mother, wife and children and what you will, when you have come, and you will receive them. You shall have whatever you persuade me to give."

Excerpt from Alexander's letter to Darius, Arrian, *Anabasis* 2.14.8

Unfortunately, Alexander's ambition to engineer a real-life re-enactment of the tearful reunion of a captured lady with her lord from one of his favourite works of literature was cruelly thwarted by the untimely death of Stateira. Nothing daunted, however, Alexander simply took advantage of a subsequent opportunity to indulge his chivalrous bent, as is reported by Curtius 6.2.5-8 shortly after Darius' death:

Alexander was not satisfied by the swarm of artists that he had gathered from Greece, since captive women were bidden to sing songs in the vernacular fashion that were dissonant and repellent to the ears of their visitors. Among them the king himself caught sight of one who seemed sadder than the rest in ashamedly resisting those who looked to lead her forward. She cut a fine figure that was accentuated by her bashfulness. Her eyes were downcast and her visage veiled inasmuch as was allowed, causing the king to sense that she was of too refined a pedigree to be exhibited amongst the entertainments in the revelry. Therefore she was asked about her ancestry and she said that she was the granddaughter of Ochus, sometime sovereign of Persia. His son had fathered her and Hystaspes had been her husband, who was a kinsman of Darius and had himself led a large army. The king still retained in his mind some modicum of his former morality. Thus out of respect for the lady's royal roots and so celebrated an ancestor as Ochus, he not only released her from captivity, but also bade that her fortune be refunded and even that her husband should be sought, so that the king might hand his wife to him when he was brought.

Figure 8.2. The death of the wife of Darius (1696)

The Persian royal ladies were deposited at Susa at the end of 331BC in the aftermath of Gaugamela according to both Diodorus and Curtius:-

Alexander's Lovers by Andrew Chugg

After this Alexander left Darius' mother, his daughters and his son in Susa, providing them with persons to teach them the Greek language…

Diodorus 17.67.1

If Darius' daughters were to be taught to speak Greek, then presumably Alexander was concerned to ensure their marriageability to Greek speaking husbands. If so, then an education in Greek customs might well have seemed equally appropriate, which tends to bolster the credibility of the associated story given by Curtius:-

Alexander also left the mother and children of Darius in the city of Susa. And it chanced that the king had been sent a present of Macedonian clothing and a great deal of purple material from Macedon together with those women whose work they were. He bade that these be entrusted to Sisygambis, for he lavished every honour upon her and even dealt her the devotion due from a son. And he bade that she should be made aware that, if the clothing met with her approbation, she might have her granddaughters familiarised with its production and he had lent her ladies who could give instruction. But the welling up at these words of her tears exposed that her spirit spurned such a presentation, since there is nothing that Persian ladies consider more humiliating than to have to set their hands to sewing. Those that had presented the gifts reported Sisygambis' distress and it appeared proper to express regret and proffer solace. Therefore Alexander visited her in person and explained: "Mother, in these garments that form my dress you behold not merely a gift from my sisters but also work of their own creation. Thus I have been misled by the practices of my nation. I implore you to be careful not to interpret my ignorance as insolence. Wherever I have been aware of your customs, I have, I hope, observed them with diligence. I know, for instance, that amongst you it is forbidden for a son to be seated within sight of his mother unless she has sanctioned it. Hence on each visit to you I have held back until you have gestured that I might sit. Though you have repeatedly wished to do me homage through proskynesis, I have not allowed you to do this. And I apply to you the title due to Olympias as my most darling mother."

Curtius 5.2.17

There are already strong hints in this passage that Alexander intended ultimately to link Darius' family with his own. It had after all been a notably successful political tactic of his father, Philip, to take a fresh wife from among the royalty of most of the nations he had vanquished in order to help in securing their loyalty.

Alexander left Susa around the end of December 331BC. He was engaged in conquering Bactria, Sogdiana and India for about six years. During this period nothing is heard of the Persian royal women. However, the King emerged from the searing cauldron of the Gedrosian desert with his exhausted army at the end of 325BC and he had reached Persia by the spring of 324BC. By this time he had conceived a firm plan to link himself and his senior courtiers with the Persian royal family and their aristocracy through the tight bonds of matrimony. It was, therefore, upon Alexander's eventual return to Susa in the summer of 324BC that the princesses re-entered history in the context of their sumptuous nuptials. That they were fated to be brutally murdered barely a year later casts a chill shadow over the splendour of the proceedings.

Alexander's decision to marry Darius' daughter, Stateira was clearly principally motivated by political considerations, particularly the pressing need to reconcile the Persian and Macedonian hierarchies in order to stabilise and unify the new empire. This is fairly explicitly stated as one of Alexander's objectives in his Last Plans (Diodorus 18.4.4): *to found cosmopolitan cities and expatriate populations out of Asia into Europe and contrariwise out of Europe into Asia, so as to lead the largest landmasses into loving kinship and communality through intermarriage and consanguinity.* The lost primary sources must have spelt out the political motivation, for Plutarch repeated it as fact in his Moralia:-

But Stateira, the daughter of Darius, [Alexander] married for imperial and political reasons, since the union of the two races was highly advantageous.

Plutarch, Moralia 338D

The political *entente* is even more explicit in the decision to wed nearly a hundred of Alexander's most senior officers and companions to daughters of the Persian aristocracy on the same occasion. Furthermore, Arrian mentions a statement by Aristobulus that Alexander also married a daughter of Artaxerxes III Ochus, who was a predecessor of Darius on the Persian throne. It seems the mood of reconciliation extended to the former Persian royal house, which may still have headed a powerful Persian faction:-

He also held weddings at Susa [in 324BC] for himself and for the Companions; he himself married Darius' eldest daughter Barsine, and, as Aristobulus says, another wife as well, Parysatis, the youngest daughter of Ochus… To Hephaistion he gave Drypetis, another daughter of Darius, sister to his own wife (for he desired Hephaistion's children to be cousins of his own).

Arrian, Anabasis 7.4.4-8

Barsine means Stateira in this passage. This may be a simple mistake by Arrian or his source (probably Aristobulus), but another possibility is that some Persian appellations, though treated as names by the Greeks, were actually royal titles or honorifics. Parysatis shares that name with an earlier Achaemenid princess, the illegitimate daughter of Artaxerxes I who reigned in the late 5th century BC. She was the mother of Cyrus the Younger, for whom Xenophon fought. Her story is mainly sourced from Plutarch's *Life of Artaxerxes*. There is also an outside chance that either Arrian's text or the manuscript of Aristobulus that he was using was corrupted regarding the name of Ochus' daughter, because *parasatto* means "to stuff or cram in beside" in Greek.

Hephaistion's union with Drypetis is a particularly clear illustration of the secondary motivation for the marriages: specifically, Alexander's desire to reward and honour his closest supporters and simultaneously to bind them ever more closely to his regime.

Alexander's Lovers by Andrew Chugg

Precisely accurate details of the festivities have fortunately been preserved for us by Athenaeus, who provides an extensive quotation from Chares, Alexander's Chamberlain. This man is a particularly credible source on this subject, since he is likely to have been closely embroiled in the organisation and performance of the ceremonies. Performance is an apt term, for this was evidently one of the greatest set pieces of political theatre in Alexander's reign:-

Chares in the tenth book of his Histories of Alexander says: "When he overcame Darius he concluded marriages of himself and of his friends besides, constructing 92 bridal chambers in the same place. The structure was large enough for 100 couches, and in it every couch was adorned with nuptial coverings, and was made of silver worth twenty minae; but his own couch had supports of gold. He also included in his invitation to the banquet all his personal friends and placed them on couches opposite himself and the other bridegrooms, while the rest of his forces, both land and naval, he entertained in the courtyard with the foreign embassies and tourists. Moreover the structure was decorated sumptuously and magnificently with expensive draperies and fine linen, and underfoot with purple and crimson rugs interwoven with gold. To keep the pavilion firmly in place there were columns thirty feet high, gilded and silvered and studded with jewels. The entire enclosure was surrounded with rich curtains having animal patterns interwoven in gold, their rods being overlaid with gold and silver. The perimeter of the courtyard measured 4 stadia [half a mile]. The call to dinner was sounded on the trumpet, not only at the time of the nuptial banquets, but always when on other occasions he chanced to be making libation, so that the entire army knew what was going on. The nuptials lasted for five days and very many persons, foreigners as well as Greeks, contributed their services; for example, the jugglers from India were especially noteworthy; also Scymnus of Tarentum, Philistides of Syracuse, and Heracleitus of Mytilene; after them the rhapsode Alexais of Tarentum gave a recital. There appeared also the harp-virtuosi Cratinus of Methymna, Aristonymus of Athens, Athenodorus of Teos; there were songs with harp accompaniment by Heracleitus of Tarentum and Aristocrates of Thebes. The singers to flute-accompaniment who appeared were Dionysus of Heracleia and Hyperbolus of Cyzicus; there came on also flute-virtuosi, who first played the Pythian melody and after that accompaniments for the bands of singers and dancers; they were Timotheus, Phrynichus, Caphisias, Diophantus, and Evius of Chalcis. And from that day forth the people who had previously been called 'Dionysus-flatterers' were called 'Alexander-flatterers' because of the extravagant presents in which Alexander took such delight. Plays were acted by the tragedians Thessalus, Athenodorus, and Aristocritus, and by the comedians Lycon, Phormion, and Ariston. There was present also the harper Phasimelus. The crowns (Chares says) brought by the ambassadors and others were worth 15,000 talents."   Athenaeus 12.538b-539a

Aelian (Varia Historia 8.7) has a very similar account, which may well itself be derived from Athenaeus' excerpt from Chares, but Plutarch provides various additional details in both the Moralia and his Life of Alexander:-

But I think I would gladly have been a witness of that fair and holy marriage-rite, when [Alexander] brought together in one golden-canopied tent 100 Persian brides and 100 Macedonian and Greek bridegrooms, united at a common hearth and board. He himself, crowned with garlands, was the first to raise the marriage hymn as though he were singing a

Stateira & Parysatis

song of truest friendship over the union of the two greatest and most mighty peoples; for he, of one maid the bridegroom, and at the same time of all the brides an escort, as a father and sponsor united them in the bonds of wedlock.

Plutarch, Moralia 329e

At Susa he brought to pass the marriage of his companions, took to wife himself the daughter of Darius, Stateira, assigned the noblest women to his noblest men, and gave a general wedding feast for those of his Macedonians who had already contracted other marriages. At this feast, we are told, 9000 guests reclined at supper, to each of whom a golden cup for the libations was given. All the other appointments too were amazingly splendid, and the host paid himself the debts, which his guests owed, the whole outlay amounting to 9870 talents.

Plutarch, Life of Alexander 70.2

Figure 8.3. The Susa marriages (late 19th century engraving after Andreas Müller)

The sum quoted by Plutarch is very specific and presumably derives from a primary source (probably Cleitarchus in view of the matching sum in Curtius 10.2.11). It equates to around 25 tonnes of gold. It is fashionable to heap scepticism upon such figures, but in this instance it is no more than commensurate with Alexander's wealth and reputed largesse. The enormous scale and opulence of the proceedings might easily account for such vast expenses, but they seem in fact to be linked to reports that many of Alexander's crack troops had got themselves hopelessly mired in debt at this time, debts which the king found it expedient to clear (Curtius 10.2.9-11, Diodorus 17.109.2, Arrian 7.12.1, Justin 12.11.2-3). Nineteenth century reconstructions of the Susa marriages, largely based on these accounts, are shown in Figures 8.3 &

8.4. Hephaistion and Drypetis may be identified, seated to Alexander's right in the former.

There are several further brief references to the Susa marriages from the other ancient historians of Alexander. Justin suggests that the weddings of Alexander's Companions were intended to dilute criticism of Alexander's own marriage:-

After [executing corrupt governors Alexander] married Darius' daughter Stateira; at the same time he presented to the Macedonian noblemen unmarried girls selected from the best families amongst all the conquered peoples, so that any recrimination against the king might be lessened by their complicity in his action. Justin 12.10.9-10

However, Justin is simply projecting Roman Republican sensibilities onto an inappropriate context. Alexander's father, Philip, had regularly taken brides from subject peoples[329]: it was an established Macedonian royal prerogative and should not have given rise to any serious criticism.

Neither it appears was the policy new in 324BC: Alexander had apparently also arranged marriages to local girls for his companions when he had married Roxane a few years earlier (early 327BC). Although this is only mentioned in the obscure contexts of the Metz Epitome and the surviving Contents List for a lost section of Book 17 of Diodorus, the fact that it occurs in both places shows that it must have been recorded in the lost *History Concerning Alexander* by Cleitarchus, which was written in the early 3rd century BC:

Chorienes convened a banquet and introduced his own maiden daughters as well as those of his friends as dancers at the dinner. The most remarkably radiant among them was Roxane the daughter of Oxyartes. Enraptured at the sight of her and filled with desire, Alexander asked who she was and who her father was. On discovering that she was the daughter of Oxyartes, also a diner at the dinner, the king took up his cup and tipped a libation to the gods, then began to declaim: "Much that befalls many men and women commonly occurs against expectations. Thus countless kings have sired sons on women won in war or dispatched daughters to distant domains to seal an alliance with wedlock." Then the king focused upon the foreigners: "In my view the Macedonians are not a better breed than you and nor, even if you would come into alliance with us as losers, do I believe you to be unworthy of intermarriage with us. I am going to make such [a union] myself and I shall have a care that the other Macedonians do the same also." He himself having exhorted his Friends with these words, each of them led away a virgin that he wedded at the banquet. Oxyartes and the rest of the foreigners were happy beyond their hopes for this to happen. Metz Epitome 28-31

How Alexander, enamoured of Roxane, daughter of Oxyartes, married her and persuaded numbers of his friends to marry the daughters of the prominent Barbarians.

Contents List for a lost Section of Book 17 of Diodorus

---

[329] Nicholas Hammond, *Philip of Macedon* (London, 1994), p. 171.

Stateira & Parysatis

Diodorus implies that a certain amount of arm-twisting and bribery may have been involved in persuading some of the Companions to take on Persian spouses at Susa (as perhaps also in Bactria). There is some evidence that many of the Companions abandoned their "barbarian" wives soon after Alexander's death (although a few, such as Seleucus, maintained these unions and used them to father heirs of mixed race for regions of Alexander's empire):-

> *[Alexander] then proceeded to Susa, where he married Stateira, the eldest daughter of Darius, and gave her younger sister Drypetis as wife to Hephaistion. He prevailed upon the most prominent of his Friends to take wives also, and gave them in marriage to the noblest Persian ladies.*
> Diodorus 17.107.6

Figure 8.4. The Susa marriages (by André Castaigne 1899)

Curtius (whose main account of the Susa marriages is lost in a lacuna) makes Alexander express his motivation for the marriages in the context of an address to his foreign troops following the subsequent mutiny at Opis. He does so in terms of the unification of the Macedonian and Persian peoples, knowing that his Roman patrician readership would regard such a policy as dangerous, threatening and wild. The attributed motive is probably accurate (it may well be sourced from Cleitarchus) and reaction to it would have been more mixed among Alexander's followers at the time. A modern perspective would probably be sympathetic to Alexander's objective of interracial harmony in this regard.

> *"Later on when I wished to extend my bloodline further, I took Darius' daughter as a wife and saw to it that my closest friends had children by our captives, my intention being that by this sacred union I might erase all distinction between conquered and conqueror..."*
> Speech attributed to Alexander by Curtius 10.3.12

We hear nothing more of the Persian queens until the aftermath of Alexander's untimely demise a year later. Perhaps this is because they continued to reside at Susa, whilst the court moved about with the king to Opis, Ecbatana and Babylon. In the light of subsequent events, it would hardly be surprising if Alexander had operated a conscious policy of keeping his Bactrian and Persian wives geographically separated. Furthermore, Plutarch implies that the queens were not at Babylon when Alexander expired and Curtius speaks of the disastrous tidings reaching Sisygambis and her granddaughters in the context of their dissemination beyond Babylon:-

And the lamentation was not confined within the walls of the city, since such terrible tidings had irrupted into the region round about and thence percolated through a prodigious part of Asia on the near side of the Euphrates. Word rapidly reached the mother of Darius too, who was dolorous over Alexander's demise. Therefore she ripped away her raiment, replacing it with garments for grieving, tearing her tresses and flinging herself to the floor. Settled with her was the second of her granddaughters, but lately bereaved of Hephaistion, whom having married she now mourned, so that the communal despondency accentuated her personal pain. But solely Sisygambis herself suffered for the injuries to her entire kindred: she wept in turn for the ills that had befallen her and her granddaughters. And these fresh frets evoked the pining of the past. You might have thought the woebegone woman had just lost Darius and was about to conduct the last rites for two of her own sons: she wept for both the dead and the living. Who now would be the guardian of her girls? Who would be the Alexander of tomorrow? They were prisoners once more and robbed of their royal rank all over again. After Darius had died, they had discovered a defender, but in the aftermath of Alexander it was clear that none could be found to care for them. In this context she was conscious that her eighty brothers had been slain in a single day by that most savage sovereign, Ochus, and that the felling of their father had augmented the massacre of so many sons. Of the offspring that she herself had borne, but a single one of seven survived. Darius himself had prospered for a little while, merely that he could meet with a more pitiless passing. So, ultimately, Sisygambis succumbed to sorrow. Veiling her head and turning away from her granddaughter and grandson, who sank down in supplication at her knees, she spurned both sustenance and sunlight and she was deceased five days after determining to die. Assuredly her death is tremendous testimony for the tenderness of Alexander towards her and for his virtuous treatment of all those taken in his wars: for she, who allowed herself to live beyond Darius, was ashamed to outlive Alexander.

Curtius 10.5.19[330]

The suicide of Sisygambis is among the most startling testaments to the potency of Alexander's charisma. It would seem that even some of his erstwhile enemies came ultimately to cherish him. Machiavelli says that ideally a prince should be both loved and feared[331] and Alexander is surely the consummate paragon of this philosophy of double-edged leadership.

---

[330] C.f. Diodorus, 17.118.3; Justin, 13.1.
[331] Niccolo Machiavelli, *The Prince*, 17.

Stateira & Parysatis

With both their husbands and their grandmother dead, Stateira and Drypetis found themselves bereft of protection and exposed to the vengeance of their enemies. Their principal antagonist soon struck. It would appear that Roxane made a pact with Perdiccas, whereby she traded her support of his regency for the foul murder of her rivals:-

Now, Roxane was with child, and on this account was held in honour among the Macedonians; but she was jealous of Stateira, and therefore deceived her by a forged letter into coming where she was, and when she had got there, slew her, together with her sister, threw their bodies into the well, and filled the well with earth, Perdiccas being privy to the deed and a partner in it.

Plutarch, Life of Alexander 77.4

9. Epilogue

The Fate of the Family

In the aftermath of Alexander's death the surviving members of his family were prominent among the victims of the protracted series of civil wars between his generals and successors. As has been related, his wife Stateira was an immediate casualty on the orders of Queen Roxane. Next in order Alexander's half-sister Cynane was slain by Perdiccas' brother Alcetas in 322BC. Then Alexander's half-brother Philip-Arrhidaeus and his wife Adea-Eurydice, Cynane's daughter, were executed by Olympias in 317BC, whilst Cassander contrived for Olympias herself to be stoned to death by the families of her victims barely a year later. Glaucias foully murdered Roxane and Alexander's thirteen-year-old son, Alexander IV, at Cassander's instigation in 310BC. Before another year was spent Alexander's other, illegitimate son, Heracles, last scion of his loins, had been strangled at the treacherous hands of Polyperchon. Following the perfidious murders of her nephews, Alexander's sister, Cleopatra, suddenly found herself almost the last survivor of the Temenid dynasty. Having been courted by almost all the Macedonian generalissimos for the sake of her symbolic power, she spurned the rest and sought the salvation of the Temenid line in a marriage with Ptolemy. However, her home in Sardis lay within the sphere of influence of Antigonus, who had become Ptolemy's fierce antagonist in the Wars of the Successors. Discovering her plans, he secretly arranged for her assassination by a female death squad.[332] Thus by 308BC, fifteen years after Alexander's demise, the legitimate and direct Temenid line had almost been extirpated.

There were, however, several prominent and interesting survivors. Another of the wives of Philip II, Nicesipolis, bore him a daughter named Thessalonike. In a deft political move, Cassander married this half-sister of Alexander after capturing her at Pydna. Their progeny, three sons, were all future kings of Macedon.[333] Furthermore, Alexander's sister Cleopatra had seemingly borne a son, Neoptolemus, and a daughter, Cadmeia, to Alexander of Epirus, the brother of Alexander the Great's mother, Olympias. They were thus simultaneously Alexander's cousins and his nephew and niece. Neoptolemus became king of Epirus after his father's death, but was killed by Pyrrhus in 297BC. Of Cadmeia little is known.[334]

Furthermore, there is a significant possibility that Ptolemy was Alexander's illegitimate half-brother. At any rate, the rumour that Philip had conducted a

---

[332] Diodorus 20.37.3-6.
[333] N.G.L. Hammond, The Miracle that was Macedon, London, 1991, p. 91.
[334] Plutarch, Life of Pyrrhus, 5; N.G.L. Hammond, Epirus, Oxford, 1967, p.558.

Epilogue

sexual liaison with Ptolemy's mother, prior to marrying her off to Lagus (after she had become pregnant), is cited by Pausanias, Curtius and the Armenian Alexander Romance.[335] If it is true, then even that most renowned Cleopatra, the seventh Egyptian Queen of the name, successively the spouse of Julius Caesar and Mark Antony, even she may have been a distant relative of Alexander. Perhaps that helps to explain why she named one of her sons after him and strove indefatigably to re-create his empire.

The Destiny of the Domains

It is misleading to suggest, as some have, that Alexander's Empire disintegrated after his death. In fact, even the Indian provinces remained under Macedonian control until twenty years after his passing. Coin evidence shows that Macedonian dynasties held sway in Bactria for several centuries. The generalissimos in the west continued nominally to act as vassals of a central Temenid monarchy until some years after the royal line had actually ceased to exist. Only in 305BC did Antigonus and Demetrius feel strong enough to declare themselves kings in their own right. By the third decade of the third century BC three great Macedonian houses had achieved pre-eminence, a situation that was to persist until the triumph of Rome. These were the Antigonids in Macedonia itself, the Seleucids in Syria and Mesopotamia and the Ptolemies in Egypt, Palestine and the Islands. However, these dynasties frequently intermarried and shared a common social and cultural identity. It is therefore debatable whether Alexander's Empire truly fractured or merely acquired several interlinked nodes of control and became what we call the Hellenistic world. That world, which brought about an effusion of ancient art and science and ascended to a cultural peak unsurpassed until relatively modern times, was Alexander's principal legacy.

An Everlasting Fame

In the course of his tragically curtailed life Alexander consciously pursued and won a glamorous fame, which has shone brightly through the intervening millennia and which promises him a kind of immortality of memory. Nevertheless, his reputation has always been dogged by controversy, though curiously for different reasons in different eras. He divided Roman opinion, because he seemed to represent an exemplar of monarchy, which was detestable to the supporters of the Roman Republic, but a propaganda gift to the imperialist Caesars.

Today some accuse him of megalomania, because of his pursuit of divine honours and his claim to be descended from the gods. Yet in the former case he

---

[335] Pausanias 1.6.2; Curtius 9.8.22; Armenian Alexander Romance (trans. Wolohojian), Section 269; Aelian in the Suda, sv. *Lagos*, and Plutarch, Moralia 458A-B say Ptolemy was illegitimate.

was merely pursuing his emulation of Achilles to its logical conclusion and in the latter he was simply asserting a widely accepted ancestry long claimed by his family. In Greek religion it was not a heresy but rather a tenet of faith that mortals might achieve divinity through supernatural acts of prowess. The legend of the Dioscuri (the Heavenly Twins, Castor & Pollux) would be a classic case in point. Alexander's contemporaries only questioned whether his deeds and accomplishments were sufficiently supernatural as to attain divinity. Their eventual answer was that from soon after his death and for many centuries thereafter he was widely worshipped in perfect sincerity as a god, most especially in Egypt.

Alexander is sometimes condemned for causing widespread death and destruction among his most fanatical opponents in India. Yet we still have no better answer to fanatical enemies in our own age. Fanatics continue to seek the destruction of themselves and other people rather than relent on any aspect of their dogmatism in our own day just as much as in his. It is certainly true that Alexander became the nemesis of many treacherous and fanatical people, but on the other hand he usually sought to befriend defeated enemies who behaved chivalrously and kept faith with him. Certainly, Alexander was the antithesis of pacifism, but who can afford the luxury of turning the other cheek when confronted by fanaticism?

Furthermore, there is clear evidence that Alexander saved many lives that would otherwise have been lost in the continual local warfare that was a feature of the era: it is specifically stated in Diodorus 17.113.3-4 that Alexander *heard embassies from those who had disputes with their neighbours* and *sent everyone away content, so far as he was able.*

By modern standards the range of Alexander's sleeping partners may seem exotic, because it encompassed men, women and a eunuch. But the modern perspective has been modulated and moulded by the rise of the monotheistic and ascetic religions, which have taught that procreation is the only morally acceptable purpose of sex. This kind of theology scarcely existed in Alexander's time. Instead, using myths such as the relationship between Zeus and Ganymede, Greek religion encouraged liaisons between men and youths as a way of preserving society from the twin curses of illegitimate offspring and violated brides. Ironically, in his own time Alexander was considered a model of sexual propriety and restraint, especially in comparison with his rapacious father. The only reason some of his relationships were frowned upon by some of his contemporaries was because they were with foreigners.

In the final analysis, perhaps, the main reason that Alexander has remained an especially controversial figure is that he has continued to be extraordinarily renowned. Contentiousness appears to go with the territory of fame. According to Plutarch (Moralia 181F), when Alexander himself was told that someone was speaking ill of him, he responded, "It is kingly to be maligned for doing good."

Appendix A: The Nature of Alexander's Divinity

Introduction

Despite W. W. Tarn's tendentious and legalistic attempts back in the 1940's to defend Alexander from charges of having arranged his own apotheosis,[336] the evidence is compelling that Alexander was at least complicit in his assumption of some species of divinity in his lifetime and that he sought to encourage his post-mortem divinisation by ordering that his corpse be conveyed "to Ammon" in Egypt.[337] Yet Tarn was not only mistaken in trying to litigate away the very extensive evidence for Alexander's filial relationship with Zeus, but the actual terms in which Tarn viewed the issue are so far from the reality as to amount to a perversion of history. For Tarn regarded it as axiomatic that if Alexander did pursue any form of divinity, then this was necessarily and by definition a wicked policy. Indeed, it would be hard to demonstrate that anyone since has strenuously objected to that implicit axiom. Thus we have a revised situation today where Alexander's complicity in his apotheosis is less doubted, but is just as much cited as a reason to condemn him. It is the purpose of this account to reveal unrecognised strands of evidence, which characterise the nuances of what actually happened more clearly than before, whilst also demonstrating that the morality of the matter is far more equivocal than has been supposed. This was particularly the case given the context of ancient hedonistic polytheism, which contrasts so radically with the modern ideal of monotheistic asceticism.

A. B. Bosworth provided more astute analyses than Tarn's concerning Alexander's divinity in the 1970's and 80's.[338] In his article on "Alexander and Ammon" he concludes by referring to the oracles that Alexander received in early 331BC from Siwa, Miletus and Erythrae:

"In the winter and spring of 331 Alexander had impressive and authoritative testimony that he was the son of Zeus. His conviction of divine sonship, however, predated these oracles and in the case of Miletus at least, gave rise to them. The models for his claim were Heracles and Perseus. There is no hint that it was his Pharaonic titulature, son of Amon-Re, that engendered the idea of divine filiation. Alexander's concept seems to have originated in Greek mythology, and in particular the peculiar status of heroes like Heracles, blessed with both divine and human fathers, seems to have afforded the basis for

---

[336] W. W. Tarn, Alexander the Great, Vol II, Sources & Studies, 1948, pp.347-373.
[337] Curtius 10.5.4; Diodorus 18.3.5 & 18.28.2-3; Justin 12.15.7; Metz Epitome 119; Lucian, *Dialogues of the Dead* 13.
[338] Bosworth, A. B., "Alexander and Ammon", Greece and the Eastern Mediterranean in Ancient History and Prehistory, ed. K. H. Kinzl, Berlin 1977; Bosworth, A. B., Conquest & Empire, Cambridge 1988, Appendix D, The Divinity of Alexander.

Alexander's own claims. It is therefore in the Hellenic world that we should look for their origins."

I would hardly disagree with any of this.[339] In fact it is quite insightful. Yet it is also adduced on rather tentative evidence – principally a far from incontrovertible argument that the oracles from Asia Minor were independent of that from Siwa and must therefore have been inspired by public knowledge of Alexander's desires. Bosworth also fails fully to explain exactly where Alexander found the origins of his ideas on his divinisation "in the Hellenic world". Yet this is a point of acute interest, because it should be expected to relate closely to his overall motives and inspiration in the conduct of his campaigns. It is the purpose of this account to air a new argument from various other strands of evidence, which firstly confirms that Alexander's policy on his deification was known from at least the beginning of his reign, and secondly uncovers the origins of that policy in Greek literary and legendary precedents. Finally, I will reveal exactly how the policy was implemented during Alexander's lifetime.

Analysis

A suitable point with which to begin is a statement attributed to Alexander himself that has long been interpreted as a compliment for the philosophy of the Cynics, but which could equally have been intended as an indication of the type of pseudo-religious veneration of his person that Alexander wished to inspire. The context was Alexander's meeting with the Cynic philosopher Diogenes of Sinope in Corinth during the session of the Council of the Hellenic League just after the fall of Thebes in 335BC as is related by Plutarch in Chapter 14 of his *Life of Alexander*.

And now a general assembly of the Greeks was held at the Isthmus, where a vote was passed to make an expedition against Persia with Alexander, and he was proclaimed their leader. Thereupon many statesmen and philosophers came to him with their congratulations, and he expected that Diogenes of Sinope also, who was tarrying in Corinth, would do likewise. But since that philosopher took not the slightest notice of Alexander, and continued to enjoy his leisure in the suburb Craneion, Alexander went in person to see him; and he found him lying in the sun. Diogenes raised himself up a little when he saw so many persons coming towards him, and fixed his eyes upon Alexander. And when that monarch addressed him with greetings, and asked if he wanted anything, 'Yes,' said Diogenes, 'stand a little out of my sun.' It is said that Alexander was so struck by this, and admired so much the haughtiness and hauteur of the man who had nothing but scorn for him, that he said to his followers, who were laughing and jesting about the philosopher as they went away, 'But verily, if I were not Alexander, I would be Diogenes.'

---

[339] Curtius 4.7.8 agrees that Alexander's purpose in visiting Siwa was driven by his belief that his creation was attributable to Zeus.

Appendix A: The Nature of Alexander's Divinity

The spin that Plutarch puts on this quotation is transparent: Alexander spoke out of admiration for Diogenes. But there is also a secondary meaning that should be unmistakeable for anyone familiar with the works of Homer. Alexander himself ranks high among the latter, for he kept a copy of the Iliad beside his bed throughout his campaigns, eventually ensconced in Darius's finest casket, and Dio Chrysostom says he knew the work by heart.[340] Of course *Diogenes* is a perfectly familiar Greek name, just as "Smith", or "Tailor" or "Baker" or "King" are familiar English names, despite also being professions or titles. However, in Homer *Diogenes* is used as the epithet of several of the Greek heroes. In this context, the term retains its literal meaning of "sprung from Zeus" or more emphatically "Zeus-born".[341] It is an epithet that Alexander must have coveted passionately, not only due to his fondness for Homer, but also because legend claimed that Alexander's ancestry on both his mother's and his father's side was ultimately traceable back to Zeus.[342] This tradition, incidentally, was why Zeus featured prominently on the coinage of ancient Macedon (usually enthroned on the reverses). Furthermore, insofar as Alexander was himself to fulfil his ambition of rivalling the fame of his ancestors Achilles and Heracles, he would have considered it highly desirable to attach such an epithet to his own name and have it publicly recognised.

It seems that Plutarch himself noticed this secondary meaning, for he actually drew attention to it in his other treatment of the subject in his Essay On The Fortune or Virtue of Alexander in *Moralia* 331E-332C:

Alexander... made Onesicritus, the pupil of Diogenes the Cynic, chief pilot of his fleet. But when he came to talk with Diogenes himself in Corinth, he was so awed and astounded with the life and the worth of the man that often, when remembrance of the philosopher came to him, he would say, 'If I were not Alexander, I should be Diogenes,' that is to say: 'If I did not actively practise philosophy, I should apply myself to its theoretical pursuit.' He did not say, 'If I were not a king, I should be Diogenes,' nor 'If I were not rich and an Argead'; for he did not rank Fortune above Wisdom, nor a crown and royal purple above the philosopher's wallet and threadbare gown. But he said, 'If I were not Alexander, I should be Diogenes'; that is to say: 'If it were not my purpose to combine foreign things with things Greek, to traverse and civilize every continent, to search out the uttermost parts of land and sea, to push the bounds of Macedonia to the farthest Ocean, and to disseminate and shower the blessings of Greek justice and peace over every nation, I should not be content to sit quietly in the luxury of idle power, but I should emulate the frugality of Diogenes. But as things are, forgive me, that I imitate Diogenes-Heracles, and Perseus, and follow in the footsteps of Dionysus,[343] the divine

---

[340] Strabo, *Geography* 13.1.27; Plutarch, *Alexander* 8.2; Dio Chrysostom, *4th Discourse on Kingship* 39.
[341] We have, for example, "diogenes Patrocles" (meaning Zeus-born Patrocles) in the Iliad 1.337 (and elsewhere) and also "diogenes, son of Laertes, Odysseus" at Iliad 2.173, 4.358...
[342] E.g. Plutarch, *Alexander* 2.1.
[343] The Loeb translator fails to realise that the use of the term Diogenes before the name of Heracles here is in its sense of an epithet as in Homer, but this is confirmed by the fact that Heracles, Perseus and Dionysus are all famously sons of Zeus.

author and progenitor of my family, and desire that victorious Greeks should dance again in India and revive the memory of the Bacchic revels among the savage mountain tribes beyond the Caucasus. Even there it is said that there are certain holy men, a law unto themselves, who follow a rigid gymnosophy and give all their time to God; they are more frugal than Diogenes since they have no need of a wallet. For they do not store up food, since they have it ever fresh and green from the earth; the flowing rivers give them drink and they have fallen leaves and grassy earth to lie upon. Because of me even those faraway sages shall come to know of Diogenes, and he of them. And I also, like Diogenes, must alter the standard of coinage and stamp foreign states with the impress of Greek government.'

That Plutarch also awards the epithet of *Diogenes* particularly to Heracles and Perseus (as authentic sons of Zeus) is the significant point, because Alexander's motive for visiting Siwa is very clearly explained as a desire to emulate these particular individuals amongst his putative heroic ancestors by Arrian, *Anabasis* 3.3.1-2 and also by Strabo 17.1.43 (citing Callisthenes, Alexander's court historian, as his source). Events suggest that Alexander specifically intended to seek evidence that he could qualify to use their same *Diogenes* epithet.

There are many further indications in the surviving evidence that *Diogenes* was the precise title under which Alexander himself claimed his oft-vaunted relationship with Zeus-Ammon.[344]

1. In Pseudo-Callisthenes 1.32.9, the author explains that the ancient Alexandrians named the five districts of their city (ΑΒΓΔΕ) from the first letters of the words in a short verse:

Ἀλεξάνδρος βασιλεύς γένος Δίος ἔκτισε πόλιν ἀείμνηστον

Which roughly translates: *Alexander the king, the Zeus-born, founded an ever-memorable city.* The order of *Dios* and *genos* is flipped relative to *Diogenes*, but the meaning is exactly the same. Since the Zeus-born epithet is used alongside Alexander's title as king, it is reasonable to infer that it had a similar official origin and status. The putative author/compiler of this source, who is mistakenly named as Callisthenes in some manuscripts (hence its attribution to "Pseudo-Callisthenes"), was very probably a citizen of Alexandria at the beginning of the 3rd century AD (or earlier), so he is an excellent source on the way that Alexander was remembered in the city that he had founded, as has also been asserted by P. M. Fraser.[345]

---

[344] There is evidence that some also emulated the priest at Siwa in flattering Alexander with the title of "Son of Ammon", e.g. Athenaeus 12.538B reports the dedication of a crown by Gorgus to Alexander as precisely the "Son of Ammon". But this was sourced from Ephippus, who was hostile to Alexander; this is why it is necessary carefully to distinguish between Alexander's own official usage of *Diogenes* and the less restrained antics of his flatterers.
[345] P. M. Fraser, Ptolemaic Alexandria, Vol. I, Oxford, 1972, p.4.

Appendix A: The Nature of Alexander's Divinity

2. Alexander's Callisthenes used the *Dios genos* terminology at least twice. Firstly, Strabo 17.1.43 in his account of Alexander's visit to Siwa (and related oracular pronouncements) quotes Callisthenes writing of Alexander as having sprung from Zeus (ἐκ Διὸς γενέσεως τοῦ Ἀλεξάνδρου). Secondly, Plutarch, *Alexander* 33.1 reproduced part of Alexander's speech to the Thessalians before Gaugamela as originally recorded by Callisthenes. In this address Alexander asks that if he is really sprung from Zeus (*Diothen esti gegonos*) that the Greeks should be protected and strengthened. Callisthenes' account was the official record of the campaign, which must have been read (probably prior to publication) by Alexander himself. The fact that two independent fragments of Callisthenes' lost record of the expedition essentially agree on the language that Alexander used to describe his relationship with Zeus strongly suggests that this is truly the official terminology of the regime. This language is precisely consistent with the actual official title being *Diogenes*.

3. Arrian too uses the *Dios genos* terminology to describe Alexander's relationship with Zeus in the context of his closing remarks at *Anabasis* 7.29.3:

I do not think that even his tracing his origin to a god was a great error on Alexander's part, if it was not perhaps merely a device to induce his subjects to show him reverence. Nor does he seem to me to have been a less renowned king than Minos, Aeacus, or Rhadamanthus, to whom no insolence is attributed by the men of old because they traced their origin to Zeus. Nor does he seem at all inferior to Theseus or Ion, the former being the reputed son of Poseidon, and the latter of Apollo.

The form of the Greek here is *Dia... genesis*. This shows that even Arrian, who was distinctly coy about the whole matter of Alexander's deification, recognised that genesis from Zeus was the standard terminology for Alexander's claim. Arrian does also use "Son of Ammon" at *Anabasis* 4.9.9, but this was in the specific context of the Siwa visit.[346] It seems likely that the priest at Siwa greeted Alexander as the son of Ammon-Re, as Plutarch relates in his *Life of Alexander* 27.5. *Sa Re* or "Son of the Sun" was a standard component of the pharaonic titulary; so such a greeting was probably stipulated by Egyptian etiquette. Alexander simply chose to translate this as *Diogenes* for official purposes, including Callisthenes' history of his campaigns and, as we shall see, at least one inscription.

4. Curtius 8.10.1 actually states that Alexander was described as a *Diogenes* by his subjects:

When Alexander entered within the bounds of India, he was met by the minor kings of the local nations, who acceded to his governance, recalling that he was the third Diogenes *who*

---

[346] See also Lucian, *Dialogues of the Dead* 12 (Philip & Alexander) and 13 (Diogenes & Alexander).

had reached their lands. They knew of reputed visits firstly of Dionysus and secondly of Heracles, but Alexander had actually manifested himself before their gaze.

The Latin of Curtius states that Alexander was greeted by the local kings in India as the *tertium Iove genitum* to visit their land, but it is virtually inescapable that this is a literal translation of "third *Diogenes*" in the Greek of Curtius' source. That source was very probably Cleitarchus, since the episode is echoed in Section 34 of the Metz Epitome, which is also demonstrably Cleitarchan in its source tradition.[347]

Elsewhere Curtius uses *Iovis stirpem* (6.10.27) meaning "Zeus ancestry" or *Iovis filium* (6.11.5, 6.11.23, 8.5.5, 8.8.14, 8.10.29) meaning "Son of Zeus", but all these usages might derive from the *Dios genos* terminology in the original Greek of Cleitarchus. The Greek term Diogenes literally means, "having a genesis from Zeus", but it was employed by the Greeks with a nuanced range of differing degrees of directness for the genesis process. In the case of Heracles, and even more so for Perseus and Dionysus, it literally means "Son of Zeus", but it could equally be used simply to mean "descended from Zeus" in the sense that someone among a person's ancestors had been a son or daughter of Zeus. The term is illustratively rendered in a broad spectrum of colourful ways by modern translators of Homer (Murray & Wyatt render it as "sprung from Zeus" or "Zeus-born" in the Loeb, whereas Lattimore variously uses "seed of Zeus" or even just simply "illustrious"). Of course, the directness of the relationship is absolutely key to judging how controversial Alexander's claims were at the time. *Diogenes* itself should really not have been particularly controversial in principle, because Alexander's family had always claimed descent from Zeus on both his father's and his mother's side. However, the matter of Alexander's adoption of Persian dress shows that his very conservative troops and the traditionalists among his officers and courtiers were easily outraged by tiny compromises relative to customary practise. Alexander seems simply to have worn the Persian Great King's purple tunic with a central white stripe and specifically omitted the trousers and the long-sleeved jacket, such that his apparel would still have looked entirely Greek to modern eyes. Nevertheless, the matter caused bitter and enduring resentment among his Macedonians.

5. There is one early confirmation that Alexander was actually called Diogenes that is statistically hard to gainsay. In his *Moralia* 717C, Plutarch asserts that Alexander the King and Diogenes the Cynic died on the same day. The identical story is given by Diogenes Laertius in his short biography of Diogenes of Sinope:

---

[347] The original source may have been Onesicritus, Alexander's chief pilot, whose account served as the principal source for Cleitarchus, at least for the period of the Indian campaigns.

Appendix A: The Nature of Alexander's Divinity

Demetrius in his work On Men of the Same Name *asserts that on the same day on which Alexander died in Babylon Diogenes died in Corinth. He was an old man in the 113th Olympiad.* Diogenes Laertius, Excerpt from Book VI, Chapter 2.79

There are about 10,000 days on which Diogenes might have died following his meeting with Alexander at Corinth in 335BC, so the chance that both of these prominent individuals expired on precisely the same day may be reckoned at about 1 in 10,000. Alternatively, Demetrius (or his source) had read that *Diogenes* (meaning Alexander) died on 10th June 323BC and wrongly assumed that Diogenes the Cynic was meant. This latter explanation is statistically far more probable, for such assumptions are very commonly made even in cases of lesser ambiguity (for example, the confusion between Oxathres and Oxyartes at Diodorus 20.109.7).

Although the extract from Diogenes Laertius is specific about Diogenes dying in Corinth, that does not avoid the point, because if Demetrius assumed that *Diogenes* was Diogenes the Cynic, then he would have known from other sources that he was based in Corinth and could easily have accreted that detail to the information from his source on the date of Diogenes' death (or the error could thus have been compounded by some still earlier source in the chain of transmission.) Diogenes Laertius also recorded that Diogenes the Cynic died aged "nearly 90", but the *Suda* says that he was born under the thirty tyrants (404BC), so he would only have been 81 in 323BC. Evidently somebody has made some kind of mistake about the death of Diogenes the Cynic. The use of *Diogenes* as an epithet for Alexander provides a single point resolution for the entire conundrum. It rescues us from otherwise having to believe in the gigantic coincidence of the greatest king and the second most prominent philosopher of the age (after Aristotle) having died within the same 24-hour period in Babylon and Corinth respectively, and also having to disbelieve the other evidence on Diogenes' age at his death.

6. Finally, there is inscription evidence for Alexander having been called *Diogenes* in his lifetime. This presents itself in the form of a votive relief dedicated to the hero Hephaistion, which was found at Pella and stylistically dates to the last quarter of the 4th century BC. It is of modest proportions (0.53m x 0.61m x 0.06m). The depiction is of libation scene (as shown in Figure 3.1). A young beardless man stands restraining his horse, for he has reached the end of a journey. He proffers a bowl into which a young woman, who greets him, is about to pour the wine of the libation (from her *oinochoe* which she holds in her right hand). Her left hand holds a small cylindrical vessel, a *libanotris* (censer), but their gazes do not meet. The man deliberately looks away from the woman, perhaps signifying the isolation of the dead soul. Most interestingly for our present analysis, the relief bears the following inscription at its lower margin:

ΔΙΟΓΕΝΗΣΗΦΑΙΣΤΙΩΝΙΗΡΩΙ

This translates: "To the hero Hephaistion from Diogenes". Now it has naively been supposed that this was the dedication of an ordinary individual named Diogenes, who had some unknown reason to be grateful to Hephaistion, Alexander's Chiliarch. However, it is an explicit matter of record that Alexander arranged for shrines dedicated "To the Hero Hephaistion" to be erected throughout the empire after the Hero's death[348] and Pella is a very likely location for one such establishment. The early Hellenistic date of this piece and its provenance are perfectly consistent with the foundation of such a shrine and if we were to venture to translate the supposed "name" of the commissioner of the sculpture in its inscription, we would get: "To the Hero Hephaistion from the Zeus-born." It is therefore far more cogent to infer that, in referring to Hephaistion by the title of Hero awarded to him by the Oracle of Ammon, the dedicator of this elegant votive piece referred to himself by the title awarded to him by the same Oracle. That is to say, this relief was a small element in the original decoration of a modest shrine to Hephaistion that was constructed on the orders stated to have been issued by Alexander himself in the context of Hephaistion's funeral at Babylon a month or so before the king's death.

A sceptic might argue that the sculpture is rather modest to be a commission by so wealthy a king as Alexander, but there are obvious explanations in the circumstances as to why the commission could not but be modest. Firstly, Alexander only received permission from the oracle at Siwa for Hephaistion to be honoured as a Hero, rather than as a full deity. Therefore it would have been disrespectful to the gods themselves for the individual shrines to Hephaistion to be grander than the shrines dedicated to fully-fledged deities. Secondly, the news of Alexander's death must have arrived in Macedonia whilst the shrines he had ordered for Hephaistion were still in preparation. There would have been scant political incentive to expend more than token resources upon their completion and decoration. Indeed it is often supposed that few if any were ever completed, although the very existence of this piece strongly suggests that one of them was established at Pella at least.

Given that it has been demonstrated that there is a large and diverse body of early evidence that Alexander was referred to as *Diogenes* in his lifetime, it would be perverse to suppose when we encounter *Diogenes* in what is probably the only surviving inscription naming Hephaistion that anyone but his king and lover is meant by the term, especially when the sources state that Alexander personally commanded such dedications.

It also merits note that there is one other inscription, found at Delphi and dating to a couple of years after Alexander's death, where the king acquires an Homeric divine appellation. However, in this instance it was the *Dios*

---

[348] Arrian, *Anabasis* 7.23.6-8; Plutarch, *Alexander* 72.2; Diodorus 17.115.6; Hypereides, *Epitaphios* col. 8.21-22; Justin 12.12.12.

Appendix A: The Nature of Alexander's Divinity

(shining/divine) epithet that Homer uses for Achilles that was adopted.[349] It seems that the *Diogenes* epithet was upgraded to *Dios* in a kind of transfiguration following Alexander's death. This may help to explain why the lifetime usage of *Diogenes* was not more prominently advertised by the post-mortem histories: it had already been superseded by a more senior grade of divinity.

Conclusions

We can conclude firstly that Alexander was known to be desirous from the beginning of his reign (or earlier) of winning for himself by virtue of outstanding deeds the divine appellations of his Homeric heroes and ancestors. Secondly, the fact that he was greeted as literally the son of the Sun god, Ammon-Re, when he visited Siwa, presented a perfect opportunity for him to encourage his courtiers and other supporters officially to accord him the epithet of *Diogenes*, since the gods themselves had evidently endorsed it.

Conservatives then and now have misconstrued the Homeric inspiration that motivated this behaviour and have accused Alexander of megalomania, of believing himself literally the son of Zeus and of rejecting Philip as his parent. Actually, however, Alexander never repudiated Philip as his biological father. Bosworth reaches this conclusion after investigating the point in some depth. He especially cites the parallel case of Heracles, whom Greek theology regarded as having enjoyed a kind of dual paternity such that both Amphitryon and Zeus were recognised as his father: hence the terminology "Diogenes-Heracles" in *Moralia* 332B.

So what *is* the true moral status of recognising Zeus, the king of the gods, as your heavenly father? An atheist might have some grounds to accuse Alexander of impiety, were it not that an atheist would not really believe in the meaningfulness of the concept of impiety in the first place. Conversely, it would be hard for Christians to find fault with Alexander's attitude without implicitly condemning themselves, since it is a core tenet of Christian faith that God is the heavenly father of each of us:

"Our Father which art in Heaven…"

Alexander pursued ambitious religious ideals in a world where practically everyone believed in the validity and worth of those religious ideals. I find it hard to conclude that he was wrong to do so. It would be the same as criticising a talented individual for being too ambitious nowadays. Opposition to personal ambition is the traditional stance of conservatives, who dislike any threat to the status quo.

---

[349] The first section of block a in the inscription found at Delphi recording honours for Archon of Pella; this section should be dated to (shortly) after Archon's death in 321BC according to *Greek Historical Inscriptions 404-323BC* by PJ Rhodes & Robin Osbourne, Inscription 92, pp.466-470.

Appendix B: The Structure and Decoration of Hephaistion's Pyre

The Cleitarchan account of Hephaistion's pyre at Babylon must mainly be derived from Diodorus 17.115, which is anyway by far the most detailed description in any source. However, other ancient writers also alluded to its magnificence, novelty and exceptional cost: in the Cleitarchan sources this amounted to 12,000 talents, although this perhaps included the subsequent erection of a permanent memorial. A silver talent constituted 6000 drachms, each weighing ~4.2g, so this sum exceeded 300 tonnes of silver, equivalent to about 25 tonnes of gold in Alexander's day. Arrian and Plutarch give a figure of 10,000 talents, which is not seriously divergent, but which may indicate that they employed a source other than Cleitarchus on this point.

Plutarch, *Alexander* 72.3, adds that Alexander desired that Stasicrates should be its architect. This seems to be the same man who is elsewhere attributed with having restored the Temple of Artemis at Ephesus, designed Alexandria in Egypt and proposed a plan to carve Mt Athos in Thrace into a giant representation of Alexander with an entire city nestling in his left palm, although this last concept was rejected by Alexander himself. Whereas the name Stasicrates has the literal meaning of "one who triumphs over strife", he is elsewhere called Deinocrates (Vitruvius, *De architectura* 2, *praefatio* 1-4; Valerius Maximus 1.4 ext 1), which means "Master of Marvels" or Cheirocrates (Strabo 14.1.23), which is "Master of Hand-Skills": these apt appellations were presumably nicknames or possibly honorific titles.

Diodorus describes a structure erected upon a base of bricks a stade (=400 cubits) square and supporting itself upon palm trunks with the bricks having been gleaned by demolishing a ten-stade stretch of the city wall. He states that it comprised precisely thirty quadrangular chambers and that its exterior faces were decorated in six horizontal bands with the addition of an array of sirens hollowed out to accommodate human singers at its summit, which reached a height of 130 cubits.

Unfortunately, the precise form of this structure is not instantly unveiled by Diodorus' words. The matter of the configuration of the thirty chambers is especially obscure. C. Bradford Welles in the Loeb translation of Diodorus 17 suggests 30 transverse compartments each 22 feet wide and 220 yards long. Some have supposed that this edifice was a box-like tower with sheer sides, but major pyres are normally stepped pyramidal structures in Roman art. For example, they feature on coins, notably a denarius of Antoninus Pius (Fig. 3.13 in the Hephaistion section). Furthermore, the stability of a simple rectangular structure a stade wide and 130 cubits tall that was entirely constructed of wood is dubious, for the force exerted upon its windward side in even a moderate breeze would have been stupendous. It might also be inferred that Stasicrates'

Appendix B: The Structure and Decoration of Hephaistion's Pyre

inspiration was the ziggurat in Babylon, which probably also had seven pseudo-step-pyramidal stages. This concept is illustrated in the reconstruction of the pyre in the late 19th century engraving reproduced as Figure 3.12, where Hephaistion's pyre echoes the ziggurat depicted on the distant horizon of the panorama.

The solution to the conundrum probably lies in the geometrical significance of the number thirty, for it is otherwise a great coincidence that $30=4x4+3x3+2x2+1x1$. Hence a square pyramidal structure comprising a four by four array of sixteen chambers on its foundation course, three by three on it first storey, two by two on its second and a single chamber at the summit precisely fits the description. This arrangement is illustrated in Figure 3.15, which shows that this suggests that each chamber measured 100x100x30 cubits, assuming that the final 10 cubits of height were provided by a plinth for the corpse. Diodorus' ensuing description of the decoration would be congruent with two bands per storey, excepting the topmost, where the sirens would match the full height of the crowning chamber. It is a strong confirmation of the width of the individual bands of decoration that Diodorus specified the overall height of the torches in the second frieze as fifteen cubits. The lower band of decoration on each storey might well have been projected outwards so as to give the impression of seven steps. Such projection might incidentally be helpful in accommodating the large reported total of sixty quinquereme prows per side at the base level of the decoration.

It will be informative to examine the iconography of the decorations in some detail, so I shall proceed from the base to the summit in the given order beginning with the galley prows in the first band. It is stated that each had a pair of archers on its catheads and five cubit tall fighting men on its deck. Olga Palagia has speculated that these vessels might represent Hephaistion's command of Alexander's Mediterranean fleet in 332BC (Curtius 4.5.10) and has noted that ships readied for a naval battle also appeared in the fourth decorative tablet on Alexander's funeral carriage (Diodorus 18.27.1).[350] But in fact the clue to decipherment of the symbolism probably lies again in the number of prows, for there were precisely sixty on each side of the structure, which matches the "sixty fighting ships" with which Alexander sailed across the Hellespont (Diodorus 17.17.2).[351] Hence we may infer that the armed men whom Diodorus notes to have been standing in each prow were probably actually Alexander and Hephaistion, with the former in the act of casting the famous spear, whereby Asia was won (see also Justin 11.5.10). Certainly Hephaistion was a key

---

[350] Olga Palagia, *Hephaestion's Pyre and the Royal Hunt of Alexander*, pp. 167-206 in "Alexander the Great in Fact and Fiction", edited by A. B. Bosworth & E. J. Baynham, Oxford, 2000.
[351] Probably this was only a section of Alexander's total fleet at the time, for Arrian, *Anabasis* 1.11.6 gives 160 triremes, Justin 11.6.2 has 182 ships and Curtius 4.5.14 gives Alexander a fleet of 160 vessels a couple of years later; indeed, Arrian's account states that Parmenion led the main crossing from Sestus to Abydos, whereas Alexander crossed from Elaeus at the tip of the Hellespont directly opposite Troy nearly thirty km further south.

participant in the ensuing ceremonies at Troy itself, where he played Patroclus to Alexander's Achilles (Aelian, *Varia Historia* 12.7; Arrian, *Anabasis* 1.12.1). In fact Alexander's ceremonial crossing of the Hellespont looks very much like a re-enactment of the arrival of Achilles and Patroclus at Troy with the fifty ships that Homer attributed to the Myrmidons (Iliad 2.685).

On the second level there were arrayed flaming torches with a serpent coiled about each of their hafts, which gazed up at an eagle ascending from the flames. It is hard not to see the torch itself as symbolic of Hephaistion, because he was named for the Greek fire god, Hephaistos. According to Herodotus 8.98.2 the Greeks (e.g. the Athenians) held torch races in honour of Hephaistos. Notably, Hephaistion himself bore a torch in a named representation of the Chiliarch in a lost painting by Aetion (cover), of which a detailed description has been preserved by Lucian (*Herodotus sive Aetion* 4-7). This explains exactly why each torch was wreathed, since the wreath was explicitly placed upon the badge of Hephaistion. The serpent and eagle are strongly associated with Ammon and Zeus respectively, but they might also represent Alexander himself insofar as he had been publicly recognized as the son of Zeus-Ammon. Perhaps the tableau could be interpreted as Hephaistion acting as a support and inspiration to Alexander. We should expect to find such specific and personal salutes to the deceased from the king in the iconography of the decoration of the pyre.

Regarding the hunting scene on the third tier of decoration, a fairly direct parallel survives in the hunt depicted on one of the long sides of the Alexander Sarcophagus found in the royal cemetery of Sidon in 1887 (Figure B.1). This truly wondrous work of art appears to have been the tomb of Abdalonymus, who had been appointed king of Sidon by Alexander on the recommendation of Hephaistion (e.g. Curtius 4.1.15-20). In the hunting scene the rider behind the lion may be Hephaistion; the mounted man being attacked by the lion may be Abdalonymus and the third horseman may be Alexander, since he originally wore a diadem. In all probability the hunting scenes on the pyre were also an opportunity to commemorate the prowess and dynamism of the deceased in the chase as well as his camaraderie with his king in such pursuits.

The fourth band depicted a Centauromachy or fight of the Centaurs, which refers to the mythological battle between the Lapiths and the Centaurs. Its most renowned precedent was the Centauromachy depicted in the metopes of the Parthenon in Athens, which Alexander would have visited in 338BC after the Battle of Chaeronea, probably in the company of Hephaistion. It is generally considered that the mythical Centauromachy often served to symbolize the struggle between the Greeks and the Persians, which is the most likely explanation for its inclusion on Hephaistion's pyre.

Appendix B: The Structure and Decoration of Hephaistion's Pyre

Figure B.1. The hunting scene on one of the long sides of the Alexander Sarcophagus from Sidon (from an albumen photo of the late 19th century in the Author's Collection).

The alternating bulls and lions in the fifth tier of adornment strongly recall the glazed brick reliefs of the Ishtar Gate and the adjoining Processional Way in Babylon, which were recovered by the German archaeological expeditions of Robert Koldewey in the early 20th century and used for a reconstruction displayed in the Pergamon Museum in Berlin. Alexander would certainly have seen them virtually every day he was in Babylon. The lions represent the goddess Ishtar and the bulls (technically aurochs) symbolize the god Adad. In the Babylonian Pantheon Ishtar was the goddess of love and war, whilst Adad was the god of storms. Lions also stood either side of the doorway of Alexander's catafalque, which was constructed in Babylon a little after the pyre (Diodorus 18.27.1). Similarly, a group of lions guarded one of the entrances to Alexander's probable first tomb at the Memphite Serapeum.[352] The main function of that temple was to house the mummified Apis Bulls in the famous subterranean galleries. Lion and bull motifs are also prominent in the decoration of other early Hellenistic tombs, such as, for example, Tomb No. 69 at Myra, which has a lion attacking a bull in the pediment of its façade.

A yet more widespread element of Greek funerary iconography was the panoply of arms, of which a fine example formed the sixth tier of ornamention on Hephaistion's pyre. There are numerous surviving parallels in Hellenistic artworks from tombs and mausoleums. An interesting example with which I myself have had some involvement is the starburst shield sculpture discovered embedded in the foundations of the main apse of the Basilica di San Marco in Venice (Figure B.2). In the course of associating the sculpture with a Macedonian tomb, Eugenio Polito suggested in 1998 that the spear shaft extending to the upper lefthand corner of the front face of this block is a sarissa. He did not explain his reasoning, but it may be noted that the point of the spearhead appears to extend precisely to the square upper lefthand corner, which is an original corner. Obviously the corners on the righthand edge of the block are not original, since it has been fractured away from another part on this side. However, symmetry arguments would suggest that the spear shaft should

---

[352] See *The Quest for the Tomb of Alexander the Great*, Andrew Chugg, 2007, pp. 62-66 & 134-145 (especially p.143).

have terminated at the original bottom righthand corner. The scale of the other arms shows that the intention of the sculptor was to depict them all at precisely lifesize: for example, the shield appears to be a lifesize phalangite type (diameter 70cm). If so, then the spear-shaft was around three metres in length both in art and reality, which is about correct for a Macedonian cavalry sarissa or xyston. Alexander himself wields such a weapon in the mosaic depicting his charge against Darius at Issus, which was unearthed in Pompeii and is now in the Naples Museum.

The spearhead on the block in Venice is rather similar to a spearhead discovered in a warrior grave at Aegae together with a connector circlet and a sauroter. These elements are believed to be the remains of the inorganic parts of a sarissa comprising two wooden shafts joined by the connector with a spike at one end and a leaf-shaped spearhead at the other.

The sculpture also depicts a pair of greaves in high relief, although they are now badly damaged. They are staggered in height on the block just to the right of the shield and the individual greaves are to scale: the bottom of the upper greave is at approximately the level of the lowest part of the star design on the shield. There is also a *kopis*, a single-edged hacking sword popular with Alexander's troops, which is suspended from a taselled belt on the lefthand side and is also precisely lifesize in scale. Its surface has however been seriously abraded.

Eugenio Polito assumed that the block had been imported to Venice from "the Eastern Mediterranean" and dated it to the third or early second century BC. It is sculpted from late Cretaceous limestone with rudist fossils, which may be found in the Roman Aurisina quarry seventy miles from Venice or in the vicinity of the lost pyramid at Abu Roash on the Nile, which was destroyed to provide sculptural stone in Ptolemaic Egypt.

The starburst design embossed upon the shield is perhaps its most striking feature, redolent as it is of the starburst emblem of the Macedonian monarchy, most famously emblazoned upon the lid of the larnax that held the cremated bones of King Philip of Macedon in Tomb II at Aegae. Starburst shields like this one appear on Macedonian coins and in several Macedonian wall paintings, notably in a mural depicting a Macedonian panoply in the tomb of Lyson & Kallikles located within Macedon itself. Phalangite and hoplite shields are commonly interspersed on Macedonian monuments.[353] A pair of rimless phalangite shields are depicted either side of the entrance on the façade of Tomb III at Aegae, which is probably the tomb of Alexander's son, Alexander IV, in which case it will have been constructed at the beginning of the third century BC.

---

[353] See "A Shield Monument from Veria and the Chronology of Macedonian Shield Types", Minor Markle, *Hesperia* 68.2, 1999.

Appendix B: The Structure and Decoration of Hephaistion's Pyre

In practice, the trophy of arms motif was the core symbolism for the tomb of a Macedonian warrior. It was roughly the equivalent of a cross on a Christian grave. Here is a contemporaneous quotation that makes the point:

It is fitting for the Macedonian spirit to bear witness to exploits with arms in fighting, and to fairness of the soul, so that trophies may proclaim the valour of the body, but opinions may testify to the soul's nobility.

FrGrHist 2.153 F4 = Freiburg Papyrus 7-8

Therefore, this kind of symbolism is what an expert would expect to find in closest association with the corpse of a Macedonian notable, so it is no surprise to read that trophies of arms formed the penultimate band of decoration on Hephaistion's pyre.

At the summit of the pyre there stood statues of Sirens that had been hollowed out to accommodate human singers. Clearly, there is an allusion to the Sirens of Homer's Odyssey with their impossibly lovely yet baleful voices. Only the most movingly mournful laments could be deemed worthy of the deceased. It is worth noticing that effigies of Sirens were also found among the statuary near Alexander's probable first tomb at the Serapeum in the Memphite necropolis at Saqqara: it is most likely that these were set up by Ptolemy Soter, who was undoubtedly an eyewitness at Hephaistion's funeral.

The archaeologist Robert Koldewey located a possible site for Hephaistion's pyre during his excavations of Babylon in the early 20th century (see plan in Figure 3.14). He uncovered a scorched and reddened platform beneath a mound of brick rubble close to the inner wall of Babylon due east of the "Southern Palace" of Nebuchadnezzar.[354] Koldewey even described having found the imprints of incinerated palm trunks on the platform, recalling Diodorus' description of the pyre quite evocatively.

It seems likely that it was Alexander's intention to build a mausoleum echoing the architecture of the pyre in its ashes, although this was thwarted by the king's premature demise. Among the Last Plans of Alexander, which are outlined in Diodorus 18.4 based on documents read to the Assembly of the Macedones by Perdiccas, there was an item calling for the "completion of the pyre of Hephaistion" at great expense. It is important to understand that in Greek the term used, which is *pyra*, can mean either a funeral pyre or a temple altar (i.e. a place where fire is kindled). Hence it can reasonably be used to refer both to the incinerated pyre and the altar of a permanent memorial, where a flame was to be kept alight for the Chiliarch. There is evidence for permanent memorials having been erected upon the cinders of funeral pyres in the case of other major Macedonian tombs: for example, a monument from the late 4th century BC has

---

[354] See "Hephaestion's Pyre and the Royal Hunt of Alexander" by Olga Palagia in *Alexander the Great in Fact and Fiction*, edited by A. B. Bosworth and E. J. Baynham, Oxford 2000, p. 173; R. Koldewey, *The Excavations at Babylon*, London 1914, p. 310-11.

been excavated at Salamis on the coast of Cyprus, where a funeral pyre had been built upon a brick platform and a stone pyramid was subsequently erected in its place as a permanent memorial – this might be associated with the naval battle at Salamis between Ptolemy and Demetrius Poliorketes in 306BC.[355]

Figure B.2. Macedonian arms sculpted upon two faces of a block from the foundations of the Basilica di San Marco in Venice (photo by the author.)

---

[355] Plutarch, *Demetrius* 17.1; V. Karageorghis, *Cyprus*, London, 1969, pp. 171-199.

Bibliography

Ancient Sources

Aelian, *Varia Historia* - N.G. Wilson, Loeb, Harvard, 1997

Aeschines, *Against Ctesiphon* – Charles Darwin Adams, Loeb, Harvard, 1919

Aeschylus, *Fragments of the Myrmidons*

Ammianus Marcellinus

Appian, *The Syrian Wars* – Horace White, Loeb, 1988

Aristotle, *Politics*

Arrian, *Anabasis Alexandrou* - P.A. Brunt, Loeb, Harvard, 1976 and 1983

Arrian, *Indica* - P.A. Brunt, Loeb, Harvard, 1983

Arrian, *Events After Alexander*, epitomized by Photius 92

Athenaeus, *Deipnosophistae* - Charles Burton Gulick, Loeb, Harvard, 1927-41

Curtius, *History of Alexander* - John C. Rolfe, Loeb, Harvard, 1946; John Yardley, Penguin, 1984

Dexippus, epitomized by Photius 82

Diodorus Siculus, *Universal History* - vol. VII, Charles L. Sherman, Loeb, Harvard, 1952; vol. VIII, C. Bradford Welles, Loeb, Harvard, 1963; vol. IX, Russel M. Geer, Loeb, Harvard, 1947

Diogenes Laertius, *Lives of Eminent Philosophers*

Diogenes of Sinope, *Letter 24*

Epictetus, *Discourses* – W. A. Oldfather, Loeb, 1925 & 1928

Epitoma Rerum Gestarum Alexandri Magni (Metz Epitome) – P. H. Thomas, Teubner, 1966

Euripides, *Alcestis*, trans. Gilbert Murray, George Allen & Unwin, London 1915

Heidelberg Epitome

Herodotus, *The Histories* – A. D. Godley, Loeb, 1920 onwards

Homer, *Iliad* – A. T. Murray & William F. Wyatt, Loeb, 2nd edition, 1999

Hypereides, *Epitaphios*

Isocrates, *Letter 5, To Alexander* – L. van Hook, Loeb, 1968

Itinerarium Alexandri – Karl Müller, Fragments of the Lost Histories of Alexander the Great, Paris, 1846

Justin, *Epitome of the Philippic History of Pompeius Trogus* - Books 11-12, J.C. Yardley and W. Heckel, Oxford, 1997; Justin, Cornelius Nepos and Eutropius, Rev. John Selby Watson, London, 1853; Teubner Edition

Alexander's Lovers by Andrew Chugg

Lucian, *Dialogues of the Dead* – M. D. MacLeod, Loeb, Vol 7, 1961

Lucian, *The Eunuch* – A. M. Harmon, Loeb, Vol 5, 1936

Lucian, *Imagines* – A. M. Harmon, Loeb, Vol 4, 1925

Lucian, *Herodotus sive Aetion* – K. Kilburn, Loeb, Vol 6, 1959

Lucian, *Pro Lapsu* – K. Kilburn, Loeb, Vol 6, 1959

Lucian, *Slander* – A. M. Harmon, Loeb, Vol 1, 1913

Lycophron, *The Alexandra* - George W. Mooney, London 1921

Nepos, Cornelius, *Eumenes*

Pausanias, *Description of Greece*

Photius, *Bibliotheca*

Plato, *Letters VII and VIII* – Walter Hamilton, Penguin, 1973

Plato, *Symposium*

Plato, *Alcibiades II*

Pliny the Elder, *Natural History* - H. Rackham, W.H.S. Jones, D.E. Eichholz, Loeb, Harvard, 1938-62

Plutarch, *Life of Alexander* - vol. 7, B. Perrin, Loeb, Harvard, 1919

Plutarch, *Life of Artaxerxes*

Plutarch, *Life of Demetrius* - vol. 9, B. Perrin, Loeb, Harvard, 1920

Plutarch, *Life of Demosthenes* - vol. 7, B. Perrin, Loeb, Harvard, 1919

Plutarch, *Life of Eumenes* - vol. 8, B. Perrin, Loeb, Harvard, 1919

Plutarch, *Moralia* – 17 vols by various translators, Loeb Classical Library

Plutarch, *Life of Pelopidas* - vol. 5, B. Perrin, Loeb, Harvard, 1917

Plutarch, *Life of Pericles*

Plutarch, *Life of Pyrrhus* - vol. 9, B. Perrin, Loeb, Harvard, 1920

Polyaenus, *Stratagems of War* – Peter Krentz & Everett L. Wheeler, Chicago, 1994

Polybius, *The Histories (The Rise of the Roman Empire)* - W.R. Paton, Loeb, Harvard, 1922-7

Pseudo-Callisthenes, *Alexander Romance* - Guilelmus Kroll, Historia Alexandri Magni, vol, 1, Weidmann, 1926

Strabo, *Geography* - H.L. Jones, Loeb, Harvard, 1917-32

Suidae Lexicon (The Suda), A. Adler (ed.), Leipzig, 1928-35

Theopompus

Vitruvius

Xenophon, *Cyropaidia* – H. G. Dakyns, Everyman's Library, 1914 & 1992

Xenophon, *Anabasis*

Bibliography

Modern Sources

Andreotti, R, "Die Weltmonarchie Alexanders des Grossen in Überlieferung und geschichtlicher Wirklichkeit", *Saeculum 8*, 1957

Andronicos, Manolis, *Vergina*, Athens 1984

Andronikos, Manolis, "The Royal Tombs at Vergina: A brief Account of the Excavations", *The Search for Alexander: An Exhibition*, New York Graphic Society, Boston 1980

Badian, Ernst, "The Eunuch Bagoas: A Study in Method", *Classical Quarterly 8*, 1958

Badian, Ernst, "Some Recent Interpretations of Alexander", *Alexandre le Grand: Image et Réalité, Entretiens Tome XXII, Fondation Hardt*, 1976

Berve, Helmut, *Das Alexanderreich auf prosopographischer*, Munich 1926

Bosworth, A. B., "Alexander and Ammon", *Greece and the Eastern Mediterranean in Ancient History and Prehistory*, ed. K. H. Kinzl, Berlin 1977

Bosworth, A. B., *Conquest & Empire*, Cambridge 1988

Bosworth, A. B., *From Arrian to Alexander*, Oxford 1988

Bosworth, A. B., *Alexander and the East: The Tragedy of Triumph*, Oxford 1998

Bosworth, A. B., "Ptolemy and the Will of Alexander", *Alexander the Great in Fact & Fiction*, ed. A.B. Bosworth & E.J. Baynham, Oxford 2000

Bowman, Alan K., *Egypt after the Pharaohs*, London 1986

Briant, P., *Alexander the Great, The Heroic Ideal*, New York 1996

Brunt, P. A., "Alexander, Barsine and Heracles", *Rivista di filologia e di istruzione classica* 103, 1975

Brunt, P. A., *Arrian's History of Alexander*, Loeb, Harvard 1976 (vol 1) & 1983 (vol 2)

Burstein, Stanley M., "IG II^2 561 and the Court of Alexander IV", *Zeitschrift für Papyrologie und Epigraphik 24*, 1977

Chugg, A. M., "The Sarcophagus of Alexander the Great?", *Greece & Rome*, April 2002

Chugg, A. M., "The Sarcophagus of Alexander the Great", *Minerva* Sept-Oct 2002

Chugg, A. M., "The Tomb of Alexander the Great in Alexandria," *American Journal of Ancient History*, New Series 1.2, (2002) [2003], 75-108

Chugg, A. M., *The Lost Tomb of Alexander the Great*, London 2004

Chugg, A. M, "The Journal of Alexander the Great", *Ancient History Bulletin* 19.3-4 (2005) 155-175.

Chugg, A. M., *The Quest for the Tomb of Alexander the Great*, AMC Publications, 2007

Chugg, A. M., *Alexander the Great in India: A Reconstruction of Cleitarchus*, AMC Pubs, 2008

Chugg, A. M., *The Death of Alexander the Great: A Reconstruction of Cleitarchus*, AMC, 2009

Chugg, A. M., *Alexander the Great in Afghanistan: A Reconstruction of Cleitarchus*, AMC, 2011

Fedak, Janos, *Monumental Tombs of the Hellenistic Age*, Toronto 1990

Alexander's Lovers by Andrew Chugg

Fraser, P. M., *Ptolemaic Alexandria*, Vols. I, II & III, Oxford, 1972

Goralski, Walter J., "Arrian's Events After Alexander" *Ancient World 19*, 1989

Gunderson, Lloyd, "Quintus Curtius Rufus: Historical Methods", *Philip II, Alexander the Great and the Macedonian Heritage*, eds. Adams and Borza, 1982

Hamilton, J. R., *Plutarch – Alexander: a Commentary*, Oxford 1969

Hammond, N. G. L., *Epirus*, Oxford 1967

Hammond, N. G. L., "The Evidence for the Identity of the Royal Tombs at Vergina", *Philip II, Alexander the Great and the Macedonian Heritage*, ed. Adams & Borza, Boston & London 1982

Hammond, N. G. L., *Three Historians of Alexander the Great*, Cambridge 1983

Hammond, N. G. L., *History of Macedonia III*, Oxford 1972

Hammond, N. G. L., *The Miracle That Was Macedonia*, Sidgwick & Jackson, London 1991

Hammond, N. G. L., *Sources for Alexander the Great*, Cambridge 1993

Hammond, N. G. L., *Philip of Macedon*, London 1994

Heckel, Waldemar, "IG II^2 561 and the Status of Alexander IV", *Zeitschrift für Papyrologie und Epigraphik 40*, 1980

Heckel, Waldemar, *The Last Days & Testament of Alexander the Great: A Prosopographic Study*, Stuttgart 1988

Heckel, Waldemar, *The Marshals of Alexander's Empire*, London 1992

Heuss, A., "Alexander der Grosse und die politische Ideologie des Altertums", *Antike und Abendland 4*, 1954

Holt, Frank L., *Alexander the Great and Bactria, Supplement to Mnemosyne*, E. J. Brill, 1988

Holt, Frank, *Alexander the Great and the Mystery of the Elephant Medallions*, California 2003

Humana, Charles, *The Keeper of the Bed*, London 1973

Jacoby, F., *Die Fragmente der griechischen Historiker (FrGrH)*, Berlin 1929

Karageorghis, G., *Cyprus*, London, 1969

Kebric, Robert B., *In the Shadow of Macedon: Duris of Samos*, Wiesbaden: Franz Steiner 1977

Koldewey, R., *The Excavations at Babylon*, London 1914

Lane Fox, Robin, *Alexander the Great*, London 1973

Machiavelli, Niccolo, *The Prince*, Florence 1513

Macurdy, Grace H., "Roxane and Alexander IV in Epirus", *Journal of Hellenic Studies 52*, 1932

Malherbe, Abraham J., *The Cynic Epistles*, Society of Biblical Literature, No. 12, 1977

Markle, Minor, "A Shield Monument from Veria and the Chronology of Macedonian Shield Types", *Hesperia 68.2*, 1999

Milns, R. D., *Alexander the Great*, London 1968

Bibliography

Mooney, George W., *The Alexandra of Lycophron*, London 1921

Moreno, Paolo, "Il principe infelice", *Archaeo XIII*, 7, July 1997

Moreno, Paolo, *Apelles: The Alexander Mosaic*, Skira Editore, Milan 2001

Oates, Joan, *Babylon*, London 1979

O'Brien, John Maxwell, *Alexander the Great: The Invisible Enemy*, London 1992

Palagia, Olga, "Hephaestion's Pyre and the Royal Hunt of Alexander", *Alexander the Great in Fact and Fiction*, edited by A. B. Bosworth and E. J. Baynham, Oxford 2000

Pearson, L, *The Lost Histories of Alexander The Great*, New York 1960

Rawlinson, H.G., *Bactria*, London 1912

Renault, Mary, *The Nature of Alexander*, London 1975

Rhodes, P.J. & Osbourne, R., *Greek Historical Inscriptions 404-323BC*, Oxford 2003

Romm, James (ed.), *The Landmark Arrian: The Campaigns of Alexander*, New York 2010

Ross, W.D., *Aristotle*, London 1923

Schröder, Stephan F., *Katalog der antiken Skulpturen des Museo del Prado in Madrid, Band 1*, Mainz am Rhein 1993

Stewart, Andrew, *Faces of Power: Alexander's Image and Hellenistic Politics*, California 1993

Stoneman, Richard, (trans.), *The Greek Alexander Romance*, London 1991

Stoneman, Richard, (trans.), "Palladius: On the Life of the Brahmans", *Legends of Alexander the Great*, Everyman 1994

Tarn, W. W., "Heracles Son of Barsine", *Journal of Hellenic Studies*, 1921

Tarn, W. W., *Alexander the Great II, Sources and Studies*, Cambridge 1948

Wilcken, Ulrich, *Alexander the Great*, Leipzig 1931

Wolohojian, A. M., (trans.) *The Romance of Alexander the Great by Pseudo-Callisthenes*, Columbia University Press, 1969

Wood, Michael, *In the Footsteps of Alexander the Great*, BBC 1997

Index

A

Abdalonymus 18, 78, 95, 225
Abdera 63
Abreas 42
Abu Roash 227
Abydos 11, 224
Academy 6, 56, 64, 67, 70, 97
Acarnania 16
Acesines, River 110
Achaemenids 138, 204
Achilles .. 3, 11, 21, 47, 67, 85, 86, 87, 88, 89, 92, 119, 120, 121, 122, 124, 129, 131, 132, 134, 135, 136, 137, 147, 153, 159, 177, 213, 216, 222, 225
Acropolis 6, 8, 130
Ada, Queen 14, 171, 199
Adad 226
Adea-Eurydice 145, 185, 187, 188, 211
Admetus 130, 131, 134, 136
Aeacidae 89
Aeacides 188
Aeacus 146, 147, 218
Aegae 3, 7, 69, 149, 193, 227
Aegean Sea 15
Aegus, Alexander 184
Aelian .. 2, 32, 68, 72, 86, 89, 118, 121, 122, 123, 124, 130, 132, 134, 136, 137, 157, 163, 205, 212, 225, 230
Aeolis 80
Aeschines 88, 96, 97, 230
Aeschylus 61, 87, 230
Aethicia 146, 147
Aetion .. 83, 84, 85, 164, 179, 225, 231
Aetolia 145

Aetolians 144, 145
Afghanistan iii
Africa 52, 97, 131
Against Ctesiphon 88, 96, 230
Agathocles 123, 147
Agde 192
agema 98, 99
Agis 97, 133
Ai Khanoum 106
Albanians 167
Alcestis 130, 131, 134, 136, 230
Alcetas 211
Alcibiades 65, 88, 231
alcoholism 117
Aldus 178
Alexais 205
Alexander IV .. 140, 142, 144, 145, 147, 148, 184, 186, 187, 188, 189, 190, 191, 192, 193, 194, 211, 227, 232, 233
Alexander Romance . 2, 22, 23, 59, 68, 70, 121, 156, 168, 171, 179, 180, 181, 182, 184, 212, 231, 234
Alexander Sarcophagus 18, 78, 95, 225, 226
Alexander's Friends . 1, 29, 36, 50, 102, 103, 110, 160
Alexander-Helios 80
Alexandra 146, 147, 231, 234
Alexandria .. 1, 22, 32, 70, 79, 106, 120, 146, 173, 217, 223, 232, 233
Alexandropolis 5
Alsdorf Relief 80, 81
Altars 41
alter ego 91, 92, 94, 121, 122, 129, 132, 135, 136, 137
Amastrine 180

Index

Amazons ..... iii, iv, 165, 166, 167, 168, 169, 170
Amestris 180
Ammon 22, 58, 77, 89, 94, 119, 121, 125, 129, 137, 214, 217, 218, 221, 222, 225, 232
Ampheum 9
Amphipolis 115, 190
Amphitryon 89, 222
Amyntas 21, 67, 69, 100, 111, 188
Amyntor 69, 97, 100
Anabasis.....29, 54, 55, 58, 65, 71, 75, 77, 87, 88, 91, 96, 99, 100, 101, 104, 106, 107, 108, 109, 110, 111, 112, 114, 117, 132, 138, 139, 140, 141, 154, 157, 161, 162, 171, 172, 174, 175, 176, 180, 181, 196, 198, 199, 200, 201, 204, 217, 218, 221, 224, 225, 230, 231
Anabasis of Xenophon 65
anastole 82, 193
Anatolia 144
Anaxarchus 36, 63, 64, 89
Ancyra 16
Andromache 62, 89
Andromeda 61
Andronikos, M ..81, 193, 194, 232
Anticleides 168
Antigenes 168
Antigona 101
Antigonids 212
Antigonus...78, 94, 142, 144, 145, 150, 176, 185, 186, 187, 190, 191, 193, 194, 211, 212
Antilochus 87
Antipater ..6, 9, 16, 48, 85, 90, 92, 97, 113, 126, 168, 176, 183, 184, 185, 186, 190, 194
Antipatrides 73
Antisthenes 59
Antonine period 162
Antoninus Pius 124, 127, 223
Aornus 39

Apame 138, 141
Apelles .... iv, 72, 82, 234
Apis bull 22, 226
Apollo 31, 218
Apollodorus 115, 131
Appian 112, 142, 230
Arabia 50, 52, 131
Arabs 21
Arachosia 31, 45
Arbela 23, 25
Archelaus 61
Areia 30, 45
Argead 3
Argeas 3
Argos 3
argyraspides 41
Ariamazes 33, 174, 178
Aristander 23
Aristion 96
Aristobulus .. 1, 2, 15, 94, 96, 101, 108, 111, 113, 115, 139, 141, 142, 148, 150, 161, 168, 169, 170, 197, 198, 204
Aristocrates 205
Aristocritus 205
Ariston 205
Aristonous 99, 188
Aristonymus 205
Aristotle 1, 5, 8, 37, 55, 56, 57, 58, 61, 63, 64, 65, 67, 69, 70, 71, 88, 89, 107, 149, 152, 159, 220, 230, 234
Armamaxae 196
Armenia 188
Arrhidaeus 6, 68, 71, 141, 142, 143, 145, 183, 185, 187, 188, 190, 191, 211
Arrian. 2, 9, 22, 23, 28, 29, 46, 54, 55, 58, 61, 63, 65, 69, 71, 75, 77, 85, 87, 88, 89, 91, 93, 96, 98, 99, 100, 101, 104, 106, 107, 108, 109, 110, 111, 112, 113, 114, 115, 116, 117, 118, 119, 120, 121, 122, 123, 129, 132,

133, 134, 136, 137, 138, 139, 140, 141, 142, 144, 152, 154, 157, 158, 161, 162, 163, 169, 170, 171, 172, 174, 175, 176, 178, 180, 181, 182, 183, 184, 185, 190, 196, 197, 198, 199, 200, 201, 204, 206, 217, 218, 221, 223, 224, 225, 230, 232, 233, 234
Arsames 16
Arsinoë 68
Artabazus .. iv, 138, 139, 140, 141, 142, 147
Artacama 141
Artaxerxes I 204
Artaxerxes II 138
Artaxerxes III 138, 141, 204
Artemis 123, 223
Artonis 141
Asclepius 87, 119, 129
Asia.... 6, 8, 11, 15, 25, 30, 52, 61, 65, 74, 92, 124, 141, 156, 161, 175, 184, 185, 186, 187, 198, 200, 201, 204, 209, 224
Asia Minor 7, 144, 196, 215
Assacenus 172
Assembly 5, 8, 31, 36, 38, 52, 102, 104, 131, 142, 143, 144, 162, 183, 189, 190, 228
Astis 109
Astronomical Canon 184
Astypalaea 1
Atarneus 152
Atheas 68
Athena 83, 85
Athenaeus 2, 61, 68, 71, 73, 74, 75, 79, 86, 115, 123, 157, 158, 159, 163, 205, 217, 230
Athenians 5, 6, 55
Athenodorus 205
Athens 3, 5, 6, 8, 28, 46, 55, 56, 58, 64, 67, 70, 71, 77, 79, 88, 96, 97, 118, 126, 147, 159, 187, 190, 194, 205, 225, 232

Athos, Mt 223
Atlantic Ocean 52
Atropates 169, 170
Attalus 6, 7, 8, 68, 69, 143, 188
Audata 68
Augustus 23
Aulus Gellius 4
Aurisina 227
aurochs 226

B

Babylon 23, 25, 26, 50, 62, 97, 100, 116, 118, 119, 122, 124, 127, 132, 133, 142, 144, 158, 159, 181, 182, 183, 184, 185, 209, 220, 221, 223, 224, 226, 228, 233, 234
Babylonia 25
Bacchae, The 61
Bacchus 217
Bactra 33, 34, 37
Bactria .. 1, 28, 29, 31, 34, 36, 105, 106, 111, 114, 133, 140, 154, 169, 174, 176, 178, 179, 183, 203, 208, 209, 212, 233, 234
Badian, E. .. 53, 154, 158, 159, 232
Bagoas. iii, iv, 72, 75, 85, 86, 112, 152, 153, 154, 155, 156, 157, 158, 159, 160, 161, 162, 163, 164, 232
Barbarians 177, 207
Barsine ...... iii, iv, 18, 72, 74, 113, 138, 139, 140, 141, 142, 143, 144, 145, 147, 148, 149, 150, 181, 204, 232, 234
Basilica di San Marco 226, 229
Batis 21, 153
Bazzi, Giovanni Antonio 84
Beira 172
Belerophon 156
Berlin 226
Bessus 28, 29, 30, 31, 32, 154, 162

237

Index

Bible 87, 124, 233
Bibliotheca 2, 231
Black Sea 167, 187
bodyguard 1, 7, 43, 68, 69, 98, 99, 100, 102, 103, 105, 106, 112, 133, 135, 141, 157, 183, 190
Boeotia 5
Bosphorus 169
Bosworth, A.B. 63, 64, 89, 99, 124, 163, 182, 214, 215, 222, 224, 228, 232, 234
Botticelli 84
Brahmins 42, 44
Branchidae 31, 32
Briseis 177
British Museum 79
Brunt, P.A. 58, 108, 112, 138, 148, 157, 161, 230, 232
Bucephala 41
Bucephalus 3, 4, 29, 41, 81, 156
bulls 226
Byblos 95
Byzantium 5, 187

C

Cadmeia 8, 9, 211
Calanus 63, 64
Callisthenes .. 1, 14, 22, 37, 56, 59, 61, 63, 70, 89, 106, 107, 108, 132, 217, 218
Callixeina 71, 72
camels 31
Campaspe .... iv, 72
Candace, Queen 23, 171
Caphisias 205
Cappadocia 2, 16, 184
Caracalla 81
Cardia 2, 71, 90, 144, 148, 163
Caria 6, 14, 71, 199
Carians 171
Carmania .. 46, 112, 158, 159, 163, 164

Carthage 20, 147
Carystius 73
Caspian .... iii, 29, 167
Caspian Gates 28, 167
Cassander..... 1, 73, 113, 143, 144, 145, 147, 148, 149, 150, 185, 186, 187, 188, 189, 190, 191, 193, 194, 211
Cassandra 146
Cassandria 1
Castaigne, A 10, 15, 32, 35, 40, 43, 49, 86, 176, 199, 208
Castor & Pollux 213
castrati 155
catafalque 184, 226
Caucasus 165, 217
Cebalinus 30, 102, 103
Centauromachy 225
Centaurs 225
Chaeronea 5, 56, 70, 225
Chalcidians 168
Chalcidice 3
Chalcis 73, 205
Chaldeans 50, 61
Chamberlain 106, 205
Chares 1, 4, 38, 47, 106, 107, 108, 111, 168, 205, 206
Charles le Brun 26, 199
Charmides 156
Charon 73
Cheirocrates 223
Chicago 81, 231
Chiliarch . iv, 67, 77, 83, 112, 113, 114, 115, 117, 118, 119, 131, 132, 133, 134, 153, 154, 158, 186, 221, 225, 228
Chios 15
Chitral Region 173
chlamys 3, 79
Choaspes 172
Chorasmians 169
Chorienes .. 36, 175, 177, 178, 207
Christianity 54, 129

Christians. 11, 129, 143, 152, 222, 228
Chugg, AM 226, 232
Churchill, W 54
Cilicia 16, 164
Claudius 2
Claudius Ptolemy 184
Cleitarchus 1, 2, 16, 22, 59, 74, 99, 111, 113, 121, 125, 143, 148, 154, 159, 161, 163, 166, 167, 168, 171, 172, 173, 177, 178, 179, 180, 197, 198, 199, 207, 208, 219, 223, 232
Cleitus.. 11, 13, 35, 36, 62, 63, 99, 104, 106
Cleomenes 120
Cleopatra ... 6, 7, 68, 69, 141, 143, 211, 212
Cleophis. iii, iv, 74, 165, 171, 172, 173
Codomannus, Darius 153
Coenus ... 34, 40, 41, 98, 102, 106, 111, 172
Cohortandus 174, 178
Colchians 169
Colchis 169
coma 51
Companion Cavalry 24, 25, 29, 30, 35, 99, 100, 101, 102, 104, 105, 109, 111, 112, 113, 134
Companions 16, 47, 67, 73, 98, 107, 113, 116, 119, 136, 141, 198, 204, 207, 208
comus 46
concubines 74
Cophen, River 109
Corianus 178
Corinth... 6, 8, 58, 60, 73, 82, 215, 216, 220
Corinth, League of 9, 30
Corinthian Gulf 145
Cornelius Nepos 144, 149, 230, 231
Cossaeans 50, 121, 122, 137

Cothelas 68
Craneion 58, 215
Craterus 34, 39, 40, 42, 45, 48, 73, 93, 94, 100, 102, 103, 106, 110, 113, 114, 117, 132, 134, 180, 183, 184, 185
Cratinus 205
Cretaceous 227
Crete 1
Critias 65
Critobulus 157
Crobylus 73
Cupid 84, 179
Curtius 2, 23, 59, 62, 65, 68, 70, 74, 75, 78, 91, 93, 95, 96, 98, 99, 100, 101, 102, 103, 104, 105, 106, 109, 110, 111, 113, 114, 118, 131, 138, 139, 142, 143, 153, 154, 155, 156, 159, 160, 161, 162, 164, 165, 166, 168, 169, 172, 174, 177, 178, 180, 182, 183, 196, 197, 198, 200, 201, 202, 203, 206, 208, 209, 212, 214, 215, 218, 219, 224, 225, 230, 233
Cydnus, River 16
Cynane 68, 211
Cynic Philosophers 1, 58, 87, 177, 215, 216, 219, 220, 233
Cyprus 18, 20, 229, 233
Cyropaidia.. 46, 65, 152, 157, 161, 201, 231
Cyrus 28, 46, 65, 152, 153, 159, 160, 161, 162, 201, 204
Cyzicus 205

D

Daedalian Mountains 172
Damascus 18, 139, 185
Damon 73, 92
Dandamis 59, 64
Danube, River 8

Index

Darius......2, 11, 16, 17, 18, 20, 21, 23, 25, 28, 29, 30, 31, 56, 73, 74, 89, 90, 93, 95, 97, 101, 113, 133, 134, 138, 139, 141, 153, 154, 160, 162, 164, 175, 177, 180, 196, 197, 198, 199, 200, 201, 202, 203, 204, 205, 206, 207, 208, 209, 216, 227
De architectura..........................223
Deidameia 188
Deinocrates 121, 223
Deipnosophistae...71, 74, 86, 115, 159, 163, 230
Delphi.........................10, 221, 222
Delta (of river) 22, 110, 180
Demaratus 6
Demetrio statuettes....................79
Demetrius...81, 97, 102, 103, 106, 107, 110, 142, 195, 212, 220, 229, 231
Demetrius Poliorketes........81, 194
Demosthenes..88, 96, 97, 98, 126, 133, 135, 231
Derdas 68, 169
diadem..................30, 87, 193, 225
Diadochi.............................78, 81
Dialogues of the Dead.......74, 214, 218, 231
Dicaearchus..........74, 86, 159, 163
Didyma..31
Dio Chrysostom ..58, 61, 149, 216
Diodorus......2, 7, 9, 50, 55, 67, 69, 74, 75, 78, 79, 90, 92, 93, 95, 98, 99, 100, 101, 104, 110, 111, 112, 113, 114, 116, 118, 124, 125, 126, 129, 132, 136, 137, 138, 139, 140, 141, 144, 145, 146, 147, 148, 153, 156, 158, 164, 166, 172, 176, 177, 178, 179, 180, 185, 186, 187, 188, 189, 190, 191, 193, 197, 199, 202, 203, 204, 206, 207, 208, 209, 211, 213, 214, 220, 221, 223, 224, 226, 228, 230

Diogenes 1, 57, 58, 59, 60, 62, 63, 70, 76, 78, 87, 152, 215, 216, 217, 218, 219, 220, 221, 222, 230
Diogenes Laertius.. 56, 57, 58, 59, 70, 91, 152, 219, 220, 230
Dion 64, 65, 153
Dionysius............................ 64, 65
Dionysus........... 39, 205, 216, 219
Diophantus............................. 205
Dios ... 22, 88, 163, 217, 218, 219, 221
Dioscuri 213
divine honours 47, 50, 51, 88, 212
Diyllus 96
Dodona 10
Domitian 162
Doryphorus............................ 155
drachm............................ 139, 223
Drakon 181
Drangians................................ 30
dropsy 149
Drypetis ... 93, 114, 131, 184, 204, 207, 208, 210
Duris 141, 142, 148, 168, 233
Dymnus 30, 102, 103, 105
dysentery 33

E

eagle....................................... 225
Ecbatana 28, 31, 49, 115, 116, 118, 119, 122, 130, 134, 136, 163, 164, 209
eclipse 23
Egypt . 1, 2, 21, 22, 23, 52, 79, 96, 97, 101, 118, 120, 126, 144, 149, 153, 171, 184, 191, 212, 213, 214, 218, 223, 227, 232
elephants.. 23, 39, 40, 41, 45, 184, 187, 189
English................... 3, 53, 60, 216
Epaminondas 67, 92

Ephemerides 2, 163
Ephesians 68
Ephesus 13, 223
Ephippus 1, 79, 115, 116, 123, 130, 131, 217
Epictetus 58, 87, 119, 132, 230
Epidaurians 119
Epidaurus 129
Epigoni 48
Epimenes 38
Epirotes 47, 188
Epirus 3, 6, 7, 69, 88, 145, 146, 186, 187, 188, 211, 233
Epitaphios 126, 137, 221, 230
equinox 7, 163
erastes 86, 87, 89
Eretria 168
Erigyius 70, 102, 106
eromenos 86, 87, 89, 102, 132, 158, 163
Erythrae 163, 214
Eschate, Alexandria 32
Ethiopia 23, 171
Ethiopians 174
Ethiopic 171
Eulaeus, River 48
Eumenes 2, 71, 90, 113, 114, 115, 117, 118, 119, 121, 122, 132, 137, 141, 142, 144, 148, 157, 163, 177, 185, 186, 188, 190, 231
eunuchs. iii, 18, 21, 29, 30, 72, 74, 75, 85, 86, 91, 112, 152, 153, 154, 155, 156, 157, 158, 159, 160, 161, 162, 163, 164, 196, 198, 201, 213
Euphrates, River 23, 50, 97, 98, 181, 182, 200, 209
Euripides.. 61, 130, 131, 134, 136, 230
Europa 68
Europe ... 6, 28, 52, 169, 187, 193, 204

Eurydice . 141, 145, 185, 187, 188, 211
Euxenippus 75, 155, 156
Euxine 169
Events after Alexander 2, 112, 176, 183, 184, 185
Evius 73, 114, 205
excipinon 75, 155, 156
Exiles Decree 47

F

Fortune 177
France 52
Fraser, P.M. 217, 233
Freiburg Papyrus 228
Freud, S 165

G

Ganges, River 109
Ganymede 213
Gaugamela . 23, 24, 26, 88, 98, 99, 100, 112, 133, 146, 200, 202, 218
Gaza 21, 95, 153
Gedrosia 45, 46, 53, 111, 158, 203
George the Monk 171
Georgia 167
German 226
Germany 54
Getae 8
Getty Museum 77, 78
Glaucias 49, 116, 117, 119, 190, 193, 211
Gordium 14
Grand Army 149, 184, 185
Granicus 11, 13, 36
Great King 9, 11, 13, 16, 18, 28, 37, 74, 101, 105, 112, 138, 139, 152, 153, 164, 180, 196, 200, 201, 219
Great Tumulus 149, 193

Index

Greece 1, 2, 3, 5, 6, 8, 9, 11, 14, 17, 22, 23, 26, 28, 30, 31, 32, 33, 34, 37, 39, 41, 42, 47, 48, 50, 52, 55, 58, 60, 65, 66, 67, 69, 70, 71, 74, 75, 77, 81, 82, 84, 85, 88, 89, 90, 91, 97, 99, 119, 123, 124, 126, 129, 133, 138, 139, 141, 145, 150, 154, 156, 157, 164, 168, 179, 180, 182, 185, 186, 187, 192, 196, 201, 203, 204, 205, 213, 214, 215, 216, 217, 218, 219, 222, 225, 226, 231, 232, 234
Greek 228
Greeks .. 11, 14, 22, 26, 28, 29, 32, 37, 38, 39, 42, 44, 45, 46, 47, 51, 63, 88, 93, 106, 108, 112, 138, 165, 167, 178, 186, 187, 204, 205, 215, 217, 218, 219, 225
Gregorian Calendar 163
gymnosophists 58, 63, 217
gynnis 71

H

Hadrian 2
Hagnon 73, 157, 158
Halicarnassus 14, 100, 133
Halys, River 200
Hamadan 118
Hammond, NGL 58, 59, 64, 68, 91, 94, 112, 148, 150, 154, 161, 172, 194, 207, 211, 233
Hanging Gardens 25, 50
harem 74
Harpalus 61, 70, 159
Harpocration 88, 96
Hazarapatis 112
Hecataeus 168
Hecatombaeon 3
Heckel, W 1, 71, 88, 96, 97, 98, 99, 100, 111, 114, 151, 182, 190, 230, 233
Hector 21, 89, 153
Hedicke, E 75, 76, 156
Hegelochus 105
Hegesias 21, 153
Hellenistic tombs 226
Hellenistic world 22, 212
Hellespont 11, 16, 200, 224
Hephaistion .... iii, iv, 5, 11, 18, 35, 37, 38, 39, 42, 49, 50, 57, 63, 67, 69, 70, 71, 72, 74, 75, 76, 77, 78, 79, 80, 81, 82, 83, 84, 85, 86, 87, 88, 89, 90, 91, 92, 93, 94, 95, 96, 97, 98, 99, 100, 101, 102, 103, 104, 105, 106, 107, 108, 109, 110, 111, 112, 113, 114, 115, 116, 117, 118, 119, 120, 121, 122, 123, 124, 125, 126, 128, 129, 130, 131, 132, 133, 134, 135, 136, 137, 155, 156, 159, 163, 164, 182, 184, 185, 198, 200, 204, 207, 208, 209, 220, 221, 223, 224, 225, 226, 228
Hephaistos 22, 69, 82, 225
Heracleia 205
Heracleitus 205
Heracles . 3, 18, 19, 22, 39, 52, 81, 88, 138, 139, 140, 141, 142, 143, 144, 145, 146, 147, 148, 149, 150, 151, 193, 211, 214, 216, 217, 219, 222, 232, 234
Heraclid 3
Hérault 192
Hermias 152
Hermolaus 37, 108
hero .. 3, 46, 47, 77, 78, 81, 85, 88, 118, 119, 121, 123, 129, 137, 139, 159, 169, 220, 221
Herodotus 84, 164, 168, 179, 225, 230, 231
Heuss, A 53, 233

hieroglyphics 22
Hieromnemon 147
Hieronymus 71, 140, 144, 148
Hindu Kush 31, 38
Hipparch 112, 113
Hipparchs 99
Hippokrates 181, 194
Hitler 53, 54
Holkias 182
Holt, F 54, 106, 233
Homer 3, 5, 11, 22, 23, 56, 66, 67, 85, 87, 88, 89, 115, 120, 122, 129, 131, 134, 135, 216, 219, 221, 222, 225, 228, 230
Hormuz, Strait of 46
Housman, A.E. 11
Hümmel, J.E. 84
Hunt, JM 224, 228
Hydaspes, River... 39, 41, 42, 109, 110
Hydraotes, River 110
Hymenaios 84, 85, 164
hyparch 109
hypaspists 41, 58, 98, 99
Hyperbolus 205
Hypereides 118, 126, 129, 137, 221, 230
Hyphasis, River 41, 48, 53
Hyrcania .. 29, 113, 154, 158, 165, 166, 167, 170
Hystaspes 202

I

ichneumon 97
Iliad 3, 5, 56, 61, 62, 65, 88, 89, 120, 122, 129, 134, 136, 137, 159, 216, 225, 230
Illyria 6, 8, 68
Illyrians 3, 8, 69
India. 1, 38, 44, 45, 46, 48, 56, 58, 63, 93, 94, 104, 108, 109, 110, 111, 114, 133, 144, 159, 163, 170, 176, 178, 181, 203, 205, 213, 217, 218, 219, 232
Indian Ocean 45
Indians.. 38, 39, 40, 42, 44, 59, 93, 98, 109, 110, 111, 171, 172, 212, 219
Indica..... 2, 69, 110, 144, 157, 230
Indus, River.... 1, 2, 38, 39, 41, 42, 44, 45, 53, 109, 110, 111, 157, 158, 164, 180
intermarriage 52, 179, 204, 207
Ion 218
Ionia 6, 8, 13, 14, 85, 139, 152
Ionian Greeks 8
Ipsus, Battle of 1
Ishtar 226
Ishtar Gate 226
Isocrates 58, 230
Issus 17, 65, 72, 74, 78, 90, 95, 132, 139, 140, 150, 196, 200, 201, 227
Istanbul 18, 80
Ister 168
Isthmus of Corinth 215
Italy 52, 53, 84, 164, 179
Itinerarium Alexandri........ 91, 230

J

Jaxartes, River 32, 33, 106, 155
Jerusalem 11, 20
Jews 20
Jhelum, River 39, 109
John of Nikiu 171
Josephus 20
Judas 147
Julian Calendar 3, 23, 163
Julius Caesar 212
Justin .. 2, 7, 56, 67, 68, 69, 70, 74, 75, 78, 86, 95, 118, 122, 132, 137, 139, 140, 142, 143, 147, 148, 150, 166, 167, 168, 172, 176, 182, 183, 184, 187, 188,

Index

189, 190, 193, 198, 199, 206, 207, 209, 214, 221, 224, 230

K

Kabul, River 109
Kalash 173
Karageorghis, V 229
Karnak 23, 191
Khawak Pass 31
Khyber Pass 38
Kochba, River 106
Koldewey, R .. 124, 127, 226, 228, 233
Kombaphe 181
kopis 227
Kos 14, 82, 194
Kushan Pass 38
Kyme 80

L

Lagus 212
Lane Fox, R 97, 118, 123, 124, 233
Lanike 36
Laomedon 71
Lapiths 225
Larissa 1, 68, 72, 157, 158
Last Plans 52, 204, 228
Latin .2, 74, 75, 77, 121, 155, 156, 180, 219
Lattimore, R 219
Leonnatus ... 7, 18, 42, 43, 99, 102, 183, 185, 196, 197, 198, 199
Lesbos 15
Leuctra, Battle of 5
libanotris 220
Liber de Morte 1, 2, 182
lions 226
lion-scalp 18
Loeb ... 58, 60, 112, 130, 180, 216, 219, 223, 230, 231, 232

Louis XIV 26, 199
Lucian 2, 60, 72, 74, 83, 84, 85, 90, 118, 123, 124, 129, 137, 152, 158, 164, 179, 214, 218, 225, 231
Lyceum 56, 71
Lycia 14, 26
Lycians 157
Lycolas 68
Lycon 205
Lycophron 146, 147, 148, 231, 234
Lydia 11
Lynkestis, Alexander 37
Lysimachus 81, 89, 168, 193
Lysippus 83, 193
Lyson & Kallikles 227

M

Macedon 3, 5, 6, 7, 8, 9, 13, 14, 17, 19, 21, 23, 24, 30, 33, 34, 36, 37, 38, 41, 47, 48, 55, 61, 67, 68, 69, 70, 71, 73, 74, 76, 78, 83, 88, 92, 93, 97, 98, 99, 100, 101, 108, 113, 116, 118, 125, 126, 132, 133, 134, 139, 142, 145, 148, 156, 161, 162, 163, 170, 174, 185, 186, 187, 188, 189, 193, 194, 203, 204, 205, 207, 208, 211, 212, 216, 227, 233
Macedones 228
Macedonia 48, 72, 82, 88, 113, 145, 146, 147, 150, 184, 185, 188, 193, 194, 212, 216, 221, 233
Macedonian 74, 177, 226, 227, 228, 229, 233
Macedonians.... 11, 14, 17, 18, 19, 20, 21, 23, 24, 28, 30, 31, 32, 33, 34, 38, 40, 52, 93, 98, 99, 102, 104, 108, 118, 131, 133, 141, 142, 143, 144, 145, 149,

159, 169, 173, 177, 179, 183, 184, 188, 189, 191, 206, 207, 210, 219
Machatas 68
Machiavelli, N 209, 233
Macurdy, Grace 187, 188, 233
Maedi 5
Magi 162
Magnesia 21
malaria 16, 51, 181
Malibu 77
Mallians 42, 43, 99, 110
Mandanis 59
Mantinea, Battle of 5
Maracanda 169
Marathus 200
Mardi 29
Marduk 51
Margites 88
Mark Antony 212
Markle, M 227, 233
marriage ... 6, 7, 20, 29, 36, 71, 84, 85, 93, 113, 131, 134, 138, 139, 140, 141, 143, 164, 165, 168, 169, 175, 177, 178, 179, 180, 200, 205, 206, 207, 208, 211
Mars 84
Marsyas 1, 88, 96, 148
Massaga . iii, iv, 38, 165, 171, 172, 173
mausoleum 228
Mazaeus 23, 24, 25, 29, 97, 133
Meda 68
Medeia 61
Media 101, 169
Mediterranean .. 13, 19, 21, 22, 45, 52, 89, 95, 96, 214, 224, 227, 232
Medius 1, 157, 158
Megabyzus 155
Megalopolis 97, 187
Megalopolitans 187
Megara 77
Megasthenes 1, 59

Meleager 81, 94, 143, 183
Melqart 19
Memnon ... 11, 13, 14, 15, 16, 138, 139
Memphis 22, 65, 96, 226, 228
Menidas 98
Mentor 114, 138, 141
mercenaries 2, 9, 11, 16, 17, 21, 38, 47, 55, 73, 159, 164, 196
Meroe 23, 171
Meroes 40
Mesopotamia 50, 113, 212
Methymna 205
Metron 102
Metropolis 25, 26
Metz Epitome 2, 59, 109, 173, 174, 178, 179, 180, 181, 182, 184, 207, 214, 219, 230
Mieza 5, 56, 70
Miletus 13, 31, 32, 214
Minithya 167
Minos 218
Mithrenes 197
Mithridates VI 80
Molossia 3, 68, 89
monsoon 41
Moon 23, 115, 163
Moralia ... 2, 55, 58, 59, 63, 64, 72, 73, 89, 92, 93, 94, 101, 126, 147, 158, 175, 204, 205, 206, 212, 213, 216, 219, 222, 231
Moreno, Paolo ... 82, 192, 193, 234
Müller 91, 206, 230
Munich 83, 232
Murray & Wyatt 219
Musée de l'Ephèbe 192
Musicanus 44
Mussolini 53
Myra 226
Myrmidons 87, 225, 230
Mytilene 1, 16, 106, 139, 205

245

Index

N

Nabarzanes 113, 134, 154
Naples 83, 227
Naples Museum 227
Nautaca 36
Nazis 28, 54
Nearchus 1, 2, 45, 46, 50, 70, 110, 111, 141, 142, 143, 147, 157, 158, 163
Nebuchadnezzar 50, 124, 142, 181, 228
Nectanebo II 66
Nemean lion 139
Neoptolemus 211
Nero 162
Nesaean horses 169
Nicesipolis 68, 211
Nicobule 61
Nicomachian Ethics 63
Nicomachus 30, 102, 103
Nile, River 21, 22, 23, 96, 185, 227
Nymphs, Temple of 56, 70
Nysa 39

O

Ocean 44, 45, 216
Ochus 113, 138, 141, 153, 158, 202, 204, 209
Odeschalchi Collection 81
Odysseus 146, 216
Odyssey 23, 88, 228
Oedipus 14, 165, 171
oinochoe 220
Olympia 83
Olympians 7
Olympias 3, 6, 7, 22, 68, 71, 74, 89, 92, 114, 132, 144, 145, 148, 149, 171, 186, 187, 188, 189, 190, 191, 203, 211

Olympic Games ... 3, 5, 47, 70, 83, 164
Olynthus . 1, 63, 79, 115, 123, 131
Onesicritus ... 1, 45, 58, 60, 61, 64, 94, 111, 168, 171, 216, 219
Opis 48, 49, 180, 208, 209
oracle 10, 21, 22, 31, 77, 119, 129, 221
Orchomenians 9
Oreitae 111
Orestes 92, 165
Orestis 68
Orithya 167
Orobatis 109
Orontes 188
Orsines 159, 160, 161, 162, 164
Oxathres 29, 31, 101, 180, 220
Oxhead 3
Oxiatris 178, 179
Oxus, River 31, 106, 178
Oxyartes ... 36, 114, 174, 175, 176, 178, 179, 180, 207, 220
Oxyathres 180
Oxydracae 42
Oxydrakes 183

P

Pakate 72
Pakistan 173
Palagia, Olga 224, 228
Palestine 20, 185, 212
Palladius 59, 234
Pamphylia 14
Pankaspe 72
Pankaste .... iii, iv, 72
Pantheia 201
Pantheon 226
papyri 118, 126
Paralus 96
paredros 129
Parian Marble 147, 148, 193

Parmenion 3, 7, 16, 18, 24, 31, 73, 98, 101, 104, 133, 135, 139, 140, 150, 200, 224
Paropamisus 38, 176
Paropanisadae 183
Parsagada 28, 159, 161
Parthenon 52, 225
Parthia 165, 168
Parthians 98
Parysatis .. iii, iv, 47, 113, 196, 204
Patala 44, 45, 110
Patroclus 11, 67, 85, 86, 87, 88, 89, 92, 120, 121, 124, 129, 131, 132, 134, 135, 136, 137, 159, 225
Patron 164
Pausanias ... 7, 61, 68, 69, 88, 100, 149, 189, 190, 193, 212, 231
Pearson, L 60, 61, 123, 234
Pegasus 156
Peirithoüs 92
Peleus 88, 89
Pella. 1, 6, 69, 76, 82, 88, 96, 220, 221, 222
Pellium 8
Pelopidas ... 67, 92, 118, 122, 130, 136, 231
Peloponnese... 3, 5, 144, 145, 150, 187
Pelusium 96
Penthesilea 167
Perdiccas.. 7, 9, 50, 51, 52, 94, 98, 102, 105, 106, 109, 111, 112, 113, 123, 124, 125, 131, 144, 182, 183, 184, 185, 210, 211, 228
Pergamon 140, 143, 144, 147, 150, 226
Pergamon Museum 226
Pericles 67
Perizonius 122, 130
Perrin, B 88, 231
Persepolis 26, 27, 28, 161

Perseus 22, 146, 147, 214, 216, 217, 219
Persia. iii, iv, 5, 6, 8, 9, 10, 11, 13, 14, 16, 17, 18, 19, 20, 23, 24, 25, 26, 28, 29, 30, 37, 41, 45, 46, 47, 48, 56, 63, 65, 67, 75, 78, 89, 91, 93, 95, 96, 97, 98, 100, 101, 104, 106, 112, 113, 114, 122, 123, 125, 131, 132, 133, 138, 139, 141, 142, 152, 153, 155, 156, 157, 158, 159, 160, 161, 162, 163, 164, 171, 174, 179, 180, 188, 196, 197, 198, 199, 200, 201, 202, 203, 204, 205, 208, 209, 215, 219
Persian dress 65
Persian Gates 26, 100
Persian Gulf 46
Persianisation 113
Persians ..9, 14, 17, 23, 24, 28, 29, 31, 46, 51, 63, 74, 92, 98, 101, 108, 122, 124, 133, 135, 138, 151, 159, 160, 161, 162, 177, 198, 225
Persis 26, 28, 29, 100
Peucelaotis 109
Peucestas 42, 43, 112, 188
pezhetairoi 58
phalanx 5, 17
Pharaoh ... 1, 21, 66, 171, 192, 232
Pharasmanes 169
Pharnabazus 16, 138
Pharnuches 157
Pharos 22, 120
Phasimelus 205
Phasis, River 165, 166
Pheidon 106
Pherae 68
Phila 68
Philadelphus 1, 146
philalexandros 93
Philinna 68
Philip II 3, 5, 6, 7, 8, 10, 16, 22, 36, 67, 68, 69, 70, 71, 74, 82,

Index

88, 89, 100, 125, 138, 141, 142, 143, 145, 149, 150, 152, 161, 164, 168, 185, 188, 190, 193, 194, 203, 207, 211, 218, 222, 227, 233
Philip III.141, 183, 187, 188, 191, 192
Philistides 205
Philo 168
philobasileus 93
Philonicus 3
Philotas.7, 9, 30, 31, 37, 100, 101, 102, 103, 104, 105, 108, 111, 113, 132, 133, 134, 135
Philoxenus 73
Phintias 92
Phocians 9
Phocis 187
Phoenicia 95
Phoenicians 20
Phormion 205
Photius 2, 112, 113, 176, 183, 184, 185, 190, 230, 231
Phrasaortes 161
Phrygia 14, 138
Phrynichus 205
Physcidas 68
Pinarus, River 17
Pindar 9, 55
Pir Sar 39
Piraeus 187
Pisa 5, 70
Pisidia 14, 184
Pithagoras 115
Pixodarus 6, 71
Plataeans 9, 96
Plato 6, 64, 65, 86, 87, 88, 231
Pliny 1, 2, 72, 83, 89, 158, 231
Plutarch ..2, 10, 22, 32, 46, 55, 56, 57, 58, 59, 61, 62, 63, 64, 65, 67, 70, 71, 72, 73, 75, 77, 82, 85, 88, 89, 92, 93, 94, 95, 97, 100, 101, 103, 106, 107, 108, 114, 115, 116, 118, 121, 122, 123, 126, 129, 130, 132, 136, 137, 138, 139, 141, 142, 147, 148, 154, 157, 158, 159, 162, 163, 164, 168, 169, 175, 184, 188, 194, 195, 196, 197, 200, 204, 205, 206, 209, 210, 211, 212, 213, 215, 216, 217, 218, 219, 221, 223, 229, 231, 233
Poliorketes, Demetrius 229
Polito, E 226, 227
Polyaenus... 2, 100, 122, 188, 189, 231
Polybius 2, 68, 231
Polycleitus 83, 168
Polycrates 156
Polyperchon... 144, 145, 146, 147, 150, 186, 187, 188, 189, 190, 191, 211
Pompeii 170, 171, 227
Pontos 80
Porus . 38, 39, 40, 41, 42, 109, 110
Poseidon 45, 218
Potidaea 3
Prado 81, 83, 234
Prince-Consort 135
Pro Lapsu 90, 231
Processional Way 226
proskynesis 37, 106, 107, 108, 113, 133, 134, 203
Proteas 16, 73
Proxenides 83, 84
Pseudo-Callisthenes... 2, 217, 231, 234
Ptah 22
Ptolemaios 100
Ptolemies 212
Ptolemy.... 1, 2, 31, 36, 38, 39, 42, 66, 68, 70, 78, 81, 101, 106, 108, 111, 141, 142, 143, 148, 168, 169, 170, 182, 183, 184, 185, 192, 193, 197, 198, 211, 212, 228, 229, 232
Publius Rutilius Lupus 55
Pura 46

Pydna............. 148, 188, 189, 211
Pylades...................................... 92
pyra................................. 124, 228
pyramids 227, 229
pyre..... iv, 50, 118, 119, 122, 124, 125, 126, 127, 128, 129, 137, 147, 223, 224, 225, 226, 228, 234
Pyrrhus.............. 88, 188, 211, 231
Pythia...................................... 10
Pythian melody...................... 205
Python................................... 73
Pythonax................................ 107

Q

quinquereme 189, 224
Quintillian.............................. 155

R

ravens..................................... 22
Re..................... 22, 214, 218, 222
Regency 48, 113, 187
Regent................... 5, 92, 144, 187
Renaissance 84, 164, 178, 179
Renault, Mary 164, 201, 234
Rhadamanthus 218
Rhambacia 110
Rhodes....... 11, 121, 138, 222, 234
Rhodians................. 138, 139, 182
Ricci, S 199
Richardson, R.B. 88
Romans.... 1, 2, 23, 55, 81, 82, 83, 87, 120, 124, 152, 162, 163, 171, 188, 207, 208, 212, 223, 227, 231
Rome 66, 80, 81, 84, 179, 192, 212, 232
Romeo & Juliet....................... 174
Roosevelt, F............................. 54
Roxane. iii, iv, 37, 83, 84, 85, 113, 140, 142, 144, 145, 148, 149,
164, 171, 174, 175, 176, 177, 178, 179, 180, 181, 182, 183, 184, 185, 186, 187, 188, 189, 190, 191, 193, 194, 207, 210, 211, 233
Royal Family........... 113, 134, 189
Royal Journal 163
Royal Pages....30, 37, 38, 82, 102, 108, 190
Royal Squadron................99, 100
rudist 227

S

Saatsoglou-Paliadeli, C 149
Sacae 75, 155, 156, 163
Sacred Band 5, 67
Sagalassus 14
Salamis.................................229
Samarkand........32, 33, 35, 36, 106
Samians 96
Samos.............. 123, 142, 168, 233
Saqqara..........................65, 228
Sardis.................... 13, 197, 211
sarissa......................41, 226, 227
Satibarzanes 30
satrap......6, 14, 26, 100, 159, 160, 162, 169, 177, 188
Satrap Stele 191
sauroter...............................227
Sayings of Kings................55, 92
sceptre 130, 171
Scymnus.............................205
Scythia....................... 168, 169
Scythians....33, 34, 106, 155, 160, 168, 169
Second World War 28
Seleucids 212
Seleucus 94, 99, 113, 185, 208
Serapeum................65, 226, 228
serpents 225
Severus................................81
Shakespeare, W.......................174

Index

Siberia 168
Sidon 18, 19, 78, 95, 133, 225, 226
Sidonians 95
Silver Shields 41
Sinope 1, 87, 215, 219, 230
Siphnos 16
Sirens 125, 228
Sisimithres 34, 174, 178
Sisygambis ... 18, 90, 91, 171, 196, 198, 199, 203, 209
Siwa ... 22, 77, 129, 214, 215, 217, 218, 221, 222
snake 146, 147
Socrates 46, 54, 64, 65
Sodoma 84, 164, 179
Sogdian Rock 174, 178
Sogdiana. 31, 33, 34, 36, 105, 106, 133, 169, 174, 175, 178, 203
solstice 41
Somatophylax ... 99, 100, 112, 190
Sophists 83
Sophocles 61
Sostratus 38
Spada 155
spado 155
Spain 52
Sparta 67, 69, 97
Spartans 5, 8
Spitamenes 31, 32, 33, 34
Spithridates 11
Stagira 5
Stasicrates 121, 223
Stateira .... iii, iv, 47, 93, 141, 184, 196, 200, 201, 204, 206, 207, 208, 210, 211
staters 83
Stewart, A 77, 79, 81, 82, 83, 171, 234
Stone, Oliver iii
Strabo 2, 56, 59, 89, 121, 144, 149, 152, 161, 162, 167, 178, 185, 216, 217, 218, 223, 231
Straton 95
Stymphaea 145, 146
Suda 32, 68, 96, 181, 194, 212, 220, 231
Sun 22, 73, 222
Susa . 26, 47, 48, 63, 93, 111, 113, 140, 141, 142, 179, 180, 201, 202, 203, 204, 206, 207, 208, 209
Susian Gates 100
Symposium 86, 87, 231
Synhedrion 30
Syracuse 64, 205
Syr-Darya 32
Syria 16, 18, 97, 112, 142, 184, 185, 188, 196, 212, 230

T

Talents . 3, 4, 6, 20, 56, 64, 70, 73, 119, 121, 122, 125, 126, 137, 147, 159, 160, 205, 206, 223
Tanais, River 32, 106
Tarentum 73, 205
Tarn, W.W. ... 53, 54, 90, 132, 141, 143, 148, 149, 152, 163, 214, 234
Tarsus 14, 16
Taurus Mountains 16
Taxila 38, 39
Taxiles 38, 39, 40, 178
Teirios 201
Temenids ... 3, 147, 151, 185, 193, 211, 212
Temenus 3, 146, 147
Tenedos 16
Teos 157, 158, 205
tetradrachm 26, 139
Thais 27, 28
Thales 59
Thalestris iii, iv, 74, 165, 166, 167, 168, 169, 170, 171
Thapsacus 23, 97
Theangela 168

Thebes . 5, 8, 9, 10, 48, 55, 67, 68, 69, 149, 168, 205, 215
Themiscyra 165
Theodorus 73
Theophrastus 1, 71, 72, 158
Theopompus 68, 82, 231
Thermodon, River.. 165, 166, 167, 168
Theseus 92, 218
Thespians 9
Thessalians 25, 55, 136, 218
Thessalonike 68, 76, 78, 129, 137, 188, 189, 190, 211
Thessalonike Relief 76
Thessalus 7, 181, 205
Thessaly ...... iii, 17, 24, 68, 71, 72, 130, 145
Third Reich 53
Thirty, The 65
Thrace 223
Thracians 8
thunderbolt 41
Thyestes 165
Tiepolo, G 199
Tigris, River 23, 48
Timocleia 9
Timotheus 73, 205
Tower of Babel 25, 124
Trampya 146
treasure 18, 20, 26, 28, 52, 89, 101, 161
Triballians 8
Trichoneium 68
trierarchs 110, 157, 158
Triparadeisos 144, 185
triremes 224
Trogus.. 2, 70, 118, 122, 140, 143, 148, 166, 198, 230
Trojans 89, 129, 137
Troy 11, 21, 85, 86, 88, 89, 90, 159, 163, 167, 224, 225
Turkey 80, 167
Tymphaea 146, 147
Tymphaeans 146, 186
typhoid 16, 49, 117, 134
Tyre 19, 20, 95, 96, 200
Tyrians 19, 20
Tyriotes 201

U

Uxians 26, 29

V

Valerius Maximus 223
Varia Historia 72, 86, 118, 123, 130, 132, 163, 205, 225, 230
Venice 83, 226, 227, 229
Venus 84
Vergina 82, 193, 194, 232, 233
Veronese, Paolo 199
Veyrier, C 199
Villa Farnesina 84, 179
Vitruvius 223
Vizier 153
Vulgate 28, 33

W

Welles, B 223
Wilcken, U 53, 234
Wood, Michael 81, 173, 234

X

Xenocrates 6, 57, 64, 70, 97
Xenophon ... 46, 65, 152, 157, 161, 201, 204, 231
Xerxes 32
xyston 227

Z

Zarangians 30

Index

Zariaspa 33
Zeno 91
Zeus .. 22, 41, 58, 77, 88, 213, 214, 215, 216, 217, 218, 219, 221, 222, 225
Zeus-born 216, 217, 219
ziggurat 25, 50, 124, 224
zona-belt 79

www.ingramcontent.com/pod-product-compliance
Lightning Source LLC
Chambersburg PA
CBHW020751160426
43192CB00006B/299